BUSINESS
CASE STUDIES
for Advanced Level

Ian Marcousé

with

David Lines

PEARSON EDUCATION LIMITED
Edinburgh Gate, Harlow, Essex CM20 2JE, England
and Associated Companies throughout the World.

First published 1990
Second edition 1994
Eighth impression 2000
ISBN 0 582 24481 1

Design and page make-up by Jordan Publishing Design

Printed in Singapore (CNC)

The publisher's policy is to use paper manufactured from sustainable forests.

We are grateful to the following for permission to reproduce copyright material and information:

Coca-Cola of Great Britain and Ireland for information in 'The Coca-Cola Story' (Case study 4); Ewan McNaughton Associates for the two 'Daily Telegraph' headlines in 'The Winter of Discontent' (Case Study 69); Findlay Publications Ltd for an extract based on an article in the journal *Machinery and Production Engineering* 17.2.89 in 'Production Management' (Case Study 41); Häagen-Dazs UK in 'Häagen-Dazs Dedicated to Perfection' (Case Study 1) and 'Häagen-Dazs UK – A Classic Product Launch' (Case Study 9); Hanson plc and ICI for information in 'Hanson – Asset Stripping or Business Building?' (Case Study 68); McDonald's Restaurants Ltd for extracts based on information from McDonald's *Behind the Arches* by John F. Love in 'McDonald's – Marketing Hamburgers' (Case Study 2); NFC plc for information in 'The Employee Buyout and the Millionaire Mechanic' (Case Study 64); The Observer for the headline 'Hanson's secrets start to unfold' from *The Observer* 23.6.91 in 'Hanson – Asset Stripping or Business Building?' (Case Study 68); Pepe UK Ltd for an extract based on information in *Pepe Jeans Launch and Annual Reports* in 'Pepe Jeans – From Rags to Riches' (Case Study 81); Times Newspapers Ltd for an extract from *The Times* 5.2.82 in 'The Rise and Fall of Laker Airways' (Case Study 95).

We are indebted to the Associated Examining Board for permission to reproduce question 1, paper 2 Business Studies, A Level examination June 1993 and to use modified versions of marking schemes for A Level Business Studies. (We wish to state however, that any answers or hints on answers are the sole responsibility of the authors and have not been provided by the Board, also that the marking schemes were not the ones used by the AEB in the actual examination), also to the University of Cambridge Local Examinations Syndicate (UCLES) for the case study entitled "Boomtime for Bankcheck" from the November 1993 Business Studies Guidelines for Assessment.

We are grateful to the following for permission to reproduce photographs and other copyright material:

Bartle, Bogle and Hegarty/Häagen-Dazs UK, page 39, Body Shop International plc, page 217; Camera Press Ltd, pages 188, 197 and 278; *The Daily Telegraph*, page 194; *The Evening Standard*, page 280, *The Financial Times*, pages 187, 224, 232 and 274; *The Independent*, page 92 McDonald's Restaurants Ltd, page 20; National Motor Museum, Beaulieu, page 202; *The Observer, Sunday*, page 246; Octopus Publishing Group Limited, page 156; OKI (UK) Ltd, pages 110 and 111; FS Palazzini for material from *Coca Cola Superstar*. Publ. Coca Cola pages 25, 26 and 27; Ingram Pinn, page 62; Popperfoto, page 206; Quadrant Picture Library, pages 261 and 276; Rex Features, London, page 191; Survival Game UK Ltd, page 209; Times Newspapers Limited, 1987/8 pages 234 and 267.

Cartoons by Martin Shovel.

CONTENTS

Case Studies

CONTENTS

ACKNOWLEDGEMENTS

There are many people to thank for their help with the writing and preparation of this Second Edition. At John Ruskin college, my colleagues Nigel Watson and Roger Raymond provided constructive criticism and encouragement. Many of our students have tested draft cases or given feedback on aspects of the book. My thanks to them all, though Sunil Tanna, Yin Fan Kit, Dipali Chakravarti, Robin Burgess and Imran Qureshi were particularly helpful.

Others have provided snippets of invaluable help. The incomprehensible jargon in 'A Day in the Life of Teresa Travis' is thanks to Angus Low; details of Fulham Ladies Football Club come from Fulham's Gary Mulcahey, my daughter Claire and her friend Ronnie; several of the visual ideas came from the Low family.

The research into employment law was conducted by my wife, Maureen. My own researches owed much to the resources of the City Business Library. At Longman, both Sophie Clark and Helen Parr have contributed greatly. The comments of David Lines have also been valuable.

I would also like to make up for some omissions to the Acknowledgements to the First Edition. I should have thanked David Whitehead for providing my first opportunity to appear in print. The other unsung hero of the First Edition was Leda Barrett. This delightful student was the one whose kind words prompted me to write to Longman in the first place to propose the book.

Many people have worked to eliminate mistakes from the 96 cases, questions and answers. Despite their and my efforts, some errors will surface, for which I both apologise and accept full responsibility.

Ian Marcousé

The Second Edition is dedicated with love to Maureen, Claire and Jonny.

HOW TO USE THIS BOOK

To the student reader

Business Case Studies provides four ways to help you succeed in your exams:

1   There are twenty-five studies of actual, "classic" business case histories, such as Coca-Cola and Body Shop. Not only can these provide you with practice in exam technique, but they can also enrich your essay writing. The study of the collapse of Rolls Royce, for example, shows the importance of careful cash flow management and the problems of being over-reliant upon a single, new technology product. The material in these studies can be quoted in exam essays as the basis for analysing the question set. The "classic cases" are listed on page 15.

2   Many of the other case studies are written in such a way as to help explain, or reinforce, difficult topics such as working capital or business ethics. So even if you do not produce written answers, reading the texts should be helpful.

3   On page 9, the Chief Examiner of Nuffield A level Business Studies provides an account of the thinking behind the setting and marking of exam case studies. This is followed up (on page 285) with a past A level exam paper, two actual candidates' exam answers, plus the Chief Examiner's comments on their strengths and weaknesses.

4   Most A level courses include a project component. This book can help you to identify possible topics for a research assignment. Some of the case studies are based upon projects for the Cambridge A level course, including "Fat Sam's Franchise" and "Stock Control and Analysis".

To teachers and lecturers

This book aims to provide case studies on a wide enough range of topics to enable you to find ones that fit your syllabus needs. Some are aimed exclusively at single topics – usually harder ones such as investment appraisal or the use of financial ratios. Others give broad coverage within a main syllabus section, so that if you start your course with personnel management, for example, you will find a number of relevant case histories. These broader studies should help prepare candidates for Modular examinations. In addition, exam boards see case studies as a means of promoting integration, so many of the studies follow that philosophy.

Within each case study section, the materials are placed in an approximate order of difficulty. The earliest are pitched at the level of good GCSE students. Overall, there has been a conscious decision to make the case study questions demanding. This is because of the likelihood that the text and questions will be discussed in class before being tackled in writing. As some users felt that the First Edition did not provide enough cases of intermediate difficulty, this Second Edition has attempted to fill that gap.

The timings provided are viewed as being appropriate for exam/test conditions. When students are working collaboratively, they will need extra discussion time.

An index of study timings is provided on page 13.

Twenty-five of the cases are "classic" business stories. They have been researched with a view to providing students with background material to enrich homework essays and exam answers. They also provide valuable stimulus to class discussion. It is recommended that students should cover all of these.

On pages 16 and 17 is a tabular display of the concepts contained within each of the studies. So if you have just covered exchange rates, you can see which exercises examine that topic. The table also shows the other main elements within each exchange rate case study, to help you decide on the one most appropriate for your students.

In addition to this display, each study has a number of "key concepts" listed beneath the title. These are topics that are central to the study but not explained in the text. So students would need to have covered them previously before tackling the study in question. This display acts as a warning to help you avoid setting impossible tasks for your students.

One other point to check before giving students a study is the level of numerical difficulty. An approximate categorisation is provided to each study on page 14. Terms such as "hard" must be seen in the context of the widely differing mathematical demands of the various exam boards; so "hard" would be "demanding" for students of Cambridge Linear, and unnecessary for those preparing for the Cambridge Double Module, London or the AEB exams.

Answers to the questions are supplied in the *Answer Guide* (ISBN 0582 244765). Particular care has been taken over the numerical answers, for which detailed workings are provided. Possible answers to the written questions are also given.

Note to the Second Edition

Business Case Studies has been expanded to 96 cases in this Second Edition: twenty-six new texts plus seventy from the original book.

The twenty-six new case histories have been written with four main factors in mind.

1   The need for more cases that fit neatly into a business module, such as marketing or production.
2   The widespread request for an increase in the number of transitional cases, to help bridge the gap between GCSE and A level.
3   The new syllabus requirements of the SCAA subject core.
4   The need to keep abreast of the developments in Business Studies theory.

The order in which the cases appear in the book has been changed to fit in with the new curriculum core. This created the need for the sections on Operations Management and Objectives. Within each section, the cases are in approximate order of difficulty.

The second edition has two other changes from the First:

1   the removal of the five exemplar student answers; these have been switched to the Answer Guide

2   the addition (on pages 301–304) of a list of Sources of Information for Business Assignments; this provides many sources of secondary data for project work.

THE EXAMINER'S VIEW

To most candidates the external examination process appears very harsh and remote. Scripts are bundled off and sent to some unknown, and thus somehow slightly sinister individual. The examination board controls the system, which in a way resembles a production line with the raw material of answers at one end, and grades at the other. In between there is waste. It is the fear of being part of that waste which every year haunts so many young people.

In fact, while the process is by necessity remote, it is neither harsh nor unfair. Indeed it can be argued that its very remoteness ensures objectivity. Examiners are fully aware of the pressures on candidates, and they much prefer to discover what students know and understand than find out what they don't know or simply can't remember. Indeed every effort is made to ensure that the papers are as fair to all candidates as possible and only those who are the best prepared get the best grades.

Without doubt the only way to reduce the pain of examinations is to be one of those best-prepared candidates, and that means not only possessing plenty of theoretical knowledge, but also applying it to the different requirements of the examination boards.

The Examination Boards requirements

Examination boards use different types of papers in order to assess different skills. Essays have a place because they reveal a candidate's ability to express thoughts in a coherent and logical way. Coursework is often set as a means of testing a candidate's ability to research and analyse a subject without a time constraint, and the other pressures of a conventional examination.

Cases are used in business studies because they test theoretical knowledge in an unfamiliar context, which is one of the best ways to discover what a candidate really understands about the subject.

All the boards which offer Business Studies Advanced and A/S level examinations use case studies as part of their assessment pattern, although the length and complexity of each case varies, and may even be issued to candidates some time before the date of the examination. In September 1994 the case study requirements of the main Boards were as shown overleaf.

Case studies are also central to GNVQ as part of the assessment of the portfolio. It can easily be seen then that in order to achieve a high grade a knowledge of case studies is absolutely vital. So, what are the skills being tested?

Business Studies Advanced and A/S Level Requirements (Sept '94)

Exam Board	AEB		Cambridge				London*			JMB	NISEAC
			Linear		Modular		Nuffield		Linear		
	A	A/S	A	A/S	A	A/S	A	A/S	A	A	A
Paper 1	50% 3 hours A: compulsory short answer questions B: data response	50% 1.5 hours Structured questions	40% 3 hours Numerate areas	60% 2 hours 3 questions from 2 sections A: numerate B: essays	2.5 hours Double module CASE STUDY	2.5 hours Double module CASE STUDY	40% 2¾ hours A: CASE STUDY B: questions, 2 from 3, 1 compulsory	80% 2¾ hours A: CASE STUDY B: questions 2 from 3, 1 compulsory	40% 2.5 hours CASE STUDY	40% 3 hours Short answer questions	50% 3 hours A: short answer B: 4 structured questions from 7
Paper 2	50% 3 hours A: CASE STUDY B: essays	50% 3 hours A: CASE STUDY B: essays	35% 3 hours CASE STUDY	40% 2 hours CASE STUDY	Research assignment	Research assignment	40% 2 optional modules from 6 ½ hours each	20% Portfolio of coursework assignments	30% untimed 3 coursework assignments	40% 3 hours A: CASE STUDY (1.5 hours) B: essays (1.5 hours)	50% A: CASE STUDY B: data response
Paper 3			25% untimed Practical project		3 optional modules pre-issued case studies†		20% untimed Portfolio of coursework assignments		30% untimed project	20% untimed 2 coursework assignments	

Notes: † The 'Economic Environment of Business' is examined via a data response paper.

* London also offers an alternative to pilot centres only in association with NDTEF

The skills tested by case studies

Case studies assess certain skills which are less apparent than in other forms of examination. So, when using the cases in this book, practise the skills outlined below, because they are the ones the examiners are looking for and the ones which will attract the highest marks.

Analytical and evaluative skills

All case studies contain numerate and non-numerate data, but not all of it is relevant. Some is vital, some is useful and some is of no use whatsoever. One of the most important skills to apply is the ability to distinguish between these three types, putting them in some sort of order of importance and then reacting to them in an appropriate fashion.

There may even be too much information, in which case it has to be filtered down to manageable levels. Alternatively there may not be enough, and then intuition and intelligence must be combined in order to fill the gaps. Whichever combination of circumstances exists, it is never enough simply to take the case study at its face value.

Application skills

Text book theories are all very fine, but knowing when to apply them, and when not to, is a special skill which case studies assess well. For instance, the text books may say that people are better motivated by a democratic leader, which is generally, but not always correct. On board an oil rig in the North Sea, for instance, the safety of all the personnel rests on the knowledge that orders can be given and then obeyed. A 'democratic' debate in such an environment could be positively dangerous.

A case study will define particular circumstances, and it is very important that those circumstances are taken into account when answering questions. Theories exist to be applied, but their application must be made carefully and with due consideration to the context. Nevertheless, it is vital not to fall into the trap of writing 'common sense' answers rather than ones which are firmly rooted in theoretical knowledge.

Creative skills

As in real-life business it is not always the obvious or conventional path which leads to success. Although assessed case studies clearly require a firm base of academic theory, it does not necessarily mean that a candidate has to be restricted to that alone. Often someone who really thinks about what the facts imply as much as what they obviously say will earn more marks. The use of examples from other sources is always a good idea, and can often move an answer from the ordinary to the very good in just a line or two.

Communication skills

Clearly business depends on the ability of one person to be understood by another.

The ability to write lucidly is therefore central, and will be assessed.

Using diagrams as illustrations is a good idea, but they should not be over-elaborate. So long as they get the basic idea across, making them pretty simply takes too long to justify the time spent.

Skills of numeracy

In a similar way to communication skills, in business the ability to carry out numerate manipulation is important. Marks will not be awarded simply for the mechanics of the operation, but they will be available for anyone displaying a knowledge of techniques and a recognition of which ones are appropriate in differing circumstances.

In carrying out numerate operations it is vital to be systematic, so that even if the final answer is wrong, the examiner can see the steps which were made and why they were made, and can give credit accordingly.

Skills of perception

Case studies provide examples to support theories. Clearly the examiner has a pretty good idea of the area of the syllabus which she or he wants to examine. It may be, for instance, the areas of motivation or marketing, production or the economic environment. Questions will be asked which require a candidate to apply theoretical knowledge to the case in a fairly straightforward way, rather like a doctor examining a patient and applying her theoretical knowledge to that individual's particular symptoms and arriving at a diagnosis.

However, the candidate may also be required to work from the case study towards a theory: to look at the particular example and then use it to generalise about all businesses. This would be the equivalent of our doctor examining a person with a bad cough who smokes, and then using the example as an illustration of the general principle that cigarettes damage people's lungs.

This shift from the specific to the general is demonstrated in the last question of the Stable Finance case study on page 286. It requires students to examine the impact of good motivation on all organisations using the case material to illustrate their answers.

Learning how to apply theoretical concepts and use case evidence effectively is a difficult skill to acquire, but it is vital because it shows applied thinking about the subject. After all, one of the strengths of business studies is that it is far more than a just a sterile, book learning exercise, and good examination responses will demonstrate that.

A summary of what is needed

In order to do well in case study work, a candidate must:

- know the basic theory
- be able to apply the theory to the special circumstances of the case study
- be creative and imaginative within these special circumstances
- be able to use the material in the case to illustrate theories found in textbooks.

CASE STUDY TIME ALLOCATION

NUMERICAL DIFFICULTY

The studies are divided into 4 categories: those with no maths requirement (N); those with easy calculations (E); those with demanding maths (D); those that are hard (H);

The first 3 categories include questions that might form part of any Business Studies exam; those termed 'hard' are suitable only for the syllabuses with a clear maths bias.

1	Häagen-Dazs dedication to perfection	N	49	Mrs Ahmed's cousin	N
2	McDonald's – marketing hamburgers	E	50	Factory safety	D
3	The Russian Lager	E	51	Teamworking – Theory & practice	N
4	The Coca-Cola story	E	52	Putting Herzberg into practice	N
5	Adding value to sugar	N	53	A day in the life of Teresa Travis	N
			54	The new laser scanning system	N
6	Even Levi's can make mistakes	E	55	The McKline dispute	N
7	Let the buyer beware	D			
8	Avoiding a price war	H	56	A case of elementary decision trees	D
9	Häagen Dazs UK – a classic product launch	N	57	Panda Wok	N
10	The product portfolio problem	E	58	Problem of pollution in a chemical plant	N
			59	Panetteria Italiana	E
11	Marketing Research	D	60	Economic change as an external constraint	N
12	Price elasticity and profits	D			
13	The marketing plan	D	61	An ethical dilemma	E
14	Dispute over marketing strategy	H	62	The medicine business	E
15	Bombay pizza	D	63	The change in government	E
			64	The employee layout and the millionaire mechanic	E
16	Constructing a business plan	D	65	The oil crisis	N
17	Working capital	D			
18	Budgeting in Harrogate	E	66	The Bhopal Tragedy	E
19	Investment decision making	D	67	A pressure group triumph	N
20	Credit factoring	D	68	Hanson – asset stripping or business building?	E
			69	The winter of discontent	N
21	The Sting	D	70	The 3 in 1 washing machine	E
22	Publishing Confessions	D			
23	Investment within financial constraints	D	71	A small business start up	E
24	The mini-merger	E	72	Ford's Model T – the birth of modern industry	E
25	Too good to be true	E	73	Porsche cars	E
			74	The Prince and the turnstile	D
26	The sofabed saga	D	75	The Survival Game	E
27	Takeovers and published accounts	D			
28	Liquidity crisis	D	76	Farley's Salmonella crisis	D
29	A Problem of stock control and production scheduling	D	77	The black hairdressers	D
30	BS 5750 and the quality fanatic	D	78	Body Shop International	D
			79	Fat Sam's franchise	D
31	Deciding on factory location	D	80	Marlboro and market power	D
32	Bringing in quality circles	N			
33	Stock control and analysis	D	81	Pepe jeans – from rags to riches	D
34	Finding a European location	D	82	SolarTile – a mini-multinational	E
35	Workforce performance and the Skoda supplier	N	83	Chocolate soldiers – the Rowntree takeover	E
			84	Money from the tap	H
36	Just-in-time production – the Japanese way	E	85	Good management practice in retailing	D
37	Personnel management and cost controls	E			
38	Kaizen-continuous improvement at OKI	E	86	Wedgwood's fight for survival	D
39	Time-based management	N	87	Interest rates and the growing business	E
40	Profit and manpower planning	D	88	Fashion goes west	D
			89	Overtrading in jewellery	E
41	Production management	N	90	Statistical analysis	H
42	Personnel management	N			
43	Money and motivation	E	91	De Lorean cars – 'from cow pasture to production'	D
44	A BMW at twenty three	N	92	The Ford Strike – 1988	D
45	Boomtime for Bankcheck	N	93	The Irish Sawmill	D
			94	Rolls Royce – the gamble that failed	D
46	The Trench	N	95	The rise and fall of Laker Airways	E
47	Management structure	E	96	The new design team	H
48	British management techniques under fire	N			

THE CLASSIC CASE STUDIES

Each of the following is a fully researched account of a real business situation or problem. As such, these cases can provide useful material for essay writing in addition to case study practice.

KEY TO MAIN CONCEPTS

CONCEPT	CASE STUDY NUMBER
Objectives and Strategy	
Company objectives	5 8 36 47 57 58 59 60 64 65 68 73 80 86 95
Internal & external constraints	28 32 36 57 59 73 82 85 86 91
Decision making	8 11 14 16 27 32 33 35 56 75 79 84 85
Corporate strategy & plans	25 29 36 38 41 47 52 53 58 60 64 65 68 80 83 84
Ethics	9 27 46 61 68 80
Contingency plans & SWOT analysis	41 57 69 86
Marketing	
Marketing Objectives/model	6 14 79 80
Marketing strategy	1 2 4 6 7 8 9 10 11 13 14 65 73 75 84 89 95
Marketing & portfolio planning	1 10 13 28 39 70 80 93
Marketing mix	1 2 4 5 7 13 14 28 71 75
Pricing & elasticity	3 8 9 12 14 59 60 67 72 73 80 88 91 93 94 95
Advertising and branding	2 4 9 13 14 61 62 70 71 80 83
Distribution	1 4 5 7 13 14 71 85 88 93
Market research	3 4 6 7 9 11 28 71
New product development	1 6 9 10 11 12 28 39 61 70 82 91 94
Market segmentation	6 10 14 28 39 40 73 77 78 84
Sales forecasting	3 11 13 16 77 79 90 96
Finance	
Cash flow	15 16 20 28 29 36 63 70 71 74 84 87 88 89 94 95
Investment appraisal	19 22 85 88 93
Qualitative factors	16 19 22 31 76 91 93
Contribution	8 12 14 19 30 33 82 84 96
Break-even	3 7 22 31 50 70 71 73 77 79 93
Profit	7 8 12 15 16 24 30 33 40 52 59 60 61 70 71 74 75 77 79 82 85 89 90 94 96
Published accounts	16 17 24 27 28 55 76 83 88 93 95
Reliability of accounts	21 25 27 88 93
Ratio analysis	21 25 26 27 28 60 68 76 78 85 88 93 95
Working capital management	17 20 21 24 28
Raising finance	16 17 20 28 62 68 71 74 78 81 82 83 85 87 88 89 91 95
Budgeting and cost control	18 20 21 68 74 89
People in Organisations	
Types of remuneration	35 42 43 46 48 49 50 52 54 62 64
Management theorists	35 41 44 45 48 49 52 54 55 72 74 91
Them and us & single status	32 37 41 48 52 55 64 92
Teamworking & empowerment	30 32 38 43 48 51 52 55 64
Quality circles	32 52 86
Hierarchy/span of control	47 48 52 64 89

1 HÄAGEN-DAZS DEDICATED TO PERFECTION

Concepts needed: Production orientation, Product life cycle, Marketing mix

In the 1950s a New York manufacturer of an ice cream brand called Ciro's decided to extend its distribution from ice cream parlours to supermarkets. Reuben Mattus had spotted that rising affluence plus freezer ownership encouraged consumers to buy ice cream all year round. Not surprisingly, this distribution strategy was soon imitated by larger rivals. They were able to offer incentive deals to the retailers that Mattus could not match, so sales of Ciro's slipped back.

Thwarted by his competitors, Mattus decided to try a different approach. Using fresh cream, all natural ingredients and with less air blown into the mix, he produced an ice cream with a finer flavour and texture. To distinguish it from other ice creams, he gave his new product a Scandinavian sounding name and packed it into pint pots instead of the usual 2 litre packs. In 1961 the first Häagen-Dazs ice cream was sold in New York delicatessens.

With its high ingredients' cost and small-scale production, the price of Häagen-Dazs had to be high to be profitable. This was off-putting to shopkeepers, who feared that customers would refuse to buy it. So Mattus visited shops personally, giving staff a taste of the product and promising to buy back any product that did not sell. By removing the shops' financial risk, gaining distribution became more possible. Slowly but steadily Häagen-Dazs spread to New York grocers, then supermarkets and later to national store chains.

Without the desire or the finance to promote the product through advertising, Mattus relied upon word of mouth to generate customer demand. Fortunately, Häagen-Dazs customers loved talking about the product. By the mid-1970s the ice cream's popularity was such that remaining Ciro ice cream products were phased out to turn the production capacity over to Häagen-Dazs. Mattus developed the theme 'Dedicated To Perfection' as a focus of staff training, materials purchasing and production control. He was determined that growth would not be at the expense of the product quality that he had sought and found in 1961.

At the same time Mattus's daughter came up with the idea of creating a 'dipping store' in which vanilla ice cream bars were hand-dipped in melted milk or plain chocolate to create a hand-made choc ice. From this 250 Häagen-Dazs stores were developed in America, each offering an opportunity for people to sample the products they could then buy from supermarkets.

By the early 1980s Häagen-Dazs had become established as *the* super-premium ice cream throughout America. In 1983 the company was sold off to the Pillsbury Company, with a condition of sale being that the company's quality standards would always be maintained. Pillsbury, the multi-national owners of Burger King, were looking to develop Häagen-Dazs internationally. In 1984, after signing an agreement for it to be manufactured in Japan, Häagen-Dazs grew to become that country's best selling super-premium ice cream.

Three years later, with sales levelling off in America, Pillsbury started to look seriously at the European market. Little progress had been made by 1989, however, when Pillsbury was itself bought up by the British company Grand Metropolitan. The American firm with the Scandinavian sounding name was now British owned, and was soon to launch its product in Britain (see Case Study 9).

Meanwhile, by 1992 American sales were slipping under pressure from a strong competitor. Ben and Jerry's produced high quality ice cream at high prices, but differentiated itself from Häagen-Dazs by containing bigger chunks of chocolate, almonds or toffee. It also had a livelier image, as epitomised by the name of one of its flavours, Cherry Garcia. Häagen-Dazs responded to Ben and Jerry's success by introducing comparable products within a new range called Exträas. This revitalised Häagen-Dazs sales. For thirty years, the company's dedication to perfection had been enough to succeed; modern markets might require still more.

Sources: *The Financial Times; Häagen-Dazs UK Ltd.*

Questions
(35 marks; 60 minutes)

1 Outline the incentive deals a firm might offer in order to achieve retail distribution for its products. **(6)**

2 Comment on the marketing mix used by Häagen-Dazs. **(8)**

3 **a** Sketch a fully labelled product life cycle diagram to show the stages in the development of Häagen-Dazs in America, using the dates provided. **(8)**

  b What may have prevented the product from growing more rapidly in America? **(5)**

4 Discuss whether Mattus was too production orientated in his development of Häagen-Dazs. **(8)**

2 McDONALD'S – MARKETING HAMBURGERS

Concepts needed: Marketing strategy, Marketing mix

In 1954, a salesman of milkshake machines paid a call on a customer in Southern California. It was a small drive-in restaurant that sold a limited range of products at unusually low prices. The salesman (Ray Kroc) was impressed with its assembly-line production method, and even more by the queues of customers. Although the hamburgers sold for just 15 cents each, this one outlet had annual sales over $300,000.

Kroc saw the potential of the business, and offered the owners an arrangement which would give him sole rights to franchise their name, production method and logo throughout the United States. The owners (Richard and Maurice McDonald) would receive a quarter of all Kroc's franchise income, which was to be 1.9% of all the franchisees' sales revenue. The golden arches which formed part of Kroc's original restaurant design structure were turned into the familiar 'M' trademark.

During this period, customer demand stemmed from McDonald's low prices, rapid service, and dedication to service and cleanliness. Its appeal was to families at a time when rival drive-ins attracted the smaller teenage market. Growth proved rapid, and by 1960 the 225 McDonald's franchises provided annual sales of almost $50 million. In 1961, Kroc bought the McDonald brothers out for $2.7 million. Had they held on to their 0.5% royalty they would have earned over $400 million by the late 1980s.

Following the buyout, the McDonald's Corporation profits flourished due to increasing numbers of outlets, and new contracts that took a much higher percentage of the franchise operator's income. However, annual sales per store were static at around $200,000 so the individual franchises needed ways to boost their own revenues. Some focused on the limited menu (and were responsible for creating the Big Mac in 1968 and the Egg McMuffin in 1973), while others concentrated on publicity.

In Washington, a clown character was being used with success on local television: renamed Ronald McDonald he became used nationally from 1965. Franchise operators found that T.V. advertising caused immediate sales increases, and that it helped overcome the traditional takeaway sales slump during the harsh northern American winter. So they agreed to contribute 1% of McDonald's $260 million sales in 1966 to a national advertising fund. This helped sales per store to jump to $275,000 from around $200,000 in the early 1960s.

It was at the local level, too, that sales promotions originated. Some became enormous successes nationally, including a mint-green Shamrock Shake sold on St. Patrick's Day, and scratch cards yielding instant prizes of Big Macs. Better promotions were capable of boosting short-term sales by 6%, and adding some novelty to the customers' visit.

Throughout this period of local initiative the McDonald's Corporation made surprisingly little contribution to the marketing effort. Only in 1968, at a time when rivals such as Burger King were closing the gap on McDonald's, did they form a marketing department. Its head decided to base his objectives on Ray Kroc's view that 'We're not in the hamburger business, we're in show business'.

Advertising agencies were invited to compete for the account by answering ten questions, including whether McDonald's possessed a 'unique selling proposition'. One agency replied no, McDonald's had only a unique sales personality, for its proposition differed 'depending on whether we're talking to moms, dads, or kids'. The agency recommended building up personality into one of warmth, fun, relaxation – and won the account.

The new campaign focused on the emotional pleasures of eating out: family togetherness, fun, and a sense of reward. Prolific use of television advertising was seen as the key to doubling revenues per store to $620,000 by 1973.

Although other factors were involved, the importance of advertising was also evident in Britain. The first British outlet to open (in Woolwich, London in 1974) started poorly. In its first year its revenue of $300,000 was too small to prevent losses of $150,000. The second outlet proved no better. Yet when profitable West End stores justified television advertising, the situation turned into one of runaway success. By 1986 the U.K. operation was so profitable that it cost the Corporation $38 million to buy out its British subsidiary.

During the 1980s, the enormous scale of the world-wide McDonald's operation was making local initiative harder to incorporate into the marketing process.

It was the Corporation itself that devised the hugely successful introduction of Chicken McNuggets in the early 1980s, and the massive T.V and promotional campaigns throughout the decade. By 1985, McDonald's controlled 20% of the $45 billion fast food market in the United States and enjoyed rapid growth in its many overseas markets. Ray Kroc had died the previous year, but his successors saw no need to change the McDonald's system.

Source: *'Behind The Arches'; J.F. Love.*

Questions
(35 marks; 60 minutes)

1 Outline how the franchisees benefited from their link with McDonald's. **(8)**

2 Until his death, Kroc focused much of his own attention on the maintenance of high standards of in-store quality, service and cleanliness. How important was this compared with other parts of McDonald's marketing strategy? **(9)**

3 Judging by the recent McDonald's advertisements that you have seen, how far do you think the firm's advertising strategy has moved away from its 1968 guidelines? **(8)**

4 What was the percentage increase in McDonald's United States dollar sales between 1966 and 1985? **(4)**

5 Large corporations can often only obtain feedback from customers at arm's length, through market research. What are the advantages and disadvantages of receiving it via franchise operators? **(6)**

3 THE RUSSIAN LAGER

Concepts needed: Market research, Pricing, Revenue, Break-even analysis

Project Steps was the codename for Allied Ales' new lager brand. Many in the marketing department thought it their most promising prospect for years. The idea had emerged from a series of group discussions among young, frequent lager drinkers. They had sounded tired of the usual pub offering of German, American or Australian beers, and when one suggested a Russian lager ('like ice'), others reacted well.

Since then the product had been tested quantitatively among a quota sample of 300 people. They had been shown a test advertisement and a variety of possible pack designs. Separate research had tested brand names on a random sample of 200 men. These surveys had given encouraging findings, convincing most in the company that the correct name and advertising was:

'Petersburg from Russia. Like Ice.'

Next came the pricing research, which was designed to show what price premium, if any, drinkers were prepared to pay for the distinction of a lager imported from 'St Petersburg, the Capital of Imperial Russia'.

The results showed the following:

Price per pint (in relation to main rivals)	Projected sales per year (50 pint barrels)
+ 20p	1,300,000
+ 12p	1,600,000
+ 6p	2,000,000
+ 2p	2,400,000
same	2,600,000

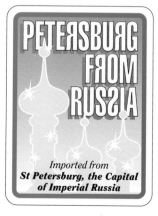

Imported from
**St Petersburg, the Capital
of Imperial Russia**

A bitter argument broke out among the five members of the development team. Some were convinced that a 6p premium was right, while others advocated the full 20p difference.

Another issue that remained to be resolved was how large an advertising budget to set. Most felt that £6 million would provide a sufficiently heavyweight T.V. campaign. Two of the team worried that this would take too large a chunk out of the £160 million sales anticipated (at pricing of + 12p). Certainly it was true that there were a lot of costs to cover, with production overheads of £20 million and variable costs of £70 per barrel. Decisions would have to be made in the near future.

Questions

(40 marks; 60 minutes)

1   Outline the factors that would affect a firm's choice of whether to use qualitative or quantitative research.   **(6)**

2   **a**   Distinguish between random and quota samples.   **(3)**

    b   What problems do market research firms face in obtaining accurate random samples?   **(5)**

3   **a**   Use the projected sales value of £160 million to calculate the selling price per pint of beer.   **(5)**

    b   Calculate whether a 6p price premium or a 20p premium would generate the higher revenue.   **(3)**

4   Calculate the break-even output and safety margin at a 6p price premium.   **(4)**

5   How might a firm make sales projections based on quantitative research findings?   **(6)**

6   Consider what other information the marketing team should examine before deciding what price to set.   **(8)**

4 THE COCA-COLA STORY

Concepts needed: Marketing strategy, Market research, Product life cycle

Coca-Cola was first sold on 8th May 1886 by a pharmacist called John Pemberton. He had devised the syrup as a headache remedy, but found that it mixed well with soda water. The first advertisement for the drink appeared in the *Atlanta Journal*: 'containing ... the wonderful Coca plant and Cola nuts'. The name proved memorable but Pemberton wanted a stylish trademark. He found it when his book-keeper wrote the brand name with a flourish in an accounts ledger. That script was registered as a trademark in 1893 and has been used ever since.

Yet it was not Pemberton who created the Coca-Cola business empire. In 1886 only nine drinks were sold per day at just 5 cents per glass. So he sold the name, the formula and the manufacturing equipment to a wealthy trader, Asa Candler, for $2,300. In 1892 Candler founded The Coca-Cola Company, and his capital plus his understanding of distribution ensured that the drink spread rapidly. Candler's marketing strategy was to sell the drink through soda fountains rather than through shops. So the syrup was transported in (red) barrels from Atlanta, and mixed with soda in a glass at the point of sale. By 1899 sales had progressed to 281,055 gallons.

Then came the real revolution. Two young lawyers saw the opportunity for Coca-Cola to be made more widely available by selling it in bottles. In 1899 they arranged to meet Candler and asked him for a bottling contract for the whole of the United States. To their surprise he agreed – and set a price of 1 dollar on the contract. This established the franchise structure that has operated throughout the world ever since. The Coca-Cola Company supplies a concentrated essence to bottling firms that turn it into syrup, add carbonated water, then bottle and distribute it. So the Atlanta head office is responsible only for producing and delivering the concentrate, and for marketing the brand. The new approach generated sales growth to 6,767,822 gallons by 1913.

6,000,000 drinks a day

The original 1899 bottle had no special shape or design. By 1913 the success of Coca-Cola encouraged many imitators to offer 'Cola Sola' or 'Pepsi Cola' in similar bottles. So the owners of the Coca-Cola bottling franchises contacted various glass manufacturers to hold a competition to design a distinctive new bottle. In 1916 the characteristic glass Coca-Cola bottle – still used today – was patented and launched. Sales pushed ahead still further, to 18.7 million gallons by 1919.

That year two other important events occurred. The Candler family sold the company for $25 million to a group led by Ernest Woodruff, whose son Bob became Coca-Cola's chief executive for the next 40 years. He was responsible for turning this soft drink into a world-wide symbol of the 'American Dream'. Helping him finance that was the other event of 1919 – the onset of Prohibition in the United States. For although it is remembered mainly for its encouragement of the illegal production and sale of alcohol, the law-abiding majority turned to soft drinks. Coca-Cola sales grew ever faster, and its distinctive name and bottle made it increasingly possible to sell it at a price premium.

Bob Woodruff's approach to leadership was to set standards and strategies, and to ensure that everyone knew they were being followed as firmly at the top as elsewhere in the organisation. He viewed the company as a force for good, not just a force for profit. For example he insisted that Coca-Cola delivery drivers 'must always set a good example in the way they drive'. He tried to give a sense of purpose, of mission, to all his employees, as can be seen in his three short 'commandments':

1   Absolute loyalty to the product and the Company.

2   All partners must earn a good salary.

3   Simplicity of the product (one drink, one bottle, one price).

If the third point is reminiscent of Henry Ford, the first two are more akin to the style of the Marks and the Sieff families at Marks and Spencer.

That third statement was stuck to until the 1950s. So for over 40 years Coca-Cola meant just one product. This narrow focus may have been important in the company's success, because the drive to diversify often attracts a firm's most talented executives, and much of its investment capital. Only when Pepsi gained market share during the 1950s as a result of the launch of a larger pack size did Coke allow itself to break its rule. From then on, The Coca-Cola Company redefined itself as a soft drinks company, which encouraged it to launch Fanta in 1960 and Sprite in 1961.

The 1960s might have seen the end of the apparently unstoppable rise of Coke. Not only was it a 70 year old product at a time when youth and experimentation were fashionable, but also the product had developed a rather staid, middle-aged image. The following advertising slogans show how this had come about:

'The friendliest club in the world'	1946
'For home and hospitality'	1951
'Refreshment through the years'	1951
'Sign of good taste'	1957
'Happy pause for the youth of all ages'	1958

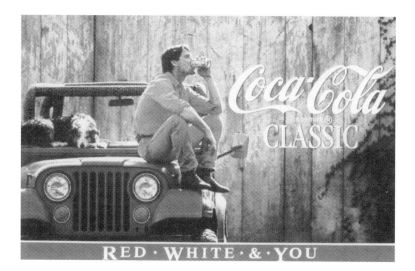

At the end of the 1950s Coca-Cola appointed a new, younger advertising agency. During the 1960s the marketing strategy became increasingly youth orientated. This not only meant new catchphrases such as 'Things go better with Coke', but also visual imagery became focused on young people having fun together.

By 1984 world-wide sales of The Coca-Cola Company were worth $7.4 billion (representing about 283 million cans per day). It was the biggest soft drinks producer in the world by a considerable margin. Yet its market share had slipped from 22.5% to 21.8%, while that of Pepsi had increased by 0.1%. Coke's new Chairman considered this a threat, especially as research showed that younger people were particularly prone to favour Pepsi. His worry was that he was presiding over the classic break within a product's life cycle between growth and decline. So a new formula drink was concocted, and then tested in great secrecy among a staggering 190,000 sample. The taste of the new Coke appeared to beat the old by 61% to 39%, so its launch was prepared.

In April 1985 it was announced to a horrified public that, after 99 years, Coke was to be relaunched with a 'Great new taste!' An immediate rush to try the new formula was followed by a barrage of criticism. Within a few days 'USA Today' published an opinion poll that showed 59% of consumers preferred the old Coca-Cola, 25% Pepsi, and only 13% the new Coke. The new was derided for being sweeter and less fizzy – 'like a Pepsi left open'. The outcry forced the company to backtrack, so on 10th July it announced that the old Coke would be reintroduced as Coca-Cola Classic.

Pepsi had gloated over Coke's original decision, as it appeared to confirm their long standing claim that in the 'Pepsi Taste Challenge' their product was preferred to Coke. Yet the whole episode proved more beneficial to Coke than Pepsi. The wave of nostalgia for 'the real thing' plus the publicity about the sweetness of both new Coke and Pepsi strengthened Coca-Cola's traditional image. By the end of 1985 Coke's share of the United States cola market had grown by four percentage points.

From 1886 to 1986 Coke's sales progress was almost uninterrupted. Health trends were met by low calorie or caffeine-free versions and changing consumer habits by family-sized bottles, multipacks, or automatic vending machines. The key to the firm's success has always been in the magic of its image, as captured in the two slogans: 'The real thing' and 'Coke is it!'. For just as Levi's are not just **a** pair of jeans, Coke is not just **a** cola. The brand name, the logo, its status as the original, and its distinctive bottle have all been woven into a decisive marketing advantage. An advantage that not only enables Coke to outsell other colas decisively, but also enables the Atlanta firm to charge a price premium. For profitability, Coke is it.

Sources: *'The chronicle of Coca-Cola'; The Conran Foundation: 'Coke!'; The Financial Times; 'Coca Cola Superstar': F.S. Palazzini*

'Coca-Cola' and 'Coke' are registered trade marks which identify the same product of The Coca-Cola Company.

Questions

(40 marks; 80 minutes)

1 How did Coca-Cola marketing strategy change over time and what were its consistent themes? **(10)**

2 Discuss the pros and cons of Woodruff's 3 'commandments'. **(10)**

3 By 1984, what was the approximate value of the world market for soft drinks? Do you think the company was right to be so concerned about its slippage in market share? **(10)**

4 Coca-Cola researched their 1980s Pepsi problem in an apparently scientific manner, yet consumer reactions were a complete surprise:

a Why may this have been so? **(5)**

b What further market research might have helped prevent this? **(5)**

5 ADDING VALUE TO SUGAR

Concepts needed: Added value, Company objectives, Marketing strategy

If you laid the 1,000 million lollipops per annum sold by Chupa Chups end to end, they would circle the globe four times. If the firm succeeds in its efforts to set up a joint venture in China, it will lay a claim to be the major lollipop multinational, as it already markets its products in 85 countries.

Chupa Chups is the life's work of a Catalan son of a pastry maker, Enrique Bernat. After working his way up to become the general manager of an overly-diversified food manufacturer, Bernat was given the opportunity to buy the business in 1955. He soon abandoned all the firm's product lines except one; he chose to specialise in lollipops. Given Spain's extreme poverty at that time, concentration on such a frivolous product was a bold step. The attraction, though, was the wide availability and cheapness of the only significant ingredient – sugar. This low input cost gave rise to the opportunity to achieve high added value, in other words a high margin between the cost of materials and the selling price. Lollipops had another financially based attraction – that year-round demand would enable continuous production to be used (chocolate, by contrast, was strongly biased away from the hot summers).

Bernat turned this financial opportunity into a marketing success by building up a highly rewarded, well motivated 400-strong sales force. This was vastly more powerful than that of the rival producers, and by 1960 Chupa was dominant. A later marketing director recalled:

> 'We were almost a monopoly ... so we created our own
> competition'

With the Spanish market saturated, Chupa looked for a way of adding more value to their modestly priced sweets. Bernat came up with an ideal way – providing a major customer benefit (fun) in a way that appeared to be difficult, and therefore expensive, to produce: lollipops that whistle. That 1962 development spawned various other, ever more musical versions. Bernat also commissioned Salvador Dali to design the distinctive wrappers that have been used ever since.

In the early 1970s, Bernat decided to take advantage of the Dictator Franco's slow opening up of the Spanish economy, by developing exports to the richer European countries. Under the brand name Melody Pops, the premium-priced lollipops became such a success that the company did not have enough plant to meet both Spanish and export demand. With long lead times on building a new factory, and caution about whether the novelty factor might make success short lived, Chupa had to choose between the home and export markets. Confident of their ability to win back the long-established home market, the managers chose to focus on exports. By the late 1970s, Chupa had to stop selling in Spain altogether.

Dozens of small competitors stepped in to supply the Spanish market – often with whistling products. For although Bernat had invented the idea, such an obvious, technically simple process cannot be patented. When extra capacity enabled Chupa to re-enter their home market, they found the going much tougher. Retailers who had been forced to buy from alternative suppliers were reluctant to return – especially while they still held stocks of the rival products. Another massive, highly expensive direct sales campaign was used to regain distribution. Through this, Chupa established a one third market share; well down on earlier levels, but enough to represent a real home base.

Those who meet Enrique Bernat report that – despite being well over 65 – he still talks with optimism about new, revolutionary ways of making ever-better lollipops. Such dedication to a single product flies in the face of text-book advice to diversify. Is his success because of this dedication or despite it?

Questions

(40 marks; 60 minutes)

1   What is added value? In what ways had Chupa attempted to benefit from it?   (8)
    What, if anything, limits a firm's ability to add ever more value to its products?   (6)

2   Chupa was short of production capacity for three years during the mid-to-late 1970s.
    How might they have tackled this problem other than in the way they did?   (8)

3   Chupa re-entered the Spanish market by using a massive direct sales campaign.
    What other methods could have been used?   (6)

4   Discuss the advisability of diversifying for a small firm.   (12)

EVEN LEVI'S CAN MAKE MISTAKES

Concepts needed: Market research, Marketing model

During the 1980s, Levi's US division was looking at ways of diversifying away from its heavy dependence on a jeans market that appeared to be saturated. They had already introduced Levi's shoes, shirts and socks, which sold quite well among people who were already buying Levi jeans. Now they wanted to move into the market for higher priced clothes, in order to attract a new type of customer to the Levi Strauss brand. As menswear had always been their biggest seller, it was decided to concentrate on the male market first.

To decide how to meet this objective, a market research company was commissioned to investigate mens' purchasing habits and attitudes to clothes (a Usage and Attitudes study). A large quantitative survey was conducted among a quota sample of 2,000 men who had recently spent at least $50 on clothing. When analysed, the survey revealed that the entire menswear market could be segmented into five types of buyer:

- Type 1 **Traditionalist** (probably over 45; department store shopper; buys polyester suits and slacks; shops with wife)
- Type 2 **Classic Independent** ('a real clothes horse'; 21% of market, yet buying 46% of wool blend suits; buys at independent stores; expensive tastes)
- Type 3 **Utilitarian** (wears jeans for work and play; 26% of the market; Levi loyalists)
- Type 4 **Trendy Casual** (buying 'designer', high fashion clothes; might buy 501s, but usually considers Levi too mass-market; 19% of the market)
- Type 5 **Price Shopper** (buys whatever and wherever the lowest prices are found; no potential for Levi; 14% of market)

As the Type 2 Classic Independent men fitted in with Levi's objective, the research company was asked to computer analyse the findings so that the behaviour and attitudes of this specific group could be split out from the rest of the sample. The large total number of interviews made it possible to have confidence in the reliability of the data from this sub-sample. It emerged that Type 2 men wanted traditionally styled, perhaps pinstriped, suits; that they liked to buy through independent clothes shops or tailors, rather than at department stores; and that they liked to shop alone, whereas others liked having their wife/girlfriend with them.

To tackle this segment of the market, Levi's decided to introduce 'Tailored Classics', a range of high quality wool

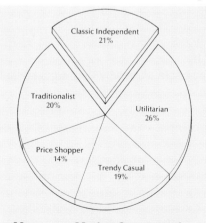

Menswear Market Segmentation

suits, trousers and jackets. The research showed that these buyers valued quality and fit rather than low prices, so they decided to price their range 10% above that of the competition. To avoid direct product comparisons – and to ensure that not too large a salesforce was needed – Levi chose to distribute through department store chains.

Having decided on this strategy, its acceptability to the target market was tested via a series of group discussions. These were conducted by a psychologist who was to look for the real motivations behind respondents' opinions or behaviour. The psychologist reported that the Type 2 men had two misgivings: first, they were concerned that the garments would be in standard fittings, and so would not provide the tailoring they wanted; second, although they could believe that Levi's could make a good suit, they still felt uncomfortable about the Levi's name. One said:

> *'When I think Levi I think jeans. If they're making suits I have to be convinced.'*

Another felt that:

> *'If I went to work and someone said: "Hey, that's a good suit, Joe, who's it by?" I wouldn't feel comfortable saying Levi.'*

The company's marketing executives responded to this by deciding to concentrate on the separate jackets and trousers in the launch advertising, and let suits 'slipstream'. The Director of Consumer Marketing felt certain that:

> *'The thing that's going to overcome Levi's image for casualness as no other thing can, is a suit that's made by Levi that doesn't look like all the other things we've made. Once that gets on the racks people will put an asterisk on the image that says: "Oh, and they can also make a good suit when they put their mind to it".'*

Soon after this decision, salesmen started contacting retail buyers. After four months of selling to the trade, it was clear that the range's sales targets would not be met. Even a price cut did little to redeem the situation, and Tailored Classics achieved only 65% of its modest sales targets.

Levi's could only find consolation if they could learn why they went so badly wrong.

Sources: *Channel 4: 'Commercial Breaks'; The Financial Times*

Questions

(45 marks; 80 minutes)

1 Distinguish between quantitative and qualitative research. **(4)**

2 Analyse the messages within the research findings that Levi's management appeared to ignore or underestimate. **(8)**

3 For what reasons may Levi have used a quota rather than a random sample? **(5)**
What factors might influence the size of sample you choose for a quantitative survey? **(5)**

4 a In constructing the pie chart shown, how many degrees within the circle should be given to the Type 2 segment? **(3)**

b The US menswear market was then worth $4,000 million. If Levi had achieved a 10% share of the Type 2 segment, what sales value would this have represented (show workings)? **(4)**

5 Discuss the decision-making process Levi used in terms of the marketing model. How well did they use it? **(8)**

6 Market research could be thought to be like an insurance policy; you pay a premium in advance to eliminate your risk of making a heavy loss. Consider the value of this statement. **(8)**

7 LET THE BUYER BEWARE

Concepts needed: Break-even, Market research, Marketing strategy, Contribution

It had all happened by chance. Melanie had been moaning to a friend about the problems of running her small design company. The friend knew of another woman (Cathy) who was thinking of selling a business. So they arranged to meet.

Cathy started the firm seven years ago, by finding a manufacturer who could mass-produce her design of baby and toddler footwear. In her first year the turnover was only £7,342 but retailers seemed to like her products, so she kept going. Two thousand pounds was spent on display stands at the Junior Fashion Fair at Olympia in the following two years, and orders began to pour in. Stockists soon included shops such as Bentalls, Children's World, and many independent babywear outlets.

By the fourth year, the Babyboots range of products had expanded to four size bands (0-6 months; 6-12 months; 12-18 months; and 18-24 months), and within each band were eight different colours, four different linings, and four different fabrics. The range has not really altered since. That year, sales were £78,780 and Cathy was making a £13,000 profit even after paying herself a small salary. Given that she did little more than take orders, pack them, carry them to the Post Office, and then phone the factory for new supplies, this was good money. Her office was (and is) a small room at the back of her house, and the stockroom the house's basement.

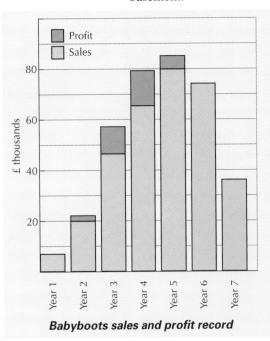

Babyboots sales and profit record

Early in the fifth year, though, Cathy had a baby and began to find it hard to find the time and energy to keep the business going. 'I realise now that I should have sold it then', she told Melanie.

Over the two years since the baby, Cathy has done nothing active to market her products. She has relied on existing customers, plus three agents who sell her goods on commission. Two operate in the South-East footwear trade on a 5% commission, but provide very little business. The third is in Scotland, and sells to chemist shops for an 8% commission. This man sold £10,000 of Babyboots last year – more than the six Bentalls department stores.

Now Melanie is trying to decide if she should make an offer for the Babyboots business, and if so, for how much? In making up her mind, she has to decide what she would do to revitalise it. For 'the books' reveal that sales slumped from £74,000 to

£35,900 in the latest year. Cathy maintains that this is a temporary result of her neglect, but could it be due to factors that would have longer term implications?

Melanie's questioning reveals that Babyboots not only have competition from a British firm (Padders), but also from Korean suppliers who sell at half the price charged by the two British rivals.

The attempt to find out more financial details is hampered by the fact that no full accounts have been prepared for this year or last. Nevertheless, the information below gives a lot of useful data – all provided willingly by Cathy. She also explains that she buys from her manufacturer at £1.55, spends three pence per display bag, and charges her customers for postage. The list price of Babyboots is £2.05, though half her customers are paying an average price of £1.95 (this includes the agents' commission).

Babyboots Sales And Profit History

	Latest Year	Year 6	Year 5	Year 4	Year 3	Year 2	Year 1
Sales £000	36	74	85	79	57	22	7
Contribution £000	–	–	20	23	17	6.5	2
Gross profit margin %	–	–	23.7	29.3	29.6	29.4	29.0
Overheads £000	–	–	15	9.3	6.4	4.4	2.4
Profit £000	–	–	5	13.7	10.6	2.1	– 0.4

Questions
(40 marks; 70 minutes)

1   List four further questions you would want to ask Cathy, if it was your money at stake. Explain the reason for each one. **(8)**

2   Outline three pieces of research you might carry out independently of Cathy in order to help to decide the potential for Babyboots (remember we are talking about your money, so don't consider massive, expensive surveys). **(6)**

3   a   Melanie estimates that she would keep Babyboots' overheads down to £8,000 per year. Using this and the other information provided, draw a break-even chart for Melanie's first year. **(8)**

    b   Use it to estimate the likely profit or loss in her first year, if she manages to halt the decline in sales, and to let her know the sales revenue she will need to break-even. **(4)**

4   Outline two marketing strategies that might boost profit in the coming year. Explain which you favour most and why. **(6)**

5   If the asking price was £12,000, would you buy the business? Outline your reasons. **(8)**

8

AVOIDING A PRICE WAR

Concepts needed: *Contribution, Profit, Price elasticity*

The Altrincham Petrol Company Limited (APC) has a prime site on a junction on the main road to Manchester. It is expensive to rent (£1,400 a week), but the Managing Director has no doubts about the site's value. At a retail price of £1.70 per gallon, this one outlet has averaged a customer every two minutes of its 18 hour day. The average customer buys eight gallons of petrol, and spends 60 pence on other goods. The garage is open for 350 days a year.

The firm buys its petrol from Shell on the following terms:

Up to 1 million gallons per annum	**£1,550 per 1000** gallons
1 to 1.25 million gallons per annum	**£1,520 per 1000** gallons
1.25 to 1.5 million gallons per annum	**£1,500 per 1000** gallons
Over 1.5 million gallons per annum	**£1,480 per 1000** gallons

Other goods sold in the garage shop have an average unit cost of 45 pence.

Of course, the firm has other overhead costs to pay for. Salaries and wages amount to £800 per week, maintenance costs £300 per week, and other bills (including electricity and rates) to £700 per week. (Assume a fifty week year.) The only other cost is that of marketing. The various promotions that Shell run cost the firm about six pence per gallon.

Now the firm faces a real dilemma. A new, very modern Jet station has opened up on the other side of the junction, and it is offering its petrol at £1.60 per gallon. In the week since it opened, trade at APC has fallen by 30%, and the Managing Director suspects that APC has traded at a loss during this week. It had been APC's intention to use the profits generated by the Altrincham garage to finance the start-up costs of a second site on the other side of Manchester. The firm already had £100,000 saved for this – and only needed another £60,000. Now, the Managing Director thought gloomily, it would never happen.

So what should they do? One option was to carry on as they were. The second was to cut their price to £1.64, which the Managing Director believed would restrict their volume loss to 10%. Or, more radically, keep their price at £1.70, and use their savings to refit the shop to turn it into an 8-till-late Spar outlet. That,

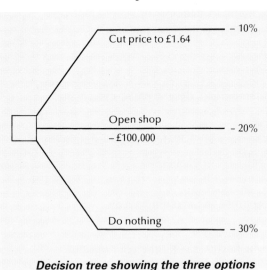

Decision tree showing the three options

Cut price to £1.64 — – 10%

Open shop
– £100,000 — – 20%

Do nothing — – 30%

he hoped, would cut the reduction in customers to 20%, and would also boost non-petrol sales to £2.00 per customer (at a unit cost of £1.50).

Questions

(40 marks: 80 minutes)

1 Explain the management's main objective, and the main constraint upon their ability to meet it. **(3)**

2 Calculate the profitability of the firm before the recent change in competition. Approximately how many months would it have taken them to raise the rest of the finance they wanted? **(10)**

3 From the evidence provided, attempt to calculate the price elasticity of the Altrincham Petrol Company's product. Show your method clearly, as there is more than one way of doing this. **(6)**

4 Calculate the three alternative strategies outlined by the Managing Director. Assuming that all costs must be accounted for fully within the first year, which strategy appears to be the most profitable? **(15)**

5 Explain how the Managing Director might test the accuracy of his estimates. **(6)**

9
HÄAGEN-DAZS UK –
A CLASSIC PRODUCT LAUNCH

Concepts needed: Market research, Distribution, Pricing strategy, Advertising ethics

In 1989, in a strategic decision to move into the fast food business, the British firm Grand Metropolitan bought up Pillsbury, the American owners of Burger King and other food brands. It is said that Grand Metropolitan only 'discovered' Häagen-Dazs after they had bought it. No time was lost, however, in developing its potential in the British market.

As a catalyst to consumer awareness of the brand, a lavishly appointed Häagen-Dazs outlet was established at London's Leicester Square in mid-1989. Long queues quickly became the norm, despite price levels 50% higher than other ice cream parlours. This was testimony to the quality of the product and proved that a gap existed in the market for a super-premium brand. Yet might it only be a market for lavish treats when out for the evening, or was there a wider, retail market opportunity? And if so, how could it best be exploited? These were questions for an advertising agency to answer.

After talking to several different agencies, Häagen-Dazs UK decided upon Bartle, Bogle and Hegarty (BBH), best known for the Levi 501s advertising. The agency's brief was to help Häagen-Dazs create a new 'gold standard' and become the ultimate ice cream in the market. At the time a premium sector existed in which Loseley and New England were the most prestigious and expensive brands. Häagen-Dazs UK decided to open up a new super-premium sector, with ice cream priced at £2.99 per half litre. This was three to four times the price of standard dairy ice cream and 50% higher than its two closest competitors.

The first task was to provide the background research upon which long-term, strategic decisions could be based. A large-scale survey showed that the target market for premium ice cream sold through retail outlets was 25–44 year olds with high disposable income but without children. These became the criteria for selecting the sample for the group discussions that followed.

These groups of six to eight men and women were prompted into discussion by each being given a half-litre tub of Häagen-Dazs Vanilla to eat as they talked. The interviewees were asked when and where they could imagine consuming the product. Usually the answer was eating it alone, as a reward or as a 'dream-like' compensation for a bad day or date. The big step forward came, however, as the group leader asked when they might share their Häagen-Dazs. Customers talked of sharing a spoon with their partner, feeding each other, and of 'mellowing out' together in front of their favourite video. Products such as Cadbury's Flake had long portrayed themselves as a self-indulgence. Häagen-Dazs now had a unique way of advertising a food product: as a sensual pleasure to be shared.

The research provided the material for BBH's account planner to write the creative brief. From this the creative department would be able to consider how best to advertise the product. It was decided that the brief should be met by the use of press media rather than television. For not only is television an expensive way of reaching affluent adults, it also lacks the subtlety of mood that BBH wanted. So the agency's media department was asked to plan a campaign aimed at affluent adults in their moments of relaxation. This led to spaces being bought in the weekend colour supplements and womens consumer press.

Meanwhile, a parallel survey had been researching into the suitability of the American pack design within the British market. In a large-scale quantitative survey consumers found the pack significantly different to other ice-cream brands. Group discussions showed that once people tried the ice cream they could identify with the package as authentic high quality. So the company and the agency decided to leave the imported packs unchanged.

On Sunday July 21st 1991 the first advertisement appeared – one of four black and white photographs that juxtaposed product messages with sensual imagery, with the slogan 'dedicated to pleasure'. The launch advertising burst lasted eight weeks and cost a little over £300,000. A further three-week campaign before Christmas took the year's spending to £450,000.

From the start, editorial coverage of the launch was considerable. Much of it represented marvellous free public relations. Some of the newspaper reporting focused upon the ethics of advertising ice cream through sexy images. Did it exploit women? Did it meet the Advertising Standards Authority yardstick of 'Legal, Decent, Honest and Truthful'? Whatever the answers, sales kept rising.

The financial impact of the advertising was dramatic, with sales doubling between June and July 1991. In 1991 as a whole, sales were five times their 1990 level. Häagen-Dazs went from a 2% share of the £50 million premium ice cream market in October 1990 to 22% by October 1991.

The diagram below relates the launch advertising bursts to Häagen-Dazs sales to retailers.

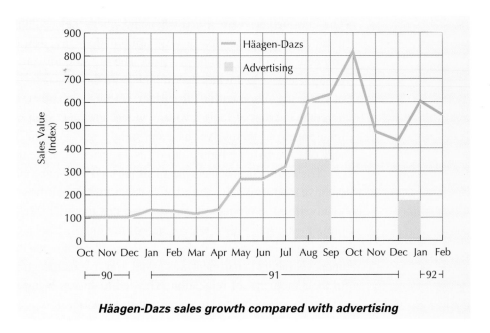

Häagen-Dazs sales growth compared with advertising

This achievement relied not only upon the advertising, but also on offering millions of product samples. Also crucial was the distribution drive started up by the Häagen-Dazs sales team. In April 1991 Häagen-Dazs was stocked in shops selling less than 20% of London's ice cream; by July this distribution level had risen to over 40%.

An innovative feature of the distribution strategy came from the earlier group discussions. Mentions of sharing Häagen-Dazs in front of a favourite film encouraged the sales team to supply refrigerated cabinets to Blockbuster Video. This proved so successful that, during one week, Häagen-Dazs was second only to *Terminator 1* as Blockbuster's biggest money-spinner. During the sales drive, some supermarket chains had turned Häagen-Dazs down, refusing to believe that their customers would buy such an expensive product. Once the advertising campaign had started, however, the same stores phoned up asking for the product. Clearly the distribution growth was both a cause and an effect of the rising demand.

Most important of all, in judging the effectiveness of the launch marketing strategy, was that sales and distribution not only went up but stayed up. Many products are highly sensitive to changes in marketing spending, with sales jumping up but then falling back once the advertising campaign or special offer has ended.

The marketing triumph of Häagen-Dazs was that customer loyalty built up so quickly. In America it had taken twenty years to achieve what Häagen-Dazs UK managed in two.

The Marketing Society voted Häagen-Dazs the 'New Product of the Year'.

Sources: *Biss Lancaster; Häagen-Dazs Report by Nick Kendall at BBH; Häagen-Dazs UK.*

Questions
(50 marks; 90 minutes)

1 How important was the role of market research in the success of Häagen-Dazs? **(10)**

2 Assess the strengths and weaknesses of the price level decided on by Häagen-Dazs UK. **(8)**

3 a Interpret the information provided by the graph within the text. **(6)**

  b The graph compares sales with advertising. Explain what other factors should be taken into account before drawing conclusions about the effect of the advertising upon sales. **(8)**

4 a What might be the key factors determining the level of brand loyalty enjoyed by a product? **(5)**

  b What benefits could Häagen-Dazs derive from high brand loyalty? **(5)**

5 Discuss whether it is ethical to promote an ice cream through sexy advertising. **(8)**

10 THE PRODUCT PORTFOLIO PROBLEM

Concepts needed: Market share, Asset-led marketing, Boston matrix

Streamer has dominated the British cider market for over fifty years. Its Sparrowhawk and Target brands have been national best-sellers for decades. The company benefited from customer loyalty, plus the inertia of the pubs, clubs and off-licences that kept on buying Streamer brands because they always had done. Up until last year Streamer held over 50% of the cider market.

The big change began two years ago, when the Chancellor of the Exchequer reduced the tax rate for cider in the Budget. With beer tax levels held constant, customers started to switch to cider. Streamer passed the tax reduction on to customers by cutting its prices, in order to boost sales volumes. A smaller rival used a different strategy, however. Devon Cider chose to develop extra strength ciders with a distinctive image, priced at the same level as equivalent beers. The extra profit margin (from the lower tax rates) was used to pay for extensive advertising. So 'Silver Light' and 'Red Streak' became household names through a blaze of television commercials. With gross profit margins four times higher than Streamer's brands, Devon Cider became a highly profitable company.

Streamer's first response had been to dismiss Devon's new brands as a minor irrelevance. However, both products appealed to the young women who had always been the main consumers of Sparrowhawk, so Streamer had to act. To the surprise of outsiders, the company's first action was to dismiss its Marketing Director. The successor immediately set to work developing a distinctive, bottled cider called 'Clear Rain' and also a more modern product to launch on draught in pubs and clubs. The latter would make the most of Streamer's distribution strengths.

Launched six months later, the draught 'Scrumpy Star' proved a great success. Its stylish advertising and fresh taste made it fashionable, and its higher price made it more profitable than Streamer's older products. The bottled product started equally well, but faltered after a large amount of product trial failed to be converted into repeat purchase. Streamer put more advertising money behind it, to try to strengthen its image, but once the campaign stopped sales fell back disappointingly.

This problem was becoming increasingly evident just as the time was looming for Streamer's annual marketing strategy review. This year, the Board decided to trim the marketing budget to £3.8 million. This would not be enough to support each of the four brands adequately, so the strategy team would have to decide how best to split up the money.

APPENDIX: *Quarterly figures for average cider sales per month (thousand barrels, seasonally adjusted)*

Period	Streamer's Brands				Devon Cider Total	Total Cider Market
	Sparrowhawk	Target	Scrumpy Star	Clear Rain		
1st Quarter 2 years ago	120	170	–	–	130	560
2nd Quarter 2 years ago	126	175	–	–	130	574
3rd Quarter 2 years ago	135	183	–	–	131	596
4th Quarter 2 years ago	137	186	–	–	138	613
1st Quarter 1 year ago	131	188	–	–	154	640
2nd Quarter 1 year ago	129	189	–	8	168	655
3rd Quarter 1 year ago	124	189	–	17	168	661
4th Quarter 1 year ago	110	182	22	24	171	670
1st Quarter this year	106	180	38	19	177	686

Questions

(40 marks; 70 minutes)

1 Identify the use made by the cider companies of each of the following marketing concepts:

   a product differentiation

   b value added. **(8)**

2 Many marketing textbooks suggest that 'asset-led marketing' is usually the most successful strategy for a firm to adopt. What does this phrase mean? What evidence is there of its importance in this case? **(8)**

3 Calculate the percentage market share for each of the Streamer brands plus the Devon Cider company for the 1st quarter two years ago, 1st quarter one year ago and 1st quarter this year. Construct a diagram on graph paper to show the main trends involved. **(14)**

4 Use the Boston Matrix to analyse Streamer's product portfolio in order to make recommendations about how the budget should be divided. **(10)**

11 MARKETING RESEARCH

Concepts needed: Marketing strategy, New product development, Market research

After preliminary market research, the Dundee Chocolate Company (DCC) decided to proceed with development of two new product ideas which the development team knew as 'Crunchieflake' and 'CoolMint' Chocolate. Samples of each were produced and blind taste tests conducted among 200 chocolate eaters.

The best of the three versions of Crunchieflake was very much liked. Sixty percent of trialists claimed they would want to buy it regularly. The most successful CoolMint Chocolate product achieved half that score. Tasters complained about the thinness of the texture and taste. However, DCC's Research & Development department were confident this problem could be overcome.

Packaging and brand names were researched next. Three versions of each were chosen by the New Product Development Manager from a range of ideas put forward by DCC's advertising agency. The three were then tested quantitatively. The results were conclusive for the CoolMint Chocolate bar, but there was some room for argument about the meaning of the Crunchieflake findings, listed below:

Research findings on Crunchieflake

	Brand Name			Packaging		
	A	B	C	X	Y	Z
Like very much	15%	22%	10%	8%	30%	21%
Quite like	38%	27%	19%	21%	25%	43%
Indifferent	28%	26%	45%	39%	33%	31%
Dislike	19%	25%	26%	32%	12%	5%

Sample: 100 regular buyers of chocolate bars

Although the management team could not decide which brand name or product to use for Crunchieflake, the research programme continued. The key survey contained questions designed to enable market share (and therefore sales) forecasts to be made. One question asked about the likelihood of product trial. Then, after the interviewee had been given a sample bar to eat, each was asked about the likelihood of regular purchasing.

The results were:

Research findings for sales forecasting

	CoolMint		Crunchieflake	
	Trial	Regular	Trial	Regular
Definitely will	36%	10%	54%	10%
Very likely to	27%	22%	26%	28%
Quite likely to	17%	29%	10%	26%
Unlikely to	8%	22%	6%	21%
Very unlikely	12%	17%	4%	15%

Sample: 200 regular buyers of chocolate bars.

The New Product Development Manager also believed that five other pieces of information had to be taken into account:

1 Solid chocolate bar sales amount to £350 million per annum. The last new brand launch achieved 'definitely try' and 'definitely regular purchasing' research ratings of 28% and 10% respectively. It now sells £6 million per year.

2 Sales of direct competitors to Crunchieflake total £480 million per annum. Wispa was the last successful newcomer, and its research results of 78%/18% turned into sales of £72 million per annum.

3 The launch of Crunchieflake would be bound to spark off a fierce round of price-cutting on Crunchie, Aero, Flake and any others determined to avoid losing market share.

4 The sales force believe CoolMint will be stocked in 90% of outlets, while Crunchieflake will only be accepted by 82%.

5 Either launch would require a national marketing budget of £8 million, so only one can be afforded from this year's total budget.

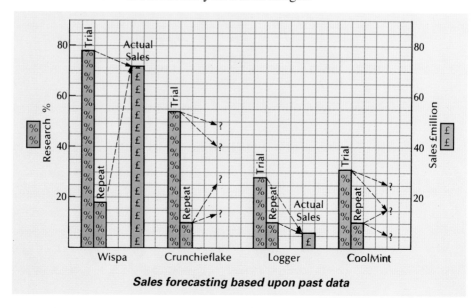

Sales forecasting based upon past data

Questions

(40 marks; 70 minutes)

1 What 'room for argument' was there about the meaning and significance of the research findings on the three test names and pack designs for Crunchieflake? **(8)**

2 To forecast sales, the researchers asked about likely trial and likely repeat purchasing. Why was that considered necessary? And what other lines of questioning would have been useful in devising a marketing strategy? **(8)**

3 Estimate the likely sales revenue for each of the products on the basis of the information available. Show your reasoning. **(8)**

4 Explain which you would recommend launching and why. **(8)**

5 The entire product testing and market research programme ended up costing DCC £1.2 million. How can such extravagance be justified? **(8)**

12 PRICE ELASTICITY AND PROFITS

Concepts needed: Price elasticity, Fixed costs per unit, Contribution, Profit

The success of the low-calorie chocolate sector amazed everyone in the industry. It had started so weakly, with a 100-calorie bar with whipped nougat filling, topped with rice and covered in milk chocolate. Produced by a small firm from Finland, it received good distribution from a curious retail trade, but achieved less than a 0.5% **market share**. When one of the biscuit companies managed a successful launch, however, the three dominant chocolate firms (Mars, Cadbury's, and Rowntree/ Nestlé) felt they had to protect their 90% market share.

In the first year after the three major firms launched their low-calorie chocolate bars, supply shortages kept prices high. Then, a series of new product launches made the marketplace increasingly competitive. One firm found that whereas a 2 pence price increase from 40 pence in the first year had cut demand by only 1%, eighteen months later a similar price rise on a 40 pence brand called 'Lo' led to a sales reduction from 50,000 units a week to 45,000. Given that its variable costs were 10 pence per unit, and fixed costs were £13,000 per week, this had quite a serious impact on the brand's profits.

In this new phase, the producers realised they had to look to improve their profitability by cutting costs rather than increasing prices. With low enough costs, they might even be able to increase profits by cutting their prices. Because **contribution** was already so high, most producers started by looking at ways of cutting their fixed and **semi-variable costs**. Only one decided to tackle variable costs first, on the grounds that:

> *'As fixed costs don't change, it must make sense to look for cuts from the variables.'*

The Finnish originator of the market sector found that its sales had slipped back sharply. Its new Managing Director was alarmed to find that its average total cost per unit was now 4 pence higher than its average selling price, leading to a £4,000 loss per week on its 100,000 units sales. When a Marketing Manager came with a proposal to double sales by improving distribution, he spluttered:

> *'Don't be ridiculous; that'll just double our losses!'*

Questions
(40 marks; 60 minutes)

1   Explain the meaning of the following terms (emboldened in the text):

      market share

      contribution

      semi-variable costs.   **(6)**

2   What actions could be taken to reduce fixed costs in such a way that sales are not affected?   **(6)**

3   Outline three factors that could lead to an increase in the average price elasticity of products within a particular market sector.   **(9)**

4   **a**   Calculate the price elasticity of the chocolate in the first year and compare it with that of the brand called 'Lo'.   **(5)**

    b   Work out precisely the serious impact on Lo's profits.   **(6)**

5   Analyse the comments made by the producer and the Finnish Managing Director.   **(8)**

THE MARKETING PLAN

Concepts needed: Setting up a marketing budget, Marketing plan, Market penetration

The launch of the low interest rate Visa card had been a great success. Rarely had a new financial product from a small bank caused such a stir. All the newspapers covered the story and it even received a mention on BBC TV News. The media story was simple: if Brooklyn Bank could offer a credit card charging an annual interest rate of 10%, why were the big banks charging 20%? Many suspected that it was a case of **market penetration** by the Brooklyn Bank and that the interest rate would rise later on. The company assured its customers that this was not so.

Three months after the launch, with the £120,000 advertising campaign completed, Bill Stein – the UK Banking Director – conducted a review. His sales target had been for 100,000 customers, a modest share of the 16 million credit cardholders in Britain. In the event 320,000 people contacted Brooklyn for an application form; half were converted into customers. Their rate of usage of the card enabled him to estimate a gross profit of £20 per customer per year.

One week before, he had commissioned a report from his data processing section to analyse all the customer application forms. This provided a full demographic breakdown – valuable material to help construct a marketing plan for the next two years.

Extracts from breakdown of customer demographics

Age breakdown		Social class (occupation)	
Category	%	Category	%
18 – 24	3	AB	40
25 – 34	23	C1	38
35 – 44	38	C2	18
45 – 54	24	DE	4
55+	12		

Bill's first task was to clarify his objectives. Brooklyn had started up in the UK with one branch to service American customers in the City of London. The successful launch of the Visa card provided a foothold among ordinary British consumers. This enabled him to consider two types of goal:

1 customer targets for the Visa card, such as 250,000 within two years;
2 targets for developing new products for the customer list built up by the Visa card, such as selling pension plans.

After discussion with his marketing manager and advertising agency, a decision was made to concentrate on the Visa card for the coming year, then develop new products the year after. This would prevent his limited staff resources being spread too thinly, and should ensure continuation of the successful start made by the credit card. He was able, therefore, to produce this brief statement of Brooklyn's marketing objective for the coming year:

'To gain 5,000 new customers per month, with minimal losses of existing customers, in order to achieve an average of 190,000 customers during the coming year.'

Having identified the objective, Bill next worked out his marketing budget. His American parent company's rule-of-thumb was that marketing expenditure should be set at 10% of the expected annual gross profit. A quick calculation persuaded him that he could not afford television advertising, so he decided to focus upon upmarket (broadsheet) newspapers.

Before further planning, Bill had to tackle a classic problem of advertising strategy: should he focus upon coverage or repetition? With a limited budget, if he used all the broadsheet dailies and Sundays he could afford no more than one advertisement every two months. By only advertising in *The Daily Telegraph* he could cover some 42% of the target market once a week for a whole year. After much thought, he decided that his product's **Unique Selling Point** (USP) was so strong as to make repetition less important than coverage.

Bill's final major decision concerned distribution. Should he be relying solely on advertising plus word of mouth to bring in new customers, or would it be wise to get a distribution outlet such as Independent Financial Advisors (IFAs) and accountants, or building societies too small to have their own credit card? He spent a week taking IFAs and building society bosses out to lunch. This convinced him of the enthusiasm of these potential distributors, but also made it clear that their commissions would take half the gross profit margin on the cards they sold. In addition, they would expect Brooklyn to provide the brochures and **point-of-sale** display materials to encourage consumer interest.

Questions

(40 marks; 70 minutes)

1 Explain the meaning of the terms emboldened in the text: market penetration
unique selling point
point-of-sale. **(6)**

2 Outline the importance to a business of obtaining a full demographic breakdown of its customers. **(6)**

3 What should be Brooklyn Bank UK's marketing budget for the coming year? (State your assumptions.) **(8)**

4 Prepare a sales and marketing plan for the Brooklyn Visa card for the coming six months, based on the evidence in the case. You will need to explain your decisions about how to proceed in the footnotes to your plan. The plan should show your sales targets, distribution plans, advertising bursts and below-the-line activity. **(20)**

14 DISPUTE OVER MARKETING STRATEGY

Concepts needed: Contribution, Marketing strategy, Distribution, Weighted averages, Market segmentation

Green's of Glasgow has been a producer of soft drinks for 150 years. Although it is Britain's third largest supplier, it has just six per cent of the U.K. market. For years, its market share held steady as the market size expanded rapidly, but now the management feel concerned. For the past 18 months its sales have been static while the market has been forging ahead. Six per cent of a £4,000 million market is worth having, but if its market share had not slipped Green's would now be enjoying £80 million more sales revenue.

The situation has led to a fierce dispute between Green's new Marketing Director, Ray Carr, and their long established Sales Director, James Day. Ray Carr believes that the distribution deal that, two years ago, brought about a merger of Schweppes interests with those of Coca-Cola is the root cause of their problem. He feels that the market power of this combine means that firms like Green's must pull out of the mass, branded sector of the market. Instead, they should concentrate on niches such as sporty-image drinks, and on their old-established minority brands such as the regional top-seller 'Spark'. The Sales Director, however, argues that it is crucial that mass market brands such as Green's Lemonade should be supported fully, as he believes that retailers are only interested in stocking a supplier with a full range of products. In other words the success of Spark relies on Lemonade and vice versa.

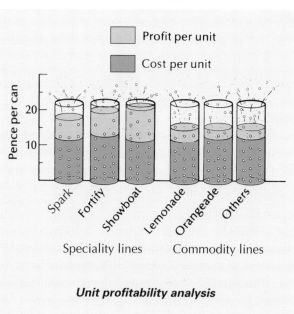

Unit profitability analysis

Ray Carr's case is built on a detailed analysis he carried out with Green's management accountant into the profitability of each canned product line offered by the firm (shown left and overleaf).

The dispute between them comes to a head when the Brand Strategy report is being compiled for the new financial year. At a preliminary meeting, other executives are horrified to find how bitter and personal the argument has become. It comes to the attention of the Managing Director, who calls both in and demands that each set out their recommendations on paper, with a view to testing which works more successfully in the marketplace. Further public discussion on the matter is banned.

Brand Profitability Analysis (cans only)

Product name	Factory gate price per unit	Cost per unit	Profit	Sales volume (million units per month)
SPECIALITY LINES				
Spark	19p	12.5p	6.5p	8
Fortify	20p	13.5p	6.5p	3
Showboat	21p	12.0p	9.0p	3
COMMODITY LINES				
Lemonade	15.3p	11.8p	3.5p	14
Orangeade	15.3p	12.3p	3.0p	6
Other mass market	15.5p	13.0p	2.5p	8
TOTAL			4.4p	42

James decides to use Ray's figures to his own advantage. He knows that the cost per unit figures include direct factory overheads; and that the canned drinks division is required to contribute £1.4 million per month to the company's distribution, sales and administrative overheads. Therefore he can produce a Contribution statement with and without the Commodity product lines. He hopes that this will go a long way towards convincing the Managing Director of his case. Yet he must not just prove Ray wrong, he also needs a plan for stabilising or even rebuilding the firm's market share. In private discussion with his area sales managers he finds out that distribution levels are slipping (see Appendix A). Apparently this is because retailers find that few people ask for Green's products by name, so they are able to save valuable shelf space by destocking them.

This leads James to believe that a twin strategy is needed:

■ Cut unit price to retailers by 0.5 pence per can while leaving recommended retail prices intact.

■ Double Green's advertising budget to £2 million, as Ray says that; 'I read while I was in the US that 7UP's advertising elasticity is 0.2, and a 20% sales increase would suit us beautifully.'

Ray's approach is typically scientific. He produces graphs showing the last few years' sales performance for each of their brands. He also hires a specialist market research agency to conduct in-depth interviews among a dozen of the country's main soft drink retail Buying Managers. The questioning reveals that the Buyers are very pessimistic about the future for firms like Green's. Indeed the Buying Manager for Sainsbury's mentions them by name as a firm that 'will probably not be around in five years'. The Buyers also reveal that they are far more interested in stocking highly differentiated products than in me-toos or weakly branded lines. So Ray is reassured of the wisdom of his strategy of concentrating sales, distribution, advertising, and new product development resources on Speciality brands.

Armed with the evidence he has collected, each sees the Managing Director for forty minutes to present his case. James leaves with a confident smile, while Ray's face betrays his concern at the boss's last remark to him:

> 'Even if concentrating on Speciality brands is right for the long term, we've still got to survive the next year or so. Your plan seems to assume that our shareholders will tolerate low profits for the 18 months or so it will take to implement. In these days of takeover mania, we probably would not survive.'

Despite the latter comment, the Managing Director asks each man to write a report detailing their objectives, their recommended strategy, and how they would use test marketing to give a realistic assessment of the impact on profitability of the actions they propose.

APPENDIX A: Green's % Volume Distribution Data

	During last 6 months	6–12 months ago	12–24 months ago	24–36 months ago
Spark % shop distribution	82%	84%	84%	87%
Lemonade % shop distribution	46%	49%	54%	56%
Any Green's product % distribution	89%	90%	91%	94%

Questions
(60 marks; 90 minutes)

1 **a** Distinguish between market size and market share. Why is it important for firms to discover this information, instead of just relying on their own sales figures? **(6)**

   b What has Green's percentage market share fallen from? **(4)**

   c The figure given for the total profit per unit is a weighted average of the data given (rounded to 1 decimal place). The mean average is 5.2 pence. Demonstrate how the weighted average figure has been arrived at, and explain how it differs from a mean average. **(10)**

2 Explain the meaning and the justification for each component of James's proposed strategy. **(10)**

3 Provide the Contribution statement that James requires to prove his point. **(10)**

4 Assume that you are Ray; write his Report to the Managing Director. **(20)**

15

BOMBAY PIZZA

Concepts needed: Cash flow forecasts, Depreciation, Profit

It was when Sunil Tanna's daughter went out with a group of Indian friends for a pizza that it struck him. In his business trips to Bombay he had never seen a pizza outlet there. If Indian teenagers liked pizza in Birmingham, why not in Bombay?

Three weeks later, while making a January visit to India for his air conditioning company, he stayed on for an extra couple of days' 'holiday'. He quickly confirmed that there was no pizza outlet in the Bombay telephone directory and spent the rest of his time researching the prices of comparable fast foods, wage rates, locations and the availability of ingredients. Sunil considered the £400 it cost as money well spent.

The following month he identified a British supplier of pizza dough-making machines and conveyor-belt ovens (which cook the pizza in three minutes and ensure that the pizza cannot burn). In total this capital equipment would cost £12,800 on delivery in Bombay, though transport charges plus Indian import tariffs would push this up to £18,000. His month's expenses were £200.

In March Sunil paid a professional chef £2,400 to devise eight pizza recipes suitable for Bombay (four vegetarian). In each case the chef drew up cards that set out precisely the method of preparation and cooking. Sunil would have to hire a good manager to run the first outlet, but he did not want to have to find (or fly out) an experienced pizza cook.

Luck did not provide a further business trip to India, so he had to pay for his own flight to Bombay to acquire a site in a busy, middle class area of the city. His strategy was to pitch his pizza prices at around Western levels, making the decor Chicago/Italian-American, using the brand name Al Capone's Pizza. This would cash in on Indian awareness of Hollywood gangster films. The site he chose required an initial payment amounting to £800, plus £200 a month rent starting immediately. All in, Sunil's April travel expenses came to £1,600.

While in Bombay in April, Sunil arranged for the design and refitting of the site to turn it into a Chicago pizza restaurant. This was completed during May at a cost of £8,000. He also hired a manager whose salary of £600 per annum commenced at the start of June. The manager immediately hired staff at the following monthly rates:

cook : £25*

2 waitresses : £15 each

delivery driver : £10

cleaner : £5

Once a delivery motorbike had been bought for £200 in early June, everything was in place for the start of the staff training programme. Unfortunately a combination of supplier and Customs delays meant that the pizza machinery only turned up in July. It was installed, tested, and did not work. It emerged that it needed a power adaptor which was ordered from England. That added £400 to the cost of the machinery, which was now due to be paid.

At last, in August, everything was ready and with £500 spent on local advertising, Al Capone's Pizza opened to a large, curious crowd. The average customer spend proved to be £5 at a cost of sales of £2. This would need to cover the monthly overheads of £680 plus the rent and wages of £320 per month.

Monthly customer figures

August	1,600
September	1,200
October	1,100
November	900
December	800
January	900
February	1,000
March	1,200
April and onwards, a monthly average of 1,200	

* Although the wage rates in this case seem incredibly low, they are exactly as researched by the real Mr Tanna.

Questions

(40 marks; 70 minutes)

1 Construct a cash flow forecast for the first twelve months of the business, that is from January–December. State any assumptions you consider necessary. **(15)**

2 On the assumption that the machinery is depreciated on a five year straight line basis, and the decorations on a 50% declining balance, calculate the profit before interest and tax during the first trading year, in other words from August–July. **(10)**

3 a How do you think that Mr Tanna developed his business next? **(8)**

   b What problems may he face in the near future? **(7)**

16

CONSTRUCTING A BUSINESS PLAN

Concepts needed: Cash flow forecasts, Profit and Loss, Balance sheets

Fresh from Poly, Karen could not wait to put her Business Studies theory into practice. Careful saving during her sandwich work year, plus a £5,000 legacy, meant that she had the £10,000 she thought necessary as equity capital. The work year had been at Thomson Holidays and that – plus her love of travel – convinced her to start up a Travel Agency. Not just any one, mind, for she believed a market gap existed for Adventure Travel in her home city of Birmingham. She had been taught to make decisions on the basis of evidence, not hunch, so she had tested out and validated her hypothesis over the past two years by visiting every one of the 140 Agencies listed in Birmingham's Yellow Pages.

Now Karen had to prepare the documentation for the Business Plan to persuade her bank to lend her the extra fixed and working capital she would need. The keys to this, she knew, were a credible Sales Forecast, a Cash Flow Forecast, a Projected Profit and Loss Account for the first six months, and an estimated six months' Balance Sheet. To forecast sales she visited comparable Agencies in London, relying on her charm and the lack of threat of competition to persuade someone to volunteer their early sales performance. Two days of being charming yielded the information given overleaf. Karen decided that averaging the figures for all three firms would give her a realistic sales forecast.

The main start-up costs were estimated by her as follows:

Purchase of 5 year lease on shop	£2,500
Fixtures and fittings (to last 4 years)	£6,000
Advertising prior to launch	£3,500

The advertising would be treated as revenue expenditure, and therefore charged in full against the Profit and Loss account for the first trading period. All the start-up costs would be paid before the start of trading, i.e. in month zero. Fixed assets would be depreciated on a straight-line basis.

Running costs would include the 90% payment of revenue to the tour operator (as Travel Agents work on a 10% commission), plus overheads amounting to £800 a month. The 90% would be paid to the tour operator in the month after being received from customers. Overheads start in month 0 and must be paid in the month they are incurred.

Sales Revenue Data For The First Year's Operation Of Three Adventure Travel Agencies

	Adventure Hols Streatham	Go-Go Travel Hampstead	Action Vacs Acton	Average of all 3
Month **1**	£2,400	£5,800	£800	**£3,000**
Month **2**	£3,400	£8,200	£2,500	**£4,700**
Month **3**	£5,800	£12,200	£4,800	**£7,600**
Month **4**	£6,400	£16,800	£6,200	**£9,800**
Month **5**	£7,200	£19,100	£7,300	**£11,200**
Month **6**	£7,400	£20,700	£7,900	**£12,000**
Months **7–12** monthly average	£8,000	£23,000	£9,500	**£13,500**

Questions
(50 marks; 90 minutes)

1 Explain the meaning of:

Equity Capital
Fixed Capital
Working Capital **(6)**

2 a Construct a cash flow forecast for months 0-6 on the basis of the above, assuming that the bank is prepared to grant a £3,000 medium-term loan (ignore interest charges). **(10)**

b What level of overdraft facility appears to be needed (if any)? **(1)**

c Outline 2 alternative methods of raising business finance that Karen might consider. **(4)**

3 Draw up a Profit and Loss Account for the period up to the end of month 6. Then use it, plus the other information available, to forecast the firm's Balance Sheet for the last day of this first trading period. **(20)**

4 Discuss whether Karen should go ahead with the enterprise. **(9)**

17

WORKING CAPITAL

Concepts needed: Working capital, Capital employed

Tracey and Neil were sure they had a winning idea on their hands. A laptop computer linked by radio waves with a head office computer. Their prototype machine worked beautifully, and some preliminary market research showed that there were many keen buyers. They had also worked out how to mass produce it cost-effectively.

The next stage was to get the finance to set up production and to launch the product. Tracey had calculated that £1.8 million would be needed for **fixed capital** (i.e. money used to buy fixed and long term assets such as machinery). More problematic was calculating the **working capital** that would be needed. Eventually, profits would provide the source of working capital. Until sales began, however, raw material stocks, wages, and many other day-to-day expenses would have to be financed by borrowings of some kind.

Both went to visit their bank manager. She was very interested, and seemed very eager to help, until she found out more about the cost estimates in the start-up period. 'You say you want £500,000 of working capital on top of the £1.8 million of fixed capital. But are you sure it will be enough? More new businesses fail through under-estimating working capital needs than for any other reason.'

So Tracey explained her estimate:

> 'I think we will need £50,000 of raw material stocks – all paid for in cash – before production starts. Production will eventually be able to turn out finished products in four hours, but in this early period we must allow one month of slow, careful testing of each part of the production. So work-in-progress (including stocks and wages) will add £120,000. After that, production will be in full swing, but the two month credit period required by our clients means we will have to fund two months of our full production costs of £150,000 per month.'

At that point, Neil butted in:

> 'In other words we expect to use £470,000 of working capital in the first few months (£50,000 plus £120,000 plus two lots of £150,000). In addition, we think we ought to have some spare resources in case something goes wrong, which is why we want an extra £30,000 of cash. So our total request is for £500,000 of working capital available, of which we plan to use £470,000.'

The bank manager smiled. She said:

> 'I think that to allow yourselves the cushion of just £30,000 of spare

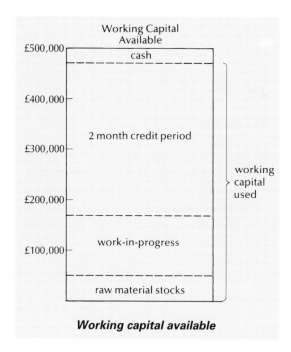

Working capital available

capital is rather risky. I'll tell you what I'll do. I will get my assistant to look at your research results more fully, and to see the magic machine at work. If he's satisfied, we will put together a finance package consisting of share and loan capital to cover the £2.3 million you have asked for.

In addition, though, I will give you an overdraft facility of £150,000. This will not increase your own working capital available, but it will enable you to buy more materials if you need to. I know it sounds daft, but it will enable you to use up to £150,000 more than your balance sheet will tell you there is available. Your own resources would allow you to spend up to £500,000 on stocks and work-in-progress. With this overdraft you can actually spend another £150,000 on top. Of course, you should try your best to restrict the amount of working capital you use, because if you have to dip into the overdraft, the interest charges will eat into your profits.'

'And if we manage to keep our working capital usage below even the £470,000 mark?' asked Neil.

'Then you earn interest at the bank, and boost your profit.'

Tracey and Neil nodded at each other, thanked the manager and left.

Questions

(30 marks; 60 minutes)

1 Distinguish between fixed capital and working capital (emboldened in the text). **(3)**

2 For what reasons might working capital requirements be higher than expected in a new business? **(8)**

3 Use the text to help demonstrate that:

working capital available = current assets – current liabilities
and working capital used = stocks + debtors – creditors. **(6)**

4 How can an overdraft increase a firm's spending power yet not increase its available working capital? **(5)**

5 Accountants have long suggested that the wise firm keeps a high working capital available while minimising working capital usage. What is the logic of this? **(8)**

BUDGETING IN HARROGATE

Concepts needed: Budgeting, Variance statements

Cleeton is a long established family firm based in Harrogate, Yorkshire. Its production of ropes and cables began in 1863 and has changed little since then. The only striking change in recent years has been the appointment of a young Finance Director, given the task of masterminding a steady increase in the firm's profitability.

Last December he brought in a new computerised budgeting system to provide managers with a monthly print-out of actual, compared with forecast, revenues and costs. At the same time, he encouraged the Sales Director to introduce a more flexible pricing policy, allowing sales representatives to offer discounts in order to get business.

Now, in April, he is reviewing his initiatives at the monthly Board meeting:

'Our policy changes have been working very well. Sales are up, market share is up and profits are up... Our new budgeting system has been especially successful, encouraging staff to keep costs down (though variable costs, I am delighted to say, have been pushed up by our buoyant sales level). With the economy of our major export market, Germany, so strong at the moment, the future looks very bright.'

Other Board members, still unfamiliar with the format of the budgeting spreadsheet, could only nod their approval.

Budget and variance statement – Cleeton Ltd.

	*								
	All figures in £000s								
	January			February			March		
	B*	A	V	B	A	V	B	A	V
Sales revenue	80	92	12	100	110	10	120	122	#
Materials	40	48	(8)	50	57	(7)	60	63	#
Other direct costs	10	12	(2)	13	15	(2)	15	17	#
Overheads	20	21	(1)	24	24	–	27	24	#
Profit	10	11	1	13	14	1	18	#	#
Year to date	10	11	1	23	25	2	41	#	#
Last year		5			20			40	

***B** = Budget   **A** = Actual   **V** = Variance

Questions

(35 marks; 60 minutes)

1 What benefits might Cleeton hope to receive from implementing a budgeting system such as the one in the table above? **(8)**

2 Identify and explain the profit variance for January given that sales volume was 15% above budget. **(7)**

3 Calculate the March figures omitted by a computer error. Instead of the numbers, the computer has printed a # symbol. **(8)**

4 To what extent does Cleeton's performance this year justify the Finance Director's statement to his Board of Directors? **(12)**

INVESTMENT DECISION-MAKING

Concepts needed: Average rate of return, Pay-back

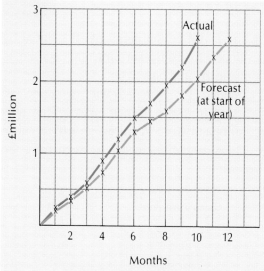

**Zentek cumulative sales revenue
Forecasted and actual**

Zentek had enjoyed a splendid financial year. At the start they had budgeted for £2.6 million of sales turnover and £1.8 million of direct costs. With £0.4 million of forecast indirect costs they would have produced a £400,000 profit. In fact, with ten months of the year completed the Managing Director had just found out that they had already met their sales targets, and she now expected the end of year profits would approach £600,000. This was especially pleasing as she knew that a Japanese competitor's first British plant would be opening within a few months, so it would be useful to have some extra funds in the kitty.

When chatting to the Finance Director about the profit forecast, she also learned that there was still £80,000 left in the capital expenditure budget for this financial year. So a memo was sent to all department heads inviting proposals for the investment of this sum.

The first bid was from the distribution department, which proposed buying four new, fuel efficient lorries as replacements for eight-year-old ones. Each would cost £20,000 and should last four years, after which time they would have a second hand value of £4,000. The new lorries should save £8,000 each per year on fuel and maintenance costs.

The only other detailed proposal came from the marketing department, requesting the establishment of a new customer services department. It would cost £80,000 to set up, and its £20,000-a-year running costs should generate extra contribution from sales amounting to:

Year 1 £20,000   Year 2 £40,000   Year 3 £80,000   Year 4 £80,000

As the year is running out, a speedy decision is needed, so the Managing Director has asked the Finance Director to write a report for tomorrow's senior management meeting.

Questions

(30 marks; 45 minutes)

Taking the role of the Finance Director, write a report to the Managing Director covering:

a Which investment is more attractive on financial/numerate grounds alone.

b Any further information you would like from each department to help you make a final recommendation.

Mark allocation: **a** 16 marks   **b** 10 marks   report format 4 marks

CREDIT FACTORING

Concepts needed: Factoring, Cash flow

SiteCo is a site investigation company. It is hired by property developers to test the soil structure on a site, to see if it is suitable to build on.

The firm started five years ago with two directors/ engineers working from one of their houses. They now employ six staff and have acquired an office and a laboratory. Their development can be seen from the following record:

	Sales Turnover £	Profit £
Year 1	16,835	174
Year 2	27,348	5,336
Year 3	82,488	1,536
Year 4	142,540	16,102
Year 5	251,310	44,531

Although delighted with their recent progress, the Directors were frustrated that they could not generate enough cash to buy the equipment they needed to cope with their expansion. So, for example, they had to subcontract sulphate testing, which was expensive and time-consuming, as an average of four trips were needed per week to the outside lab. At present the testing was costing them £175 per week. This would be cut to £25 per week if they could find the £6,000 needed to buy the machine. However, this was just one among many pieces of capital expenditure that seem pressing, and it had to join the queue.

All rapidly growing firms have a strained cash flow position, but the particular cause of SiteCo's difficulties was the Directors' inefficiency with paperwork. Both enjoyed the testing work, and the relationship with their customers, but neither liked dealing with administration or the job of chasing late payers. So the busier they were, the more reasons they found for not processing the paperwork. As a result, the last time they checked they were owed £60,000 by customers.

Now, rather than going to their bank manager to ask for their overdraft limit to be increased, they called in a management consultant. After a few days of investigation, she concluded that there was no point in looking for a solution that would have to be implemented by the current staff. Nor could she believe that the appointment of a Credit Controller would be worth the expense, as it would still be essential for the Directors to cooperate fully with the administrative system. Hence her recommendation that SiteCo should use the Credit Factoring service of one of the major banks. She suggested that they should use the full service, including 80% of invoiced amounts paid within 24 hours; sales invoice management and analysis; debt collection; and insurance against bad debts. This service would result in a charge amounting to 5% of sales turnover.

Both Directors loved the idea of someone else being responsible for debt collection, especially as their business was so dependent on good relationships with clients. Yet the cost did concern them, so they needed to be convinced that the cash flow benefit would be large enough to enable them to make several of the cost-saving investments they had planned.

Based on their sales forecast of £360,000 in the coming year, and on their current three month lag between invoicing and receiving payment, the consultant made a back-of-the-envelope calculation. She estimated an immediate cash benefit of £72,000, being whittled down to £54,000 in the following twelve months. That reassured the Directors fully, so after the bank had made the necessary checks into SiteCo and its customers, the new system became operational. Within a month both Directors were convinced that it was a great success.

Question
(30 marks; 45 minutes)

1. On the basis of the information given, how many weeks would it take for the purchase of the sulphate testing machine to pay for itself? **(4)**

2. Why do 'all rapidly growing firms have a strained cash flow position'? **(4)**

3. Outline three ways in which SiteCo's Directors might benefit from using the service of sales invoice management and analysis. **(6)**

4. Attempt to reproduce the management consultant's 'back-of-the-envelope' calculation of the cash generated by factoring. **(5)**

5. Identify and explain three types of firm that would probably not find factoring worthwhile. **(6)**

6. Analyse the effects upon the cash flow of a firm of a decision to stop using the services of a Factor. **(5)**

21

THE STING

Concepts needed: *Published accounts, Financial ratios, Overheads,*
Working capital

Sadaf bought the shares after seeing the company featured on *The Clothes Show*. She had wanted to invest part of the £4,000 inherited from her grandfather, and this company seemed just right. Brilliant clothes designers with shops in all the major high streets, Sting Plc was now expanding into Europe. At only 40p each, Sadaf considered the shares a bargain; she bought 2,000.

As the economies of Europe picked up during the spring, Sadaf felt increasingly confident about her investment. When the share price hit 56p in July, she was tempted to sell and enjoy a 40% profit.

Then in August the share price dropped back unexpectedly. Two days later the Chairman issued the following profit warning:

> '*Poorer than expected trading in Britain plus a disappointing first season*
> *in Europe has led to a profit downturn. I remain convinced that our move*
> *into Europe will be in the long term interests of your company. Full*
> *details will be available in the interim accounts, to be published within*
> *two weeks.'*

By the time the accounts arrived in the post, Sting shares were quoted at just 18p. Sadaf wondered whether to sell while her investment still had some value. So she looked at the accounts with great interest. Did the company's finances look strong enough to survive a period of poor trading, while still expanding into Europe?

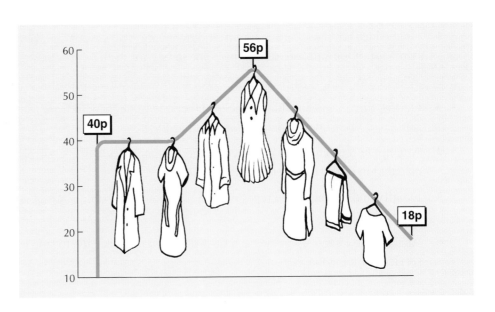

Interim Accounts for Sting PLC, Jan – Jun (unaudited)

Profit and loss account

	£m
Sales turnover	34
Cost of sales	26
GROSS PROFIT	8
Overheads	10
TRADING PROFIT	(2)
Taxation	3
NET PROFIT	(5)
Dividends	1
RETAINED PROFIT	(6)

Note: Issued share capital of 50 million 10p shares

Balance sheet (June 30th)

	£m
Property	16
Machinery	4
Vehicles	4
Stock	6.5
Debtors	4.5
Cash	1
Current liabilities	11
Working capital	1
ASSETS EMPLOYED	25
Loans	15
Shareholders funds	10
CAPITAL EMPLOYED	25

Questions

(40 marks; 70 minutes)

1 What might Sadaf conclude about the short term financial health of Sting Plc from these accounts? **(7)**

2 A recent newspaper article mentioned that Benetton's stock turnover was about twelve times per year. What does this suggest about Sting's management of its working capital? **(5)**

3 The Chairman's statement that accompanied the accounts said that: 'We intend to conduct a vigorous exercise in overhead reduction'. Give examples of items that might be affected, and outline the possible effects on the firm of the proposed cuts. **(8)**

4 a What dividend yield is Sadaf receiving on the sum she invested? **(3)**

b What real rate of return does that represent, given the current rate of inflation? **(3)**

5 Why may Sting Plc be continuing to pay a dividend even though it is making operating losses? What risks does this action carry? **(8)**

6 For what reasons might Sadaf's reliance on these accounts prove ill-founded? **(6)**

22

PUBLISHING CONFESSIONS

Concepts needed: Profit, Break-even, NPV

Barbara Macfarlane's first book (*Confessions*) had been such a success that her publishers could not wait for the next. Book reviewers had written dismissively of its 'raw potboiler' style, but its serialisation on satellite television had helped push sales to 200,000 in its first year. As her royalty had been set at 10% of the £5 cover price, Barbara was delighted with her financial rewards. The publisher's profits were also substantial, as can be discovered from the breakdown below.

Now Barbara had to negotiate the contract for her second book. She had already sent an outline of its plot to five major publishers, and all were interested. All had offered her royalties above the 10% mark, and several had also offered to pay a substantial advance. As she expected this book to take her a year to write, and it would be six months after that before the book was on sale, without an advance she would have a long time to wait.

She narrowed the offers down to just two – her existing publisher and an even bigger paperback house. The former proposed a 14% royalty with a £20,000 advance on signing the contract (i.e. now) and a further £20,000 once the script had been handed over. These advances would be deducted from her share of the initial sales revenue, so Barbara would only be paid royalties after her book had earned her the first £40,000 worth.

The other publisher offered 12%, with a £25,000 advance on delivery of the script. This seemed less attractive, but as they intended to charge £6 per copy instead of £5 it might prove more profitable for Barbara. Especially as they expected to sell almost the same number of copies as their rivals.

Cost Breakdown On 'Confessions'

One-off costs		
(Investment outlay)	Artwork	£2,800
	Proofreading	£1,000
	Typesetting	£8,200
	Editor's time	£8,000
	Launch publicity	£40,000
Running costs	Printing cost	£0.80 per copy
Delivery		£0.20 per copy
Overheads		£2,500 per month

Barbara had to make a decision on the basis of this information. Fortunately, she could remember from school that she should discount the cash flows involved. An old textbook told her that at the 8% interest rates being offered by the banks, the relevant discount factors would be:

Now	1.0
In 1 year	0.93
In 2 years	0.86
In 3 years	0.80
In 4 years	0.74

Publishers' Sales Forecasts

	Current publisher	New publisher
Within 1 year of receiving script:	80,000 copies	108,000 copies
2nd year	140,000 copies	120,000 copies
3rd year	80,000 copies	70,000 copies

Questions
(30 marks; 60 minutes)

1 Draw a chart to show the break-even point and the first twelve months' profit made by *Confessions*. State the break-even sales volume and the profit. Assume one-off costs are added to year one fixed costs. **(10)**

2 a Calculate the Net Present Value of the discounted cash flows on each publisher's proposal. (Remember that the book takes a year to write.) State which one Barbara should choose on the basis of your calculations. **(12)**

b Discuss any other factors Barbara should take into account before making up her mind. **(8)**

23 INVESTMENT WITHIN FINANCIAL CONSTRAINTS

Concepts needed: Published accounts, Financial ratios, Investment appraisal

ScanCo is a medium sized producer of X-ray machines. Last year its sales were £4.5 million at a gross margin of 60%. It expects sales growth of £0.5 million per year for the coming five years, with gross and net margins staying constant.

ScanCo's Research and Development manager has just come up with a new product idea for a portable scanner that will require an investment outlay of £400,000. Each machine will cost £4,000 to make and will be priced at a 100% mark-up on direct costs. It will be ready for launch at the start of next year. Forecast sales and overheads are given below:

Year	Sales forecast (units)	Forecast overheads (£000s)
Next year	150	600
1 year later	250	700
2 years later	250	750
3 years later	250	750

The target market for the new X-ray scanner is the oil industry, to check the accuracy of pipeline welds. The Research and Development manager decided on the sales forecast after discussion with an expert on North Sea oil technology.

ScanCo's Directors must decide whether to approve the £400,000 investment at their next Board meeting.

APPENDIX A

ScanCo balance Sheet Dec 31st

	£000
Fixed assets	1,900
Stock	450
Debtors & cash	150
Current liabilities	700
Net current assets	(100)
ASSETS EMPLOYED	1,800
Loans	720
Shareholders' funds	1,080
CAPITAL EMPLOYED	1,800

APPENDIX B

Discount factors

	4%	6%
Year 1	0.96	0.94
Year 2	0.92	0.89
Year 3	0.89	0.84
Year 4	0.86	0.79
Year 5	0.82	0.75

	8%	10%
Year 1	0.93	0.91
Year 2	0.86	0.83
Year 3	0.79	0.75
Year 4	0.74	0.68
Year 5	0.68	0.62

Questions
(40 marks; 60 minutes)

1 Explain the meaning of the following terms:

overheads

fixed assets

shareholders funds (6)

2 a Given that ScanCo's overheads were £1.8 million, what was the firm's profit and trading profit margin last year? (4)

b Comment on the firm's return on capital last year. (5)

3 a Use two appropriate investment appraisal techniques to analyse the Research and Development manager's proposal (stating any necessary assumptions). What would you recommend purely on the basis of the numerate data available? (15)

b Discuss what other factors the firm should consider before making a decision. (10)

24

THE MINI-MERGER

Concepts needed: Business organisations, Profit and Loss, Balance sheets

Jay Bhatt and Jason Alexander were, at one time, sole traders – both operating in sheet metal works. They had known each other for several years and worked at their similar trades at different locations. They eventually decided to pool their resources and knowledge, and work under one roof. They considered going into Partnership, but on advice from their accountants, and bank managers decided to form a Private Limited Company instead.

As they had similar machines, they sold off the outdated and retained the modern. This enabled them to handle double the work for half the overheads per unit.

However, their situation proved to have its difficulties:

1   Mr. Bhatt had to move his business from South Norwood to Battersea. Many of his staff were unhappy with having to travel long distances in London traffic and decided to leave.

2   Personality clashes arose between Mr. Bhatt and the staff who used to work for Mr. Alexander. There was also a lack of cooperation between the staff from the two old businesses. This problem became very clear when Mr. Bhatt demanded that every effort should be made to squeeze more credit from suppliers and give less to customers; only after months of argument did he succeed in impressing this on all the staff.

3   It became evident that Bhatt and Alexander had different objectives for the company. Mr. Bhatt wanted to maximise profits because he still had a young family to cater for and a large mortgage to pay off. Mr. Alexander's main concerns, though, were to be able to share the decision-making, and to have regular holidays with his wife. All his children had left home, so his need for profit and income was far less.

4   At present, due to lack of time, both react to crisis rather than plan ahead. They have tried, unsuccessfully, to find a manager to take over the day-to-day problems.

On a brighter note, business is good and demand for their services and skills seems endless. The progress in this, the firm's second year, can be seen in the accompanying accounts.

APPENDIX A: Profit and Loss account

Last year			This year	
£	£		£	£
302,500		**Sales**		355,640
		Cost of sales		
	108,700	Purchases	128,900	
	15,380	Machine hire	14,520	
	61,450	Salaries	64,000	
	16,800	Vehicle running costs	19,800	
	39,200	Casual labour	34,720	
241,530				261,940
+7,800		Change in value of stock		+12,000
68,770		GROSS PROFIT		105,700
		LESS: **Overheads**		
	26,000	Directors' fees	36,200	
	21,400	Rent and rates	24,500	
	5,800	Depreciation	7,800	
	10,400	Promotion/sales	13,450	
	11,350	Other expenses	12,800	
74,950				94,750
− 6,180		NET PROFIT (Pre tax)		10,950

APPENDIX B: Balance sheet (as at year end):

Last year			This year	
£	£		£	£
27,870		**Fixed Assets**		38,200
		Current Assets		
	53,200	Debtors	41,800	
	35,500	Stock	47,500	
	250	Cash	6,400	
	88,950		95,700	
		LESS: C. Liabilities		
	31,400	Creditors	43,900	
	11,600	Overdraft	−	
	43,000		43,900	
45,950				51,800
73,820		ASSETS EMPLOYED		90,000
	−	Loans	4,800	
	80,000	Share Capital	80,000	
	− 6,180	Reserves	5,200	
73,820		CAPITAL EMPLOYED		90,000

Questions

(35 marks; 70 minutes)

1 What problems might have arisen in the separate businesses to provoke the decision for Mr. Bhatt and Mr. Alexander to merge? **(6)**

2 Consider why their advisors thought it wiser to form a Private Limited Company rather than a Partnership. **(6)**

3 Analyse the connections between the second and third difficulties. **(6)**

4 At the end of last year, the firm had £250 of cash and an £11,600 overdraft. By the end of this year, the overdraft had been paid off, and £6,400 was in their bank account. So there had been a net improvement of £17,750 in the firm's cash position. Use the balance sheet to explain the causes of this improvement. **(9)**

5 From the Profit and Loss account, identify the main reasons for the improved profit performance this year. **(8)**

25

TOO GOOD TO BE TRUE

Concepts needed: Published accounts, Gearing, Business plan

In the eight years between 1983 and 1991 the share price of High Tide rose 2,900% making fortunes for the early investors. The company had been founded in 1979 by Steve Dray and Frank Thomas, quickly becoming a leading producer of self-assembly conservatories. Through the 1980s High Tide became a stock market darling, famous for its rapid rise in annual earnings per share. It even managed to keep profits rising during the recessionary years of 1990 and 1991. Yet by 1993 fame turned to notoriety for poor accounting practices, allowing the *Financial Times* to repeat an old stock market cliché: '*If a thing looks too good to be true, it probably is*'.

High Tide's troubles became public when, in late 1992, it announced accounting problems at a subsidiary. Two months later a follow-up statement warned that 1992 profits would be significantly below 1991. Further warnings followed, pushing the share price lower and lower. Eventually the company's large institutional shareholders (such as pension funds) forced the firm to appoint a new senior management team.

By September 1993 the new Finance Director and Chairman were able to quantify and comment on previous management mistakes. Accounting changes meant High Tide declared a pre-tax loss of £36.4 million for the half year to July 1993. This compared with an equivalent figure for 1992 that had, at the time, been stated as an £18.4 million profit. Now the 1992 total was recalculated at £8.2 million, changing the profit figure by £10 million at the stroke of a pen. The group, previously believed to have a positive net cash position, also revealed debts of £34.9 million, giving a gearing level of 39%.

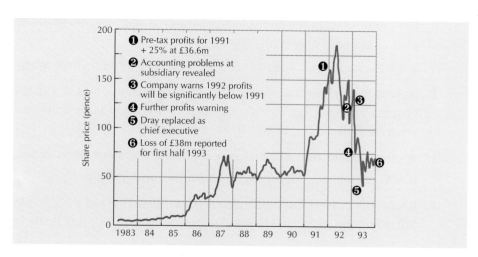

The new Finance Director described the previous accounting practices as 'very aggressive'. For example, to mask poor trading in 1992, sales were being booked early towards the end of the financial year. In other words goods that would normally have been delivered in August or even September were being rushed to customers in July. This distorted the 1992 figures for the six months to July, making sales and therefore profits look higher than they really were.

There were two underlying causes of the difficulties. One was that 'Senior management did not want to recognise that the recession had happened' and imposed unrealistic targets on the line managers. It was as if High Tide could not bear to lose its status as a super-growth company. So the managers felt forced to produce high 'profits' to meet their targets and keep their jobs.

The second cause was an expensive diversification into the start-up of two businesses in 1992, Victorian Greenhouses and Edwardian Doors. A total of £46 million was invested in Victorian Greenhouses alone, yet the two operations lost over £6 million in the first half of 1993. The new Chairman was especially scathing that his predecessors had permitted these businesses 'to commence trading without the benefit of definitive business plans, and without an adequate appreciation of the technical, production and marketing issues surrounding their early development.'

In September 1993 several of the former Board directors were encouraged to resign, including the founder Mr Dray. The firm's auditor was also replaced. The new Finance Director said that the auditor's performance 'was not perfect but they were not responsible for the worst things'. As with many fallen 1980s star performers, High Tide's self belief led it to push its accounting systems beyond prudence towards optimism or worse; its auditors proved unable to protect the company from itself.

Source: *The Financial Times; The Guardian.*

Questions
40 marks; 70 minutes

1 High Tide's experience shows that company accounts cannot always be relied on.

  a In what ways may accounts mislead the user? **(6)**

  b What are the pressures on companies that may result in misleading accounts? **(6)**

2 Approximately how much money would have been lost by a shareholder who bought £5,000 of High Tide shares when the 1991 profits were declared, and sold when Mr Dray was replaced? Show your workings. **(5)**

3 a What would you expect a business plan for a new operation to contain? **(5)**

  b What problems might result from starting up without one? **(8)**

4 It was only in 1993 that it became clear that High Tide had a gearing level of 39%. What does this mean, and how might the company reduce this figure in future? **(10)**

26 THE SOFABED SAGA

Concepts needed: Profit margins, Asset turnover, Return on Capital

The Sofabed Company Chief Executive was examining her firm's accounts in comparison with those of her nearest rival, SofaSogood. She found that margins were similar, but her return on capital (ROC) was markedly worse: 21% compared with 30%.

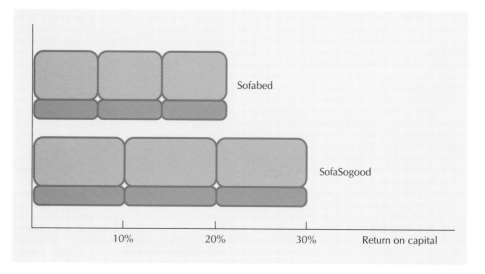

This was a worry because the current economic downturn made it likely that future trading conditions would be poor, so the weaker of the two might be forced out of business. The subject came up at the next Board meeting, where the Finance Director and the Sales Director put forward alternative methods for boosting the ROC.

The Finance Director spoke first: 'At present our net margins are 14%, which is only 1% below those of SofaSogood. So our real problem is asset turnover. I propose that we negotiate a sale and leaseback on our head office. That will bring in £400,000 that we can use to pay off some of our long term loans. Our assets employed will be cut by 25%, boosting our asset turnover and therefore our ROC.'

The Sales Director replied: 'Paying off our debts may be sensible, but I am more concerned about our margins. Two years ago they were 17%, last year 14%. What of the coming year, given the recession? Our sales staff are under constant pressure to give bigger discounts to customers. If they give an extra 7% discount our margins will be halved! So my proposal is that we should boost our advertising spending with a highly distinctive campaign, in order to make demand for our products less price sensitive. That should protect our share of this falling market.'

The Finance Director was unimpressed with this argument from Sales, as it: 'Just holds gross margins up at the expense of net margins.'

Eventually the Chief Executive decided on a third option: to open up a sixth outlet in rented premises in a different town. It would use stock from existing outlets, the same distribution lorries, advertising budget and office staff. Therefore 'our assets can be made to work much harder'.

Questions
(30 marks; 40 minutes)

1 Calculate the asset turnover ratio for:

   a The Sofabed Company

   b SofaSogood. **(6)**

2 Explain the logic behind saying:

   a 'If they give an extra 7% discount our margins will be halved.' **(3)**

   b 'Just holding gross margins up at the expense of net margins.' **(4)**

3 Outline two weaknesses of the Finance Director's approach. **(6)**

4 a Discuss how well the Chief Executive is making use of the concept of asset turnover. **(5)**

   b Assuming her plan works, and that the sixth outlet achieves sales and profits comparable with the other five, what will be Sofabed's ROC? **(6)**

27 TAKEOVERS AND PUBLISHED ACCOUNTS

Concepts needed: Balance sheets, Profit and Loss accounts, Ratio analysis

The spectacular growth record of the 'fromage frais' dairy sector looked unending. From £15 million two years ago to £36 million last year and industry analysts were forecasting £48 million this year. Little wonder that Zee Co were interested in buying a firm, English Dairy, boasting a 20% market share. English Dairy had been the first British firm to spot the product's potential, and although their share had slipped from the 50% they once held, the growth in the market size had ensured that their own sales volume had kept rising.

When he heard a rumour that English Dairy's shareholders were thinking of putting the firm up for sale, Zee Co's Chairman had immediately phoned his Merchant Bank to ask for a report. The Bank soon returned with a detailed analysis of English Dairy's three most recent years' accounts. Their summary read as follows:

---

1 The chilled dairy products market is growing in volume by 8% per annum and should reach £750 million this year.

2 English Dairy had sales last year of £6 million – all in the booming fromage frais sector. Their gross margins of 45% and net (pre-tax) margins of 10% were better than most dairy product firms.

3 In their latest accounts, English Dairy's key ratios were as follows:

Liquidity	1.7
Acid Test	0.8
Gearing	40%
Return on Assets	30%

We believe these to be encouraging.

4 With its £1,200,000 of shareholders funds, its high profitability and the value of its brand name, we recommend that you offer £1.20 for each of the 1.5 million ordinary shares. This will give their shareholders a chance to sell at a 30 pence premium over the most recent price at which English Dairy's shares were traded.

5 The purchase of English Dairy could be financed by a sale and leaseback of your £1.4 million head office, and by bank loans that we will provide. Our fees will amount to just 4% of the purchase price plus a £4,000 arrangement fee for the loans.

The Board of Zee Co found this satisfactory, and authorised the takeover to be carried out by the Merchant Bankers. The Financial Director was a little worried about the high, combined gearing level after the merger, but reasoned that English Dairy's high stock levels could be cut back – thereby generating the cash to repay some of their borrowings. **Appendix A** shows the Balance Sheet for Zee Co at the time of the bid.

With the merger completed on the financial terms outlined above, a small team of Zee Co executives went in to learn about English Dairy's business. Within a fortnight they began to realise that not all was well. The factory looked impressive, but the stockpile of finished, refrigerated fromage frais was worryingly large.

Worse came when it emerged that English Dairy had three separate distribution depots – all equally full of finished product. When Zee Co's cost accountant explained this to his marketing colleagues, they analysed English Dairy's sales figures carefully. Four days later the position was quite clear.

After its years of spectacular growth, the fromage frais market had been hit by an unexpected problem this year. The switch in consumer demand towards skimmed milk had led to such excess supplies of cream (skimmed off the milk) that the bulk supply price of cream had fallen by 20%. As a result, many manufacturers were launching real dairy cream versions of their yogurts, mousses, and ice creams. These new products took market share from fromage frais.

This setback had occurred at a very awkward time for English Dairy, since it had just completed a factory expansion programme designed to cope with a forecast of £10 million of sales next year. In order to keep their stated profit high, the company had kept production levels up, even though demand had slipped by 10%. This had led to stockpiling but because it kept the apparent fixed costs per unit down, it enabled the firm to declare what appeared a healthy profit figure. Now – too late – Zee Co had found out that the assumptions they had made were based on misleading figures. The Board considered taking legal action against the Directors and Auditors of English Dairy, but they knew this would only succeed if they could find evidence that the deception had been done deliberately. Otherwise, the defendants would just plead that they had misjudged market conditions, i.e. that theirs was an honest mistake.

Once Zee Co's accountants had finished a complete audit of English Dairy's position, they concluded that it had in fact made no profit last year, and was making substantial losses currently. As a result, English Dairy's gearing level was probably near to 80% at the time of the take-over. Now Zee Co had to try to retrieve something from their misguided investment.

APPENDIX A: Zee Co Balance Sheet

	£000	£000
Fixed Assets	12,200	12,200
Stocks	4,800	
Debtors	3,600	
Cash	400	
Current Assets	8,800	8,800
Assets Employed		21,000
Long term loans		7,000
Shares	1,200	
Reserves	12,800	
Shareholders' Funds	14,000	14,000
Capital Employed		21,000

Questions
(60 marks; 100 minutes)

1 What danger signs were there that Zee Co should have followed up more carefully before buying English Dairy? **(10)**

2 Explain the ways in which English Dairy's accounting ratios misled Zee Co and its Merchant Bank. What conclusions can you draw about the accuracy of published company accounts? **(15)**

3 **a** What was the value of the goodwill element in Zee Co's bid for English Dairy? **(5)**

   b What percentage of the extra bank loans will be paid to the bank in fees? **(6)**

4 Use the data available to help you analyse and discuss Zee Co's gearing position before and after the takeover. **(12)**

5 Outline three actions that Zee Co might take to 'retrieve something'. How might the Directors decide between the three you suggest? **(12)**

28 LIQUIDITY CRISIS!

Concepts needed: Balance sheets, Ratios, Market research, Government intervention

All through the 1980s commentators had stressed the problems of an ageing population. Annabelle was one of the first to realise that this trend would also throw up business opportunites. Her family electrical manufacturing business (Raysun) had been struggling for years and she looked forward to the wider, competitive market of 1992 with horror. She knew that their small output from a 30-year-old factory was no basis for matching the economies of scale of the major producers like Philips and Electrolux. Even worse, her father's decision five years before to stop producing branded goods left them at the mercy of the price conscious own-label buying managers at the store chains. So, appreciating that her firm could not compete in the mass market, Annabelle decided to aim her products at the only segment that was both growing and uncatered for – the elderly.

Her father took some convincing, but eventually he conceded that 'Since I retired last year, you're the boss, so your decisions count.' The next problem was how to organise and finance the required Research and Development (R & D) and market research programmes. A constraint was that years of poor trading had led to a run down of Raysun's capital stock. That meant the firm's machinery and vehicles had been allowed to get older and older, as operating losses made it impossible to finance the purchase of new fixed assets. Such actions had helped the firm survive, but now there was little of value left on the balance sheet to give a bank manager the confidence to provide a long term loan. This can be seen in the following balance sheet.

Raysun Ltd. Balance Sheet 31st December

	£000	£000
Fixed Assets		
Property leases	25	
Machinery	12	
Vehicles	15	52
Working Capital		
Stocks	60	
Debtors	88	
Cash	7	155
Creditors	55	
Overdraft	10	65
Net current assets		90
Assets employed		142
Share capital	10	
Reserves	82	
Bank loans	50	
Capital Employed		142

After discussion with her Engineering Director and Sales Manager, Annabelle decided that she would need to budget £180,000 for development spending on a vacuum cleaner for the elderly over the next twelve months. She anticipated an operating profit on her existing business of just £12,000 in that period, after deducting £8,000 of depreciation. Her father had given his agreement to a Rights Issue in which shareholders would subscribe for three new shares for each one held currently. Therefore, the remaining £130,000 would have to be squeezed out of working capital. This would have a severe impact on Raysun's liquidity position, but she felt that the firm's long standing relationship with its suppliers should make them willing to accept some temporary delays.

For nine months both strands of the policy went well. The Sales department found out that the over-70s wanted cleaners that were very light, easy to manoeuvre, and with extra long leads so that the user need bend down only once to plug it in. The Engineering department went ahead with this brief, experimenting with new, lighter plastics and with power-assisted wheels that enable the user to push the cleaner along effortlessly. By month ten, however, it was becoming clear that technical problems would delay the launch by six months, and cost a further £50,000.

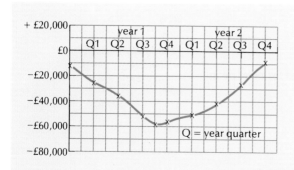

Raysun cashflow forecast for the coming two years

Annabelle carefully worked out a cash flow forecast for the coming two years, and converted it into the graph shown left. She used it (plus the market research findings included as **Appendix A**) to attempt to persuade her bank manager to increase Raysun's overdraft facility. This proved fruitless.

A frantic week followed in which Annabelle visited a series of different banks – all with the same depressing result. At the same time she had to fend off creditors who complained that they had not been paid for goods supplied 20 weeks ago. Despite her pleadings, two suppliers refused to supply any more goods on credit and one said he would instruct his solicitor to take her to court to retrieve his £2,800 debt. As she had no cash, and the week's cash inflow was only going to be sufficient to pay her wage bill, she felt powerless.

It was while she waited to see a sixth and final bank manager, nervously flicking through a local newspaper, that she noticed an article about the Regional Enterprise Board. A local politician was complaining about the 'waste of public funds involved in using Council money to prop up firms that the banks consider a bad risk.' Annabelle apologised to a puzzled secretary, and sped to the Enterprise Board's offices. They sent a business advisor over to see her factory, the R & D work, and her finances. He was impressed with the enthusiasm of all the staff he met, and with the clarity of her marketing strategy. They agreed that the financial package needed would be £20,000 of equity capital and £40,000 of loan capital.

Annabelle felt awkward about telling her father that she had to dilute his shareholding by a third, but she knew that the risks the Board was taking deserved the chance of a share in the profits of success.

To avoid being taken to court in the ten days before the Enterprise Board's committee met to approve the finance, Annabelle had to sell her VW Golf to raise the £2,800. After the successful launch of the 'Ageless' vacuum cleaner, though, she was able to look back on the struggles of the liquidity crisis with some relief and much pride.

APPENDIX A Summary Of Market Research Findings

	Age of respondents		
	60–69	70–79	80+
Q1 Last bought a vacuum			
Up to 5 years ago	34%	22%	8%
5–10 years ago	42%	39%	31%
11+ years ago	24%	39%	61%
Q2 Think vacuums are poorly designed for elderly			
Agree very strongly	20%	39%	64%
Agree strongly	24%	32%	31%
Agree	32%	23%	5%
Disagree	24%	6%	–
Q3 Would buy a vacuum designed for older people			
Yes, definitely	36%	61%	42%
Yes, very probably	31%	28%	22%
Yes, quite probably	11%	7%	12%
Probably not	22%	4%	24%

Questions

(100 marks; 2.5 hours)

1 Comment on Raysun's main strengths and weaknesses at the time Annabelle took it over. **(10)**

2 Distinguish between:

a market research and R & D

b working capital and capital employed **(6)**

3 Explain precisely how £50,000 was expected to be generated from profit, depreciation, and the Rights Issue. **(10)**

4 If Raysun's overdraft limit was £15,000, how might Annabelle have 'squeezed' £130,000 out of working capital?

Comment on your suggestions, then use ratios to help you evaluate the firm's liquidity position before and after the changes you suggest. **(20)**

5 Analyse the market research findings with a view to showing:

a How they might have helped justify Annabelle's case to her potential backers.

b How she could use them in her marketing planning for the new product launch. **(20)**

6 If you were the bank manager, what questions would you have asked Annabelle about the evidence she presented in support of her loan application? **(10)**

7 Discuss the advantages and disadvantages of council-backed Regional Enterprise Boards operating alongside private sector sources of finance. **(12)**

8 In Britain, banks rarely offer equity finance; they prefer to give loans secured against fixed assets. In Germany, by contrast, banks have traditionally sought a longer term relationship with companies by investing in the share/equity capital of the business. Use the information in the Case Study as a basis for discussing the wider significance of this difference. **(12)**

A PROBLEM OF PRODUCTION AND STOCK SCHEDULING

Concepts needed: Stocks, Cash flow, Capacity utilisation

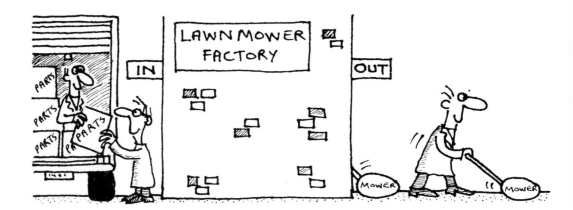

The marketing manager of a lawnmower manufacturer forecasts the following sales pattern for the coming year:

Monthly Sales (000 units)	
Jan	55
Feb	60
Mar	95
April	140
May	110
June	80
July	70
Aug	65
Sept	75
Oct	80
Nov	60
Dec	45

Maximum production capacity is 90,000 units per month and only 80,000 units of finished stock can be stored. The management aim to keep a minimum (buffer) stock level of 40,000 units at all times; so the year starts and should finish with that amount of stock. The production manager must schedule output for the coming year bearing all these factors in mind.

With a view to the longer term, though, the production manager believes she must discover whether a different strategy would be more profitable. At present, it is inevitable that the expensive factory overhead costs are being fully utilised for only part of the year. Perhaps it would be more economic to sell off some of the machinery, convert part of the factory to warehousing, and then use a full-time workforce to produce flat out all year? Surely that would be more efficient than the time-consuming and expensive process of recruiting and training temporary workers every winter.

She decided to spend more time planning out her idea, and then to discuss it with the firm's chief accountant.

Questions
(40 marks; 70 minutes)

1   What production level do you recommend for each month, bearing in mind a general requirement for stable production levels where possible (to minimise the need for temporary staff or 'double-time' overtime payments).
Use this layout to work out your answer: (12)

	Stocks at start (thousands)	Monthly sales (thousands)	Production level (thousands)	Stocks at end (thousands)
Jan				
Feb				
Mar				
etc.				

2   a   Draw a line graph of monthly sales and monthly production over the year.   (7)

   b   Shade in the areas on the graph that indicate when stocks are building up.   (2)

   c   Indicate the under-utilisation of the firm's 90,000 capacity.   (2)

3   a   Is it possible to meet the desired buffer stock target at all times?   (1)

   b   How well do you think you managed to meet the constraints placed upon you by the terms of the question?   (4)

4   What are the implications of the production manager's plan for the firm's future position regarding stock levels, cash flow, and responsiveness to changing customer demands?   (12)

30 BS 5750 AND THE QUALITY FANATIC

Concepts needed: Quality assurance, Profit, International competitiveness

The management of the Kimber Wetsuit Company (KWC) had been considering adopting the BS 5750 quality standard for some years. What clinched it was when the Ministry of Defence turned down KWC's quote for 1,000 suits for Royal Navy divers. They lost the order to BJ Diving, which had just received its 5750 certificate.

As a former professional diver, KWC's Managing Director (Jim Stewart) had always been fanatical about quality. This had helped in his development of a substantial export business, accounting for 75% of sales turnover. The level of quality that the overseas buyers looked for had been instilled by Jim into his workforce. So he found it hard to see what the British Standard could do to improve on the reliability of his wetsuits. Nevertheless he decided to hire a consultant to advise how to proceed.

The advisor spent a day following an order through from design, to materials ordering, cutting, bonding, assembly, styling, quality control and packing. Every piece of documentation was checked, as was the communication system and document storage method. The following day Jim Stewart received detailed feedback on what the firm would have to do to achieve the BS 5750 standard. He was horrified at the focus on paperwork, which included specific recommendations for at least twelve new pieces of record keeping or record storage. He told his wife after work: 'Not once did the clown mention the quality of craftsmanship or the care taken by every worker in my factory'.

After a few days, however, Jim calmed down and set about reading the documentation from the British Standards Institute, and re-reading the consultant's report. This enabled him to write his own report (shown opposite), which he sent to every member of his staff.

Jim decided that the best way to proceed was not through outside 'experts' or even as a purely management-based exercise. His approach was to be bottom-up, i.e. employee-centred.

The whole KWC staff received a huge boost when they heard, four months later, that the Navy had cancelled its order with BJ Diving on the grounds that the wetsuits delivered so far did not meet the Navy's standards. Gossip soon reached them that BJ's approach to obtaining BS 5750 had been so bureaucratic that the company was weighed down with paperwork systems. The process of producing high quality wetsuits had become secondary to producing high quality paper.

With BJ Diving rejected and KWC well on the way to its 5750 quality standard, it was no surprise when Jim received a telephone call from the Ministry of Defence. Within a fortnight KWC had the contract for producing the remaining 500 Navy wetsuits.

Report to: All members of staff
From: Jim
Subject: Applying for the British Standard 5750 quality award
Date: March 17th

1 Background

We have recently lost out on a Royal Navy order that would have added 50% to this year's sales. BJ Diving won it because they hold the BS 5750 certificate that the Navy insists upon. As we all know, our quality is considerably better than theirs, so it would be foolish of us to allow this to occur again.

2 Proposal

I intend that we should achieve the required standard within nine months. The Italian Navy contract comes up then, and it is my plan that this should form the stepping stone to a far stronger presence in the European market. The BS 5750 is the same as the internationally accepted ISO 9000, so this should help our cause.

3 Detailed requirements

In order to be successful, we will need to cover four main areas:

3.1 Management responsibility: an organisation chart will be needed to set out the responsibilities of all staff who manage or carry out work associated with the quality of the product and customer service. Quality procedures must be written down in full detail.

3.2 Contract review: each customer's requirements must be defined and documented to establish that the necessary resources are available.

3.3 Process control: requiring documentation of how the process is to be carried out. Written instructions must be given to each employee involved and the process must be monitored. (Note to all: I do not know how this may affect our policy of self-checking.)

3.4 Document control: we must produce quality and procedure manuals to be kept in designated locations. Any changes to the system must be logged in the manuals.

4 Conclusion

I am as appalled as any of you at the amount of paperwork this will generate. It will cost us a great deal and will probably be very irritating to work with. Nevertheless, if important customers want us to hold this certificate, we must not only get on with it, but also trust that our customers are not fools. I will be very surprised if we do not learn a great deal from this process, and emerge an even stronger company as a result.

Questions
(40 marks; 70 minutes)

1 Why may a customer demand that a supplier holds a BS 5750 quality assurance certificate? **(6)**

2 Jim Stewart decided to implement the BS 5750 requirements through a bottom-up approach. What is meant by that and how might it be achieved? **(8)**

3 a Before getting the Navy order, the average cost of producing KWC's wetsuits was £124, comprising £74 of variable costs and £50 of fixed costs per unit. Calculate and comment on the effect on these costs of getting the Navy order. **(10)**

b Assuming a selling price of £195 per wetsuit, also calculate the effect of the extra order on KWC's profit. **(6)**

4 Use the case as a starting point to discuss the reasons why high quality standards may be considered of particular importance in today's business world. **(10)**

31 DECIDING ON FACTORY LOCATION

Concepts needed: Location, Break-even, Contribution

In his large office in Hesketh House, London W.1., James Drayton studied the wall-map of Britain. He realised, with some surprise, that he did not know it very well. His twenty years of building up Jarton Electronics had made him familiar with the industrial districts of Japan, Taiwan and South Korea, so he felt he knew Singapore Airport better than he knew Newcastle or Glasgow. Yet having decided to build his first British factory, he knew he must adjust.

Jarton's Projects Director had already done the legwork, and the afternoon's Board Meeting was to discuss whether to choose Site A (Billingham, Co. Durham) or Site B (Rochester, Kent). As Company Chairman, James Drayton's opinion would probably be decisive. The Projects Director started the meeting by presenting a report on the financial implications of each site.

Report to: The Board of Directors
From: D. Springer, Projects Director
Subject: The Costs and Benefits of Sites A and B
Date: April 17th

1 Background and Objectives

1.1 Due to forecast excess demand next year, the Board agreed on 2nd March that a new plant should be constructed. It will produce up to 100,000 video cameras per year at a target cost of £225 each. With worries about the degree of import protectionism towards non-EC goods after the establishment of the Single Market, the Board approved a proposal that the factory should be constructed in Britain.

1.2 This report sets out the costs of each of two alternative sites, broken down into fixed and variable.

2 The Costs

2.1 Based upon the best available evidence, the costs are:

	Site A	Site B
Fixed (per annum)	£000	£000
Rent and rates	1,240	2,100
Salaried staff	3,660	4,500
Depreciation	1,900	1,900
Interest charges	1,200	1,500
Variable (per unit)	£	£
Materials and components	£89.50	£80.00
Piece rate labour	£4.00	£5.00
Delivery costs	£14.50	£5.00
Travel and expenses	£10.00	£4.00

3 Recommendations

3.1 Final conclusions can only be drawn once the marketing department has made a firm sales forecast. The above costs have been calculated on the assumption that 50% of output would be exported to Europe via the Channel Tunnel. If the proportion changes in favour of U.K. sales, site A will become more attractive than suggested above.

3.2 If sales are 100,000 units with about half being exports, site B looks more attractive.

The Chairman asked the Personnel Director for comments, and received the following reply:

'I have severe doubts about estimates such as these. I think they fail to allow for the problem of high labour turnover in the South. There's the measurable costs of staff turnover, of course, such as recruitment and training overheads. But I think it's still more important to allow for the impact on morale of having too little continuity. Both on the production and R & D side, what we need is experienced, loyal staff. In the long run, I'm sure that County Durham with its 12% unemployment will serve us better than Kent with its 5%.'

The Marketing and the Finance Directors both spoke against this view. The Finance Director's views were typical of both:

'To succeed, we need first rate top management. If we set up in the North it will be a struggle to get high-calibre people, because the best ones want to be in reach of London.'

The Personnel Director thought them ignorant and prejudiced. She was feeling rather isolated, and although the Production Director spoke up in favour of County Durham, it was evident that the majority wanted the factory in the South. She tried one last line of argument:

'Are we not being reckless by ignoring the possibility of a slump in demand for our product? After all, if sales fall sharply from 100,000 and perhaps the price slips from the £320 we anticipate, how will we cope with the high fixed costs in the South?'

This suggestion was greeted in silence, with the Finance Director appearing very angry at this stepping over what he regarded as the demarcation line between finance and the rest of the organisation. He reminded his fellow Directors that:

'Our duty is to our shareholders; it is not for us to allow emotion to cloud our judgement just because unemployment is temporarily higher in the North. At 100,000 units, site B will give us £400,000 more profit than site A. I move we vote for site B and then get on with the rest of our agenda.'

Questions

(40 marks; 70 minutes)

1   On a large scale, construct a break-even graph that shows the costs of both sites. Mark and state the point at which B becomes more profitable than A.   **(10)**

2   If you were James Drayton and had all the above information available, which site would you choose? Explain your answer.   **(10)**

3   How might the Projects Director have found out the information upon which to base the figures given on page 89? How definite would they be?   **(10)**

4   What other information should the Board be requesting before it makes a decision? Explain how each piece of information could be important.   **(10)**

32 *BRINGING IN QUALITY CIRCLES*

Concepts needed: Motivation, Resistance to change

'But we don't have a quality problem!' exclaimed the Chairman, evidently put out by Sarah's suggestion. He pointed to the very low rates of customer guarantee claim (just 1%); and to the advanced electronic testing system operated by the seven quality control inspectors. But Sarah continued to press her case for the introduction of quality circles:

> 'There's more to quality than having fault-free products. Quality circles look at every aspect of a product's design and manufacture, with a view to providing a product the customer will be more satisfied with. Plus, of course, there are other vital areas such as delivery times. Quality means good service as well as good products.'

After some more, quite heated, discussion the Chairman agreed to provide Sarah with a £20,000 budget for a one year trial of quality circles within her own department. If her hedgetrimmer production line benefited, then perhaps the main lawnmower plant would follow. She would have to report to the Board on progress in six months, and give a final assessment at the end of the year.

She began by calling a meeting of all her staff, to explain the test that was to take place, and the reasons why she had pushed for it. They were used to – and quite liked – her meetings, which often involved open criticism of her management of their section, so most were receptive to what she had to say. Some had moaned before about 'the waste of the skills and brains of the shopfloor workers' so they responded positively to a proposal to use those very attributes. The only groans came when Sarah explained that the group would meet after work, and would be unpaid. Her reasoning was that to offer to pay people would attract many who did not really want to participate, so it needed to be truly voluntary work.

By talking individually to all of her eighty-five staff over the following weeks, Sarah was able to construct a list of eight volunteers. Before their first meeting, she and they went on a weekend management training course on 'Setting up successful quality circles'. This had the desired effect of making them feel far more confident and far more motivated towards the scheme, and helped to knit them together as a team. All were especially impressed by the potential of the 'fishbone' diagram as a way of tackling problems (see overleaf).

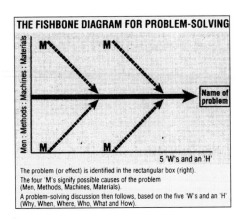

This invention of the Japanese management expert Ishikawa seemed easy to use. The problem to be solved is written in a box on the right hand side of a large piece of paper. An arrow is drawn across the sheet pointing towards the box, then the members of the circle suggest possible causes – which are put into one of the 'four M' categories: Men, Methods, Machines, Materials. Having agreed on the causes, a problem-solving discussion follows, based on the 'five Ws and an H' (Why, When, Where, Who, What and How). They were told that this technique is the one used most commonly by the two million quality circles operating in Japan.

The first week's quality circle proved a disappointment, as the topic they chose to look at (late deliveries) was so wide that they became swamped by the number of different factors. In subsequent weeks they corrected this, and then began to generate some useful ideas. The first triumph was when their idea for braking the hedge-cutting blades at the instant the user switches off was designed, tested, and then incorporated into all the firm's output. This was completed by the time the six month review took place, so Sarah felt very confident that the Board would congratulate her. In fact, she found that many Board members were worried about the implication of her work. The Production Director suggested that:

> 'The workers are already showing signs of believing that they know
> best. Two managers have reported insolence, and one has told me
> that some of his staff actually started changing the production process
> without his permission. I'd like this experiment abandoned.'

Fortunately for Sarah, the Marketing Director and the Chairman were so impressed by the improvement in the hedgetrimmer that they backed her for the other six months. She went away determined to overcome the resistance to change among the middle management, though not yet sure how to achieve this.

Source: *The Independent*

Questions

(40 marks; 70 minutes)

1   Outline the strengths of Sarah's approach to the implementation of the circle. What problems might arise if the Chairman decides that the system should be implemented throughout the business? **(10)**

2   How, precisely, could successful quality circles boost the profitability of a firm? **(10)**

3   Use the fishbone technique to tackle the problem of exam success at Business Studies. Group the causes of the problem under the 'four M' headings, and your thoughts on solutions within the categories: 'five Ws and an H'. Make your points as specifically as you can. Comment briefly on the potential of this technique as a focus for group work. **(10)**

4   Why is resistance to change such a widespread personnel management problem? Discuss how Sarah might tackle the problem of resistance to change among her fellow managers. **(10)**

STOCK CONTROL AND ANALYSIS

Concepts needed: Stock control, Contribution, Profit

Lockware Plastics is part of the Lockware Group, a medium-sized Public Limited Company. In its latest financial year, the group made a pre-tax profit of £2.1 million – a big recovery from its awful performance of recent years. The plastics division enjoyed a 10% sales increase, but this was still 46% below the levels of four years before (see below). In his recent report to shareholders, the Chairman said:

'Our recent difficulties have been due to the severity of the economic recession in our main operating markets. Now we are fit, lean and eager to take advantage of the improving world economy.'

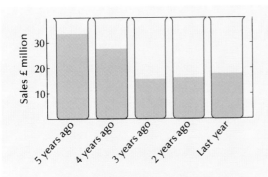

Sales revenue for Lockware Plastics during the last 5 years

Lisa had her doubts. She was stuck in a dingy plastic moulding factory, wondering how a management trainee with four weeks' experience could be expected to sort out a mess like this. The production director had evidently been surprised to see her that Monday, and had only spent twenty minutes with her before telling her to 'get the machine spares system into shape'.

It took her a day to find out that he meant the Engineering Stores section, where spare parts were held in stock in case any of the manufacturing machinery broke down. Lisa found the storeman unhelpful as she tried to learn about the system and its problems. Fortunately a young maintenance man took an interest, and her education began.

She learned that a recent stock check recorded £60,000 of machine parts held in the warehouse. As the book value of the machines themselves was only £40,000, this seemed very high. Furthermore, the maintenance man assured her that the 49 large moulding machines broke down frequently, and despite the warehouse full of supplies, the right part was often missing. Lisa was assured that there was usually at least one machine idle on any one day for just this reason. So, on the face of it, Lockware had the worst of all worlds – large stockpiles of some parts and none of others.

Lisa discussed with the cost accountant the implications of a machine being out of order. She found that if a machine was out of action for a whole week, the lost contribution amounted to £16,000 on average (production is 'round the clock' seven days a week). Due to the non-stop, three shift production, machine downtime can never be made up, so it puts back delivery times.

Already, Lisa had enough information to appreciate that she had quite an important task on her hands. She tried again to talk to the warehouseman, and this time had some success. He said:

'We've got four different types of machine here; with 498 separate parts between them. The four machines each come from different suppliers, two British, one German, and one American. If we run out of an American part, it can take eight weeks to get a replacement. The problem is that the maintenance lads just help themselves if I'm not around, so I think we've got spares when we haven't. Then they bad mouth me when they come for a spare and I haven't got any.'

He went on to explain that re-ordering was undertaken when the number of parts reached a minimum level. The level differed according to the turnover of the part; the higher the usage/turnover, the higher the minimum level. These minimum levels were not recorded anywhere. The warehouseman said proudly that he knew which parts had a quick usage and which were needed rarely. Lisa was astonished to learn that re-ordering was so dependent on his personal judgement. She wondered what happened when he went on holiday, and what chaos there would be when he retired. No less surprising was that he had the authority to re-order any number of parts, yet he had no knowledge of any budget to which he should be working.

Lisa set out to check on the efficiency of this system. She found a file of stock record cards. A typical one is shown below.

Stock Record For Previous Year – Omron Light Switch

Quantity delivered	Delivery date	Unit cost	USAGE Quant.	USAGE Date	Stock	Physical count	Date of count
3	2/1	£28			3		
			1	4/3	3		
			1	12/4	1		
			1	11/6	NIL		
			Stock check		NIL	NIL	30/6
2	8/7	£30			2		
			1	25/7	1		
			1	14/9	NIL		
2	24/9	£30			2		
			Stock check		2	1	31/12

She felt that this confirmed her suspicions of the warehouseman's competence. Especially when she heard from a maintenance man that the lack of this item had held up production on one machine for three days last September.

Lisa tried to talk things over with the production director, who was supposed to be in charge of her six week 'training programme in manufacturing'. As he still seemed unwilling to find any time for her, she decided to prove her worth by conducting a full analysis of all 498 machine parts. She found the stock records for each part for the last three years. She intended to place each part in a category that reflected its frequency of use. To virtually guarantee that no part would ever be out of stock, each part was categorised depending upon its highest (rather than its average) annual usage:

e.g.   Year 1   Year 2   Year 3
          6   4   16

The part would be placed in category 4 (below).

Category	Frequency part used in a year	Proposed minimum stock level	Proposed maximum stock level
1	0–5	1	2
2	6–10	1	2
3	11–15	1	3
4	16–20	2	4
5	21–25	2	4
6	26–30	3	5
7	31–35	3	6
8	36–40	4	8
9	41–45	4	8
10	46–50	5	10
11	51+	5	10

The categories emerged as a result of Lisa's three weeks' study of the stock record cards, as did the proposed minimum and maximum stock levels. This study also showed her the scope for increasing the efficiency of the firm's stock control system. Among the many peculiarities she found one part costing £78 that had not been used once in the last three years; fifteen were in stock, so over £1,000 had been tied up quite unnecessarily for three years.

After another week of careful calculation, Lisa was able to prove that her system would, on average, cut Lockware's stockholding from £60,000 to £36,500. Furthermore if it was implemented fully, it would ensure that parts were virtually never out of stock. The cost accountant had been able to calculate for her that machine downtime had cost £85,000 of lost contribution (and therefore profit) in the past year. Careful use of probability theory enabled her to show that her method would lead to an average of just £5,000 of lost production per year, so she appeared to have a watertight case for change.

With her six weeks nearly over, Lisa asked the personnel director (who had recruited her originally) if he would arrange a meeting with the production director for her to present her findings. This duly occurred, and Lisa impressed the personnel director and herself with her clear presentation of such complex material. The production director was less happy, however. He summoned her the following day and could barely control his fury as he told her, 'You betrayed my trust, prying without my authority, and then humiliating me in front of a fellow director. Get out and don't ever return to my patch.'

Lisa could never quite get over that, and left Lockware as soon as her year's training was completed. Five years later, she was production director for a firm with a fine growth record. It overtook Lockware's sales turnover soon afterwards.

Questions

(40 marks; 80 minutes)

1 Consider the Chairman's view that the firm was 'fit, lean and eager' to face the future. **(8)**

2 Discuss the strengths and weaknesses of Lisa's approach to solving the stock problem. **(10)**

3 Draw a graph showing the stocks of Omron light switches over the previous year (the dates will inevitably be approximate). On what grounds were Lisa's suspicions confirmed? **(12)**

4 Distinguish between contribution and profit. In what ways would the successful implementation of Lisa's scheme help to increase each of these concepts? **(10)**

34 FINDING A EUROPEAN LOCATION

*Concepts needed: Location factors, Direct and indirect costs,
Single European market*

The success of 'Stun' in the United States has already become a standard business case history. Started as an ethnic, black leisurewear business, it grew on the back of the athletics and basketball successes of its sponsored sports stars. Unusually for a fashionable sportswear firm, Stun had always used the slogan 'The value of style' to highlight that it offered the customer performance at reasonable prices. Sales of $380,000 in its first year ballooned to $56 million by year five. Now, two years later, with US sales still rising at a compound rate of 50%, the 'Stun' directors want to make a decisive move into Europe.

Their strategy is to set up a single marketing and distribution centre which will be given responsibility for covering the entire European Union. The warehousing and transport systems must be capable of handling and storing large volumes of shoes imported from Mexico. The Directors believe that the single European market's removal of costly and time-consuming border controls has opened up the opportunity of distributing goods cheaply to a market of 320 million people. Stun's rivals such as Nike and Reebok operate on a national basis, with offices, depots and staff overheads in each country in Europe. So Stun wants to gain a competitive advantage by benefiting from the economies of scale associated with a single, large operation.

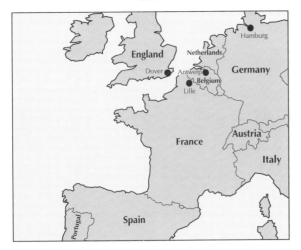

Their problem is to decide where. A consultant has collected data and provided a shortlist of four sites: Dover in Southeast England, Hamburg in North Germany, Antwerp in Belgium, and Lille in Northeast France. All four sites are near to ports that could cope with the shoes shipped from Mexico. They also have very good motorway and rail links. Yet there are many other points of difference. The consultant has set out the key points in a report; extracts from this are shown below.

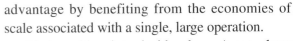

Main resource needs

Office space	10,000 sq feet	Marketing staff	45
Warehousing	80,000 sq feet	Warehouse staff	30
		Other staff	50

Main Resource (Indirect) Costs

	Dover	Hamburg	Antwerp	Lille
Office ($ per sq ft)	14	10	8	8
Warehouse ($ per sq ft)	5	3	2	2
Marketing staff ($ p.a.)	32,000	52,000	40,000	45,000
Warehouse staff ($ p.a.)	15,000	25,000	20,000	18,000
Other staff ($ p.a.)	30,000	40,000	30,000	30,000
Overhead costs ($ p.a.)	570,000	575,000	450,000	500,000
Corporation tax (%) (tax on profit)	35%	48%	40%	38%

From their research into potential European revenues, Stun's Directors forecast first year gross profits of $15 million, after allowing for direct production, distribution and marketing costs. In addition the Dover site would carry a cost penalty of an estimated $2 million for a year's time delays and charges relating to crossing the English Channel.

There are other, less quantifiable factors to consider. As more of the East European countries are allowed to enter the Community, the nearness of the German site would be most useful. Dover also has its trump cards. As the least regulated of all the member states, the Directors are aware that Britain would be the easiest location for redundancies or dismissals, should either be necessary. No less important is that senior American managers are more willing to move to England than to continental Europe. Offset against these advantages for Dover is this warning from Stun's consultant: 'Do bear in mind that Britain is a reluctant European Union member, therefore it may not join in with key future developments such as a common currency.'

Stun's Directors have a few calculations and a great deal of thinking to do.

Questions

(45 marks; 80 minutes)

1 **a** To what level has Stun's annual sales revenue grown over the past two years? **(4)**

   b What problems might such a growth rate cause in relation to factory and office sites? **(6)**

2 What are the advantages and disadvantages to Stun of operating with a single location for all its European distribution and marketing? **(12)**

3 On the basis of the numerical data available, calculate which of the four sites would be the most profitable for the company. **(10)**
State your assumptions. **(3)**

4 Discuss the reasons why Stun might choose a site other than the one identified in question 3. **(10)**

35 WORKFORCE PERFORMANCE AND THE SKODA SUPPLIER

Concepts needed: Motivation theory, Accountability

Sadiq could hardly believe it. Only fifteen months out of university and he had landed this plum project. His employer Lincoln McGee, Management Consultants, hired him straight from college in preference to eighteen other shortlisted candidates. Three months of induction training were followed by a series of assistant roles in projects run by senior partners. Now Sadiq was being sent to Liberec, 50 miles northeast of Prague. His task was to advise Floc, a supplier to Skoda cars, on the modernisation of its factory working methods and practices.

Lincoln McGee had been hired because of Skoda's threat to withdraw orders from Floc if the supplier could not guarantee performance improvements within four months. The specification laid down by Skoda is shown in Table 1.

Table 1

Problem	Measurement	Current rate	Target rate
Quality	Rejects per thousand	24.5	9.9
Lead times	Time from order to delivery	18 days	6 days
Delivery reliability	% of occasions delivery is late	23.5%	2.5%

Over the following month he came to know the Floc components factory intimately. Sadiq's excellent German made it easy to communicate with the Czech managers and supervisors, and his youthful appearance encouraged people to talk openly.

The Works Director told him that the whole assembly section of the plant had, until the late 1980s, been staffed by political prisoners. To minimise sabotage risks, production was reduced to many simple operations. The winding mechanism for a car window, for example, involved eighteen different people, each recruited and trained to complete a task as quickly as possible. Such was the specialisation that workers who could carry out their own task in nine seconds per unit might take five times longer if switched to someone else's. This mattered little in the past, as the prisoners were not allowed to be absent. Now, with paid employees carrying out these tedious tasks, absenteeism had become a major worry.

Floc did not have conveyor-belt production lines, so to ensure high output rates the payment structure was through piece rate. As each stage of production took a slightly different time and skill, a staff of fourteen salaried clerical workers was employed to set, measure and calculate the piece work payments. Recently the factory workers had elected their own representative to negotiate the sums involved. There was even talk of joining the National Engineering Union. There were two main grievances: the piece rate wage loss caused to an individual by being forced to switch from their own post to that of another, absent colleague; plus the poor health and safety position within the plant.

The Floc factory was a huge, drab site with three corrugated iron buildings linked by pot-holed roadways. The machinery in most of the plant was 30 years old and revealed little concern for health and safety. There was no extraction system for the dust and fumes caused by the mechanical and chemical processes used. Not all the machines were guarded to protect workers from moving parts. Sadiq learned that the average accident rate was 9.5 per week, with serious injuries occurring at least once a month.

Sadiq spent the fourth week of his investigations visiting Floc's suppliers and customers. He wanted to find out their opinion of the company. The suppliers were understandably hesitant about criticising their customer, but Sadiq was able to learn that the Floc production staff had never met or even spoken to the supplier factory management. The only contact was through Floc's purchasing department. Skoda, the main customer, was complimentary about Floc's helpful customer service, agreeing to replace defective parts without a quibble. Nevertheless it did criticise the erratic deliveries and unreliable quality standards.

Lincoln McGee had a four week consultancy contract, so it was now time for Sadiq to present his findings to Floc's thirteen Directors, and to make his recommendations for change. There would be one other participant at the meeting, as Mr Fraser McGee was flying out especially. So Sadiq spent a whole day preparing the slides for his presentation.

For a full two hours, Sadiq was on his feet going through a detailed account of Floc's strengths and many weaknesses. As lunchtime approached, he summarised his argument:

Main strengths:
- effective control of output and costs
- good recruitment and training procedures for the manufacturing system being used.

Main weaknesses:
- absenteeism levels running at:

Monday	11.4%
Tuesday	9.1%
Wednesday	6.9%
Thursday (payday)	2.7%
Friday	10.1%

- ratio of direct (factory) labour to indirect (staff) of 1 : 1.6 compared with 1 : 0.6 in equivalent British plants, thereby generating a very high staff overhead cost
- a prevailing attitude (culture) of interest in high volume production at the expense of product quality, delivery schedules or customer satisfaction

■ a climate of fear of detection; no-one wants to be held accountable for mistakes, so errors are hidden and decisions delayed: 'There is always a bunch of signatures on every document' says Sadiq.

With Sadiq's report over, they all went off to lunch. He felt delighted by how well the morning had gone, but knew that the hardest part had yet to come: the recommendations for action.

Questions

(50 marks; 90 minutes)

1 What are the causes of Floc's poor performance at the factors identified in Table 1? **(8)**

2 If Floc continues to operate as at present, what personnel problems might arise if Skoda requires Floc to change to higher technology production of a brand new product? **(10)**

3 What actions might the company take to reduce:

   a the level of absenteeism

   b the proportion of indirect labour? **(10)**

4 Analyse the underlying problems in terms of motivation theory. **(10)**

5 Putting yourself into Sadiq's place, what recommendations for action would you make and why? **(12)**

36 JUST-IN-TIME PRODUCTION – THE JAPANESE WAY

Concepts needed: Communications, Stock control, Productivity, Objectives and constraints

As Redlin's new Group Production Controller, Booth felt it important that he should make his intentions clear from the start. So he arranged a meeting with the seven senior and middle-managers answerable to him, to announce his commitment to Just-In-Time (J.I.T.) production systems. He put his case as follows:

'Given the low profitability of our products in recent years, plus the threat of increased competition when EU trade barriers really come down, we have to tackle our uncompetitiveness compared with the Germans and the Japanese. We have not got the demand to justify a fully automated flow production system, so we must ensure that we make the best use of our 500 staff and our financial resources by moving towards the Japanese Just-In-Time (J.I.T) method. In other words production that operates so smoothly that waste of time, labour and resources is minimised, as each part arrives just in time for the next stage of manufacture.'

Booth concentrated first on the suppliers, with three objectives in mind:

1   to minimise the need for raw material stocks;
2   to eliminate the need for goods-inward quality inspection;
3   good communications with suppliers to ensure their awareness of new product developments that may require them to redesign and retool.

To achieve the first objective, it was necessary to switch from the traditional system of infrequent deliveries of bulk orders, to very frequent – even daily – deliveries. To make that economic, one supplier had to be chosen to get the whole order instead of having competing suppliers. Before the J.I.T programme, Redlin had 330 suppliers with an average on-time delivery performance of 82%. As J.I.T. relies upon 100% reliability of supply (since virtually no buffer stock is held), Booth began discussions with the suppliers with a view to cutting their number to one hundred of the most reliable.

For the second objective, since 207 of the 330 had already achieved 100% quality, Booth could act decisively to ensure that suppliers took their materials straight to the production line, rather than through a quality control inspector. The latter could be switched to checking the quality of Redlin's finished goods.

To improve Redlin's communications with suppliers in order to meet the third objective, Booth began an education programme for each: a factory tour, conversation with the workers using those materials, and a discussion between the New Product Development engineers and the supplier. After several months of close contact, he persuaded the suppliers that if they delivered a faulty component, they would have to pay for all the costs generated. In other words, if a 25 pence switch was discovered to be faulty after it had been built into a Redlin RangeVan, and it cost £40 of labour time to replace it, the supplier would have to pay Redlin £40.25 compensation. Both sides could see that such a strong incentive to supply 100% reliability would be to everyone's long-term benefit.

Having completed the preparations for supplier reliability, Booth was in a stronger position to convince his manager of the opportunities provided. After all, if components could be relied upon totally, less labour would be needed to handle stocks, because the suppliers could deliver straight to the factory floor. The Assembly Manager also spotted that: 'Less warehousing should be needed for stocks, so perhaps we could convert half the warehouse into the assembly line extension we need so badly'.

The Group Production Controller reminded them, though, that J.I.T. would require some fundamental changes. Meticulous production planning would be needed, so that suppliers could receive their orders four days before delivery was needed. No less importantly, it would be essential to ensure that work flow in every section of the factory was uninterrupted. Previously, a temporary breakdown in one section would not stop work elsewhere in the factory, because semi-finished products were stockpiled at every stage of manufacture and assembly. Now the approach would be what the Japanese term 'Kanban', whereby good communications between production sections enable each to produce the right quantity of the right components for the next section to use. As a result, no stockpiling of work-in-progress should be necessary.

One senior production manager looked at Booth with disbelief, and said:

'We're not dealing with Japanese machine-people out there, you know! On a Monday 15% of them will be "off sick", and we won't know which 15% until 8 o'clock that morning. What if they're mostly from one section, so we can't get any production of a vital component that day? Must we send the rest of the workforce home?'

This comment emboldened others to add:

'And what about machine breakdowns? The average one takes three hours to re-start and we get at least a couple a day. After all, we've a good 180 machines on each production line.'

'I'm more worried about the power it'll give to the shopfloor workers. We'll be so dependent on each one of them that they'll have us over a barrel.'

Booth listened as one after the other criticised his proposal, then he fished some sheets of paper out of his briefcase which, without speaking, he handed to each of them. They quietened down as they looked at the contents (see below). After five minutes of silence he asked them if they accepted his view that the situation was critical, and needed drastic action. Glumly, they nodded.

Key facts on Redlin's competitive position

Redlin's market share

	UK	Europe	Rest of World
Last month	19%	8%	5%
1 year ago	23%	10%	8%
5 years ago	31%	12%	11%

Output per worker (productivity)

	Redlin	Average European rival	Average Japanese rival
Last month	24*	31	45
1 year ago	24	29	40
5 years ago	19	23	26

*Units of output per month

Stockholding per worker*

	Redlin	Average European rival	Average Japanese rival
Latest year	£9,800	£6,500	£1,800
Previous year	£9,500	£6,600	£2,700
5 years ago	£7,100	£5,800	£4,900

* Stock value divided by no. of workers

Although that meeting had ended gloomily, over the following weeks Booth saw each manager individually to discuss how they should help move towards the Japanese J.I.T. production method. Each came to realise that full cooperation from the workforce was an essential element in the process. Some saw this as a marvellous opportunity to adopt a different management style from the authoritarian one they had used in the past. Others, though, dreaded the changes involved; two sought early retirement and one asked for time off to look for another job. Booth agreed, knowing that full commitment among the management was essential.

After three months of intensive training on J.I.T. the managers felt able to implement changes. One of the first was to negotiate a job flexibility deal with the trade unions. This would overcome the problem of individual absentees holding up production. If all workers could do each other's jobs, staff could be switched as necessary. After this change was achieved, Booth experimented by doing away with a component stockpile between the grinding and the plating departments. The plating team were made responsible for ensuring that the grinders had their 'orders' at the beginning of each day – so no overnight stocks were needed. When this process was running smoothly (after two months) it was introduced step by step through the factory. After two years, the improvements began to show through in dramatic productivity and financial gains.

Questions

(50 marks; 90 minutes)

1 Outline the reasons why good communications are regarded as crucial to the success of J.I.T. **(8)**

2 How would Redlin's suppliers view the changes being introduced? **(8)**

3 Explain the significance of the figures Booth provided. **(10)**

4 What financial benefits would Redlin have received from the impact of the J.I.T. system on their stock and productivity positions? **(8)**

5 Booth overcame his management's resistance to change. What other internal constraints might he have faced in the circumstances outlined? **(8)**

6 Traditional economic theory suggests that firms make decisions on the basis of short run profit maximisation. Discuss this in the light of the above text. **(8)**

Concepts needed: Types of production, Standard times/costs, Them and us

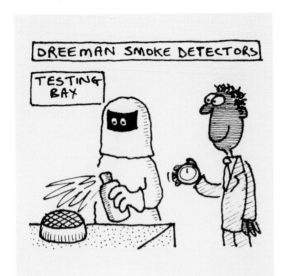

Dreeman Limited is a manufacturing firm employing forty factory and thirty administrative/managerial staff. It is a major producer of smoke detectors, which it designs, assembles, tests, and markets.

It regards itself as rather progressive in its personnel policies, with its close links with local colleges, and its single status conditions of service. So, whereas in many firms only the factory workers have to clock in, and have no sick pay and no company pension, at Dreeman the shop floor staff enjoy the same rights as the white-collar staff. This system was introduced three years ago, when four factory workers with eighty years' service between them, refused to clock in any more. Now the Managing Director believes there is much more mutual trust and respect between workforce and management.

Each year, Dreeman make over 100,000 smoke detectors, in twenty-six different models. The largest selling line – with 12,000 units – is produced continually, the remainder in batches. Having so many lines produced by batch production in the same factory and largely by the same people, makes it hard to keep track of how long it takes to produce each item. Without accurate information, it is then impossible for the accountant to decide the true production cost; this matters because 60% of the firm's direct costs are on labour. In turn, it makes pricing a hit-and-miss affair. The other need for accurate production time information is to enable the supervisor to judge the output per worker. Annual bonuses can be based on this information, as can decisions to give warnings of dismissal to those considered inefficient.

At present, Dreeman's approach is two-fold:-

1 Standard Costs are calculated when a new line is introduced. This entails a lot of work in measuring precisely how long it should take to carry out each task, plus the estimated wage, material, and fuel costs per unit. Yet it has the advantage of providing a yardstick against which shop floor performance can be measured. Unfortunately, shop floor resistance to the sight of anyone with a stopwatch means that once an item is in production, the Standard Times do not get updated. Some are as much as ten years old.

2 The second element in their costing system is time-sheets, on which the factory workers are supposed to record how long they spent on each batch of work. If

this was completed accurately, it would be possible to calculate precisely the time spent per unit on each line made. This could then be compared with the Standard Times to assess efficiency. Unfortunately, the shop floor workers regard timesheets either as pointless bureaucracy or as a threat, so they fill them in only when the supervisor pressures them – too infrequently for them to be accurate.

Now a new Personnel Manager has been given the task of setting up a computerised system of time-sheet analysis that would print out actual production times per unit. Although a computer novice, he knows enough to warn the Managing Director that: 'Computerising a defective system can only speed up the mess.'

When he starts talking the problem over with the two factory supervisors, he is surprised to find out that not even they knew how the information is used to work out production costs and prices. What is clear, though, is that shop floor resistance to the system is deep-rooted. One supervisor suggests:

'If you want a system that my crew will work properly,
you've got to make it so that it cannot be used to measure
their own performance. They can't abide snooping.'

In fact, it is the Personnel Manager's secretary who suggests the solution that is adopted. She suggests a time sheet that follows the batch round the factory floor, and is filled in anonymously by those who spend time on the batch. In that way, no-one need object to filling it in, and therefore a training session on its importance should ensure that it will be completed with fair accuracy. As she says:

'Better to have valid information on one thing than
worthless information on two.'

Questions
(40 marks; 60 minutes)

1 a Outline three main benefits to a business of operating continual/flow production, instead of by batch. **(6)**

b What is the average output for the batch-produced lines? **(2)**

2 a Explain the term Standard Times. **(3)**

b What benefits do Dreeman's wish to obtain from using Standard Times? **(5)**

c What is the significance of the information that some of the Standard Times are 'as much as ten years old'? **(6)**

3 Comment on the secretary's solution. **(6)**

4 Discuss the company's view that it is 'rather progressive in its personnel policies'. **(12)**

38 KAIZEN – CONTINUOUS IMPROVEMENT AT OKI

Concepts needed: Lean production, BS 5750, Productivity

OKI

In 1992 a company only four years old won three prestigious awards. *Management Today* magazine named it the 'Best Electronics Factory in Britain'; ICL awarded it a total quality accolade; and it became one of the first companies to reach the government's standard as an 'Investor In People'. The management was delighted, but fearful that complacency might set in. So OKI (UK) Ltd redoubled its efforts to improve, continuously.

The Japanese electronics company OKI had decided to establish a dot-matrix printer factory in Europe in 1987. After brief consideration of Germany and Spain, the project leader, Mr Kojima, decided on Britain. This was due to the success of other Japanese firms in the UK, plus the familiarity of OKI staff with (American) English. Mr Kojima settled upon Cumbernauld in Scotland for its air and sea transport and its closeness to numerous electronic component suppliers in the heart of 'Silicon Glen'.

Mr Kojima was appointed Managing Director of OKI (UK) Ltd and given the task of getting a new factory up and running within two months. Sixty experienced OKI staff were flown over to help commission a factory layout designed and developed in Japan. Meanwhile, Mr Kojima recruited new managers and supervisors and arranged for each one to spend at least a week in Japan. From the start, it was established that OKI would be a single status employer, with everyone paid on a straight salary basis.

By mid 1988 the Cumbernauld plant had 300 staff producing 2,400 printers per week. Twelve months later a doubled staff level made 6,000 printers weekly. Having coped with the pressures of rapid expansion, OKI's UK management team wanted time to think through the company's future. A series of discussions was held with managers and a hundred shopfloor representatives. All agreed that OKI should build its future around its staff rather than automation. Yet the highly competitive market for printers made it essential for costs to fall and for quality to rise each year. This pointed to the Japanese idea of 'kaizen' (continuous improvement).

OKI management translated kaizen as follows:

> *'The establishment of a process for continued improvement involving everyone – managers and workers alike.'*

KAIZEN

This became the unifying theme that ran through the company's production and personnel practices.

Ian Smith, the production manager, realised it would be hard for each individual among many to see how to contribute meaningfully to OKI's overall improvement. Therefore a system was needed to provide immediate, localised feedback on performance to each staff member. OKI now follow a two-stage process to achieve this.

1 Cell production. The factory operation is split into five cells, each with its own suppliers and 'customers' (internal and external). For instance, completed printed circuit boards (PCBs) are delivered to the final assembly line, so the assembly line is the customer. If the 'customer' finds any quality defects, these are reported back to the relevant PCB workers. An important side-effect of this system is that quality is checked several times over. In 1992, buyers of OKI's printers reported a defect rate of only 0.25% (one in 400).
2 Performance targets. Each section has a daily quality target (such as a maximum of eight reported defects per day). This is displayed on a large board to which is added, every hour, the 'customer's' report on quality performance (see the diagram below).

PCB Quality Performance Friday 24th

FAULT	MAXIMUM	ACHIEVEMENT			
		9.00	10.00	11.00	12.00 →
Loose fit	1	–	NO DEFECT	1	–
Cracking	3	–		–	–
Electrical fault	2	1		–	–
Discolouring	2	–		1	1

This system ensures that the PCB workers know within an hour if a fault has slipped through to the assembly line. The individual responsible can be traced and the cause discussed. This might lead directly to a suggestion that would improve the production process. For example, workers have suggested changing the height of work benches, criticised the quality of materials from certain suppliers and learnt to spot when machines are starting to go wrong.

Improvement need not only stem from mistakes, however, so it is important to find ways of discussing how good methods can be made better. OKI's approach to communications begins with a 5–10 minute meeting every morning. Problems concerning the previous day's production are discussed and possible improvements may emerge. Twice a year all employees have an appraisal interview with their immediate superior. This is not concerned with pay or bonus levels, but with any problems or ambitions the employee has. It is a form of more reflective communication.

Interlinked with OKI's approach to communications is its heavy expenditure on training. Within its £250,000 training area, OKI provides new recruits with full induction courses, including simulated conveyor belt production lines. Existing staff are encouraged to take between six and fifteen days of training per year, primarily focused upon learning new skills. This creates a more flexible workforce and provides the skills (such as public speaking) to foster the discussion and involvement that the management seeks. In addition to job training, the company is very proud that 126 staff are taking Further Education evening courses up to degree level – sponsored by OKI.

In 1993 OKI piloted its first suggestion scheme, among the sub-assembly workers. A rule set from the start was that suggestions would only be considered if they related to the person's own performance. Suggestions on how others could improve were not welcome. The management team – all with experience of suggestion schemes in British firms – had debated about what type of financial rewards to offer. When raised with the pilot staff, however, this was treated with surprise. The staff felt that suggestions to improve people's working life or performance were worthwhile in themselves. The scheme got off to a strong start and is to be extended to other sections of the plant.

The result of all this effort is measured in two ways within the factory: quality defects and productivity. In 1988, 75% of completed PCBs passed first time when tested. After a year an 80% target was set, which was extended to 85% in 1992. With that having been achieved, the 1993 pass rate was pushed to 89%. This progress not only reduces the chance of a faulty product slipping through to the customer, but also reduces production time and therefore cost. Instead of 25% of all PCBs needing extra work in 1988, the target for 1993 pointed to only 11% failing first time.

The factory manager likes to measure productivity in a slightly unusual way. He believes that 'the 1990s are about speed' so he concentrates on the time it takes for a printer to be produced. In 1988 it took 120 minutes from the start of the final assembly line until packing. This included 45 minutes of 'robust test printing in extreme temperature conditions'. In 1994 the assembly target will be 75 minutes,

even though the test has not changed. This approach to improvement has enabled output per worker to rise to sixteen printers per week in 1993.

When asked about the company's management approach, Mr Kojima denies that it is purely Japanese. He makes it clear that he prefers the plain speaking of his Scots staff to the respectful language of the Japanese. Yet as he sits with his blue jacket on – the same jacket as on the shopfloor – there is no doubt that he has brought Japanese thinking to Scotland; and it seems a marriage of continuous improvement.

Questions
(50 marks; 90 minutes)

1 Why might OKI's management be happy to build the company's future 'around its staff rather than automation'? (8)

2 From OKI's experience, what are the main preconditions of establishing a successful kaizen programme? (8)

3 a Calculate OKI's output per worker in 1988 and 1989. (4)

 b Assuming an average wage of £150 per week in 1988 and £200 in 1993, what was the labour cost per unit in those two years? Express the change as a percentage. (6)

4 Ian Smith tries hard to encourage a lean approach to production at the Cumbernauld factory. What does this mean and what examples of this are evident within the text? (10)

5 OKI holds the BS 5750 quality standard, describing it as 'a possible starting point for developing high quality products'.

 a Why may BS 5750 not lead to high quality products? (5)

 b How has OKI achieved the quality levels that have won them the ICL and *Management Today* awards? (9)

39 TIME-BASED MANAGEMENT

Concepts needed: Product life cycle, Communications, Just-in-time, Single European market

It was the mountain bike experience that led to the changes. Wheeler Bikes of Nottingham had been producing profitably until a flood of cheap Taiwanese bicycles saturated the market. The collapse in the market price of mountain bikes led to huge losses at Wheeler. During the worst period, four years ago, the company was close to liquidation. It survived due to ruthless cost-cutting and rationalisation.

Since then, its finances have recovered to allow a new growth strategy. The first phase was to reorganise the factory into cells. The continuous production line was replaced by a system of ten work groups, each responsible for a significant part of bicycle production or assembly. The cells represented ten of the twelve links in the chain from raw material to customer (the other two being delivery and retail sale). Reinforced by flexible teamworking and just-in-time production, the company could regard its manufacturing as fully up to date.

Now Ann Raymond, the new Managing Director (MD), wanted to go one stage further. The firm could produce quickly and flexibly within its existing model range, but new products were still taking at least 18 months to get to the market. That slow pace increased the cost of new product development and restricted the firm's ability to respond to changing customer needs. A case in point was the new Wheeler 'City' bicycle, launched earlier this month. Started 20 months ago, it was conceived when the government Minister for Transport was offering subsidies to encourage local councils to create more bicycle lanes. Yet in this launch month for the Wheeler 'City', the company's main rival announced that its 'CommutaBike' had sold an impressive 50,000 in its first six months. Worse still, the government minister was being replaced by a car enthusiast.

Ann had recently attended conferences on Time-Based Management and simultaneous engineering. She felt ready to implement change. Her first step was to call a meeting of the heads of Wheeler's six departments. Ann explained that she wanted to set time-based targets for future product development, such as ten months from idea to retail sale. The head of engineering was concerned about the effect on design quality, but accepted the need for more speed. Ann assured him that she would finance the purchase of an advanced computer aided design (CAD) system, but urged everyone to think about how to coordinate better, rather than just to work faster:

'I'm sure that the key is simultaneous engineering. For the City bike, John worked for two months on the design before Christine even started thinking about the structure and materials. If they had spent a couple of days together at the outset, surely both could have been working at the same time.'

The MD showed what she meant by sketching a diagram of the stages they went through to produce a finished prototype of the City bike.

Diagram A: Development of City bike (64 weeks)

Diagram B: Development through simultaneous engineering (38 weeks)

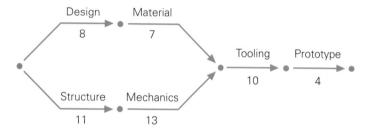

The head of engineering looked admiringly at the diagram, but was puzzled at the shorter times allowed in diagram B for tooling and making the prototype. Ann explained that this should be possible if the teams responsible for both operations were involved in the earlier stages. That would enable them to plan their work in advance.

During the following weeks the department heads went on a series of training courses. They learned not only that their MD's summary was sound but also more about how to make Time-Based Management work.

The course leaders emphasised the importance of communications. Different sections of the firm could only work simultaneously if each knew exactly what the other was doing. Otherwise there would be considerable wastage of time, materials and money.

Questions

(40 marks; 80 minutes)

1   It is widely thought that product life cycles are becoming shorter.

    a   For what reasons may this be occurring in a market such as bicycles?   **(6)**

    b   What implications do shorter life cycles have for Time-Based Management?   **(7)**

2   What may be the financial implications for Wheeler of shortening the development time for new products from 64 weeks to 38?   **(8)**

3   **a**   Explain the barriers to communications which the company may encounter.   **(5)**

    b   How should the company tackle them?   **(6)**

4   As with other elements of lean production, time-based management is about the elimination of waste. Why may this be of particular importance since the establishment of the single European market?   **(8)**

40

PROFIT AND MANPOWER PLANNING

Concepts needed: Market segmentation, Profit, Contribution

'Mercedes in Manchester!' The businessman from London could not hide his disbelief. 'Certainly,' replied the cab driver, 'I've been planning it for a couple of years now, and it starts next month.'

It emerged that the cabby owned the company the businessman had hired from, and was just standing in for an ill driver. As the drive from the airport to Ashton ground to a halt in rush hour traffic, the conversation brought out more details.

Trevor Wray had built up his car-hire business over eight years. At first, it was just him on the road, with his wife answering phone calls at home. In between fares he would drive from telephone box to telephone box, pinning his business card at eye level above the receiver, and removing any others that were there. Now he had four cabs on the road twenty-four hours a day – with ten drivers each alternating within a 12 hour shift pattern (A.M. and P.M.). Six drivers handled six shifts per week, and four did five shifts. Some even wanted to do seven shifts a week, but Manchester Council licensing arrangements prohibited that.

Deregulation of bus services in Manchester had been causing great problems, however. Many new bus companies had sprung up, causing a marked fall in the demand for taxi services during the daytime. It was different at night, as many of the buses stopped running at 6:30 pm. Yet the loss of trade in the daytime had encouraged some cabbies to switch to nights, so it was hard to operate profitably then as well. Most people expected that the situation would ease in a few months, though, as the bus firms cut back on unprofitable daytime routes.

'You wouldn't believe', Trevor continued, 'the costs involved in running four cabs like mine. Do you know that I have to pay £1,600 per annum insurance per driver? Not to mention the £12,000 overhead bill that each car must contribute to. And the Sierras only last eighteen months. By that time they've usually done 180,000 miles, and they're finished. I buy them for £8,000 and sell them for about £2,000. The cars each bring in £3,000 a month on average, but 50% of that goes to the drivers, and another 20% on diesel and maintenance, so I'm not left with enough to cover my fixed costs.'

The final straw had been a downturn in the local leisure and pleasure trade, caused by a squeeze on disposable incomes following a large increase in the mortgage rate. Hence the decision to switch from the mass market to an upmarket niche. Trevor knew that the business trade was still buoyant, and he suspected that Mercedes cars would always be in demand for special occasions.

'Of course I wouldn't have been able to afford to buy four Mercedes outright, but I found the dealer helpful in sorting out a leasing deal for me. Four £22,000 Mercedes on a three year contract for a total of £2,500 a month. Okay, the 50% rise in the insurance premiums is a killer, and I'll have to spend £20,000 on direct mailshots to local firms, but I still think I'll be better off. I thought it reasonable to charge 25% more; do you agree?' Having been reassured by the Londoner, he went on to explain that he expected monthly revenue per car to rise 50%, though his drivers would receive no more than before, and diesel and maintenance would rise by just 20%.

As they drove into Ashton, Trevor asked the Londoner about his line of work. 'Accountant', came the reply. The cabby grimaced as he realised that he should have been asking questions, not just chatting. He pulled up at the destination, and as he got out, the passenger said: 'If I were you I'd work out the figures with no volume increase. Leasing companies get rather heavy with people who can't pay their bills.'

Questions
(40 marks; 70 minutes)

1 Explain the meaning of the term niche, and discuss the importance of niche marketing strategy for modern businesses. **(10)**

2 Calculate the change that Trevor is anticipating in his profit as a consequence of his new strategy (ignore, for the moment, the accountant's advice). **(10)**

3 Outline the pros and cons of the switch to a Mercedes car fleet. **(10)**

4 Demonstrate that the shift pattern outlined will ensure that there are always four cars on the road. Make sure that no driver has to do mornings and evenings in the same week. **(10)**

41

PRODUCTION MANAGEMENT

*Concepts needed: Stocks, Theory X and Y, Company objectives,
Production management*

Scott's arrival from the United States as the new managing director came after eight redundancy programmes within the previous ten years. So the workforce of York International was understandably defensive, and job demarcation was rife. As a producer of air conditioning equipment, the firm's sales were dependent upon the highly cyclical construction industry – hence its hire-and-fire record. The poor morale among the eight hundred workers showed in the firm's poor delivery and quality performance. Sixty-one per cent of all deliveries were over twenty days late, and quality costs of £1.5 million a year were accounting for 14% of the total manufacturing bill. The major element in the quality cost was warranty claims, which implied further customer inconvenience and therefore dissatisfaction.

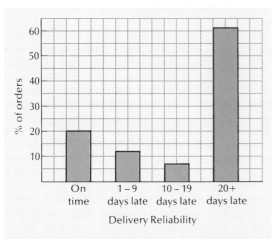

York delivery record before introduction of 'Order out of Chaos' programme

Scott's first statement to his staff was to promise no more redundancies, and to announce a three year programme for 'Order Out of Chaos'. At first, middle management was as sceptical as the workforce. The first action that made people take notice was Scott's order to the sales department to aim for steady growth. They were to refuse orders that would beat their sales targets, since that would disrupt the attempt to reorganise the production system. His second action was to set the factory the objective of establishing an efficient system of production control so that the whole production monitoring process could be computerised in twelve months' time. For Scott had quickly appreciated that York's fundamental problem was that it was locked into a chaos spiral.

Disorganisation undermined production control, which reinforced the disorganisation; and low morale had become both cause and effect. The greatest surprise for the staff was that the third step was not to dictate how this objective should be achieved, as the previous management would have done. Instead, he encouraged middle management to work in teams with engineers and shopfloor workers to decide on the correct strategy.

The building of order required certain key building blocks.

1 Training was needed on the purpose of monitoring systems, so that it was possible to obtain accurate data. Before, maintenance men would have helped themselves to spare parts from the stores; now careful recording took place.

2 Meaningful production plans were needed to schedule people's work for each

day. Variance analysis was used to check the accuracy of the planning, and major variances by individual workers were discussed openly between worker and foreman.

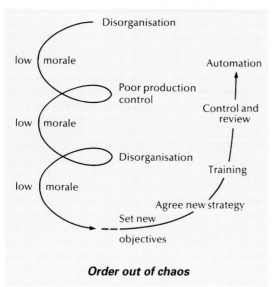

Order out of chaos

Within the twelve month target, York had production information of an accuracy that it had never enjoyed before; and production planning had emerged from the old-style crisis management. By the time the Manufacturing Resource Planning (MRP) computer was installed, Scott suspected that they had already achieved 80% of all the possible gains.

The computer monitored all material inputs and stocks, all production in each section of the factory (plus wastage) and finished goods quality and stock levels. It could also match this information with customer order quantities and delivery dates, enabling managers to anticipate when completion of a particular order would need to be speeded up. Within a year of the MRP computer's installation, on-time deliveries had risen to 85%, from 20% just two years before.

In the longer term, though, the computer's simulation capacity proved its most valuable facility. It enabled production engineers to get quick answers to questions such as '**What if** we replace the four hand-operated pressing machines with one automated one?' The computer could show not only the direct cost implications, but also the impact on work-in-progress, on factory layout, and on overheads.

Scott's managerial skill was to use such print-outs not as a blueprint, but for discussion with the relevant engineers and workers. Often it was found that there were better ways of using the existing equipment (perhaps using conveyor belt transfer of components). This encouraged the workforce to participate in decision making, and therefore to work to prove that the decision they had initiated or backed was the right one. The higher motivation of the workforce showed through in product quality. From representing 6.5% of the total manufacturing bill, the cost of guarantee claims fell to 1%.

The next stage in the company's production-led revival came with the appointment of an expert in Just-In-Time manufacturing as the production director. When interviewing, Scott made sure that candidates were not only qualified technically, but were also committed to a bottom-up approach to employee involvement. Authoritarian, top-down managers were rejected. For Scott was convinced that active participation by the workforce was essential if further changes to working practices were necessary.

Source: *Machinery and Production Engineering*

Questions

(50 marks; 90 minutes)

1   Explain why Scott felt the need to announce a programme for 'Order Out of Chaos'. **(6)**

2   How would the preparation for – and installation of – the MRP computer have
helped York's stock position? **(10)**

3   Discuss the management styles outlined in the text in terms of McGregor's
Theory X and Y. **(10)**

4   **a**   How might the computer's 'What If?' facility be used to improve further
the product and service quality received by customers? **(6)**

   b   Why would such achievements be important? **(6)**

5   In what ways could the success of Scott's approach be measured other than the
ones listed in the text? In what circumstances would such approaches be especially
important? **(12)**

42 PERSONNEL MANAGEMENT

Concepts needed: Division of labour, Trade unions, Labour turnover, Motivation

The ABC Company was proud of its reputation as a no-nonsense employer. The T.G.W.U. had once organised a six week strike over union recognition but the strikers had eventually given up. 'We want to make money, unions want to take money,' ABC's Chairman had once said.

The factory was organised with very high division of labour, in order to ensure that relatively unskilled workers could be used, yet output would be high. For the same reasons the factory was highly automated.

Now the Directors were having to admit that things were not working properly. Absenteeism (at 15%) and labour turnover (at 40% a year) were nearly three times the national averages, and were making it impossible for production to keep up with the demand for their products. Even more alarming was that the local Job Centre had told them that job-seekers were refusing to go for interviews at ABC because of its poor reputation.

The Board of Directors met to discuss the situation. The Production Director said:

> 'It's simple; we need much greater financial incentives. An extra £5 for every full week of attendance, a £500 bonus for each year of completed employment, and a £50 signing on fee.'

The Marketing Director disagreed:

> 'I think we need a new approach. Our products are pretty poor quality, and my customers complain that if they phone the factory to check on deliveries, our people are very off-hand with them. It's not just a matter of money, we need to give our workers the job satisfaction that will lead to a more responsible attitude by them'.

The Managing Director had a different solution: 'If we moved to the Northeast, the level of unemployment would mean people really want to get jobs and keep them. We could sell this factory, and with the proceeds could buy a factory in Newcastle plus management offices here in Bristol. So only Production need move.'

Question
(40 marks; 60 minutes)

1 Explain the term 'division of labour'. How might it lead to lower production costs per unit? **(6)**

2 In what ways might the ABC Company have been in better circumstances if a Trade Union had been allowed to represent their workforce? **(6)**

3 Explain the meaning of 'labour turnover'. Outline two major costs that would be caused by high labour turnover. **(6)**

4 Re-examine the Production Director's proposals. Discuss their advantages and disadvantages for the firm. **(8)**

5 Examine three other personnel-based considerations in the decision on whether to move to Newcastle. **(6)**

6 What elements might one introduce into the ABC factory production methods if one wanted to create more job satisfaction? What constraints might operate that prevent these from succeeding? **(8)**

MONEY AND MOTIVATION

Concepts needed: Profit, Remuneration, Consultation

The Walton Furniture Company is a long established, highly profitable business. Its sales turnover averages £15,000 per week. Given that it operates on a 200% mark-up (quite normal in furniture retailing), its £7,500 of weekly overheads are covered with ease. The owners have always believed that much of their success has been due to the incentive scheme they operate; the 2% commission on all sales provides a carrot of about £300 per week for the staff.

Recently, however, the owner/managers (Mr and Mrs Vine) have seen takings hit, following the departure of the only two full-time staff. Over the past eight weeks, sales have only averaged £10,500. Mr Vine believes it is just a temporary problem, as the two new full-timers find their feet. Mrs Vine decides to talk to each of the six staff members find out their views.

Joyce, a 55 year-old part-timer, has no doubts:

> *'It's the commission system that's causing the problem. Both the full-timers left because of it, and I'm totally fed up with it as well ... The problem is that you pay commission only to the person who writes out the customer's bill. So no-one wants to do any of the other jobs such as checking deliveries, chasing up special orders, or pricing new stock. You keep asking me to do these jobs because you know I'm reliable; but that prevents me from getting commission.'*

Eileen, a 22 year-old part-timer, is even more forceful:

> *'I can't stand Grace (another part-timer), because she's always robbing me of my commission. Yesterday morning, I spent two hours discussing sofas with a customer. After she'd settled on two £1,100 leather ones, she felt she should bring her husband along for a second opinion in the afternoon. And what happens? When I come back after my afternoon break I see them just leaving, and Grace has written out the bill for £2,200. So she makes £44 for doing damn all, while I do the work and get nothing. I'm still fuming, and I refuse to work with her again.'*

A shaken Mrs Vine then sees Margherita, one of the new full-timers (and the deputy manager). She is hardly reassuring:

> *'I've never known such a touchy, bitchy staff. I'm seriously thinking of quitting. I got Joyce to do some pricing this morning, and for the rest of the day she's been grumbling about Eileen getting a £1,000 order from a regular customer of hers. I can't see that £20 is worth all the fuss.'*

Questions

(30 marks; 45 minutes)

1 Remembering the commission, what profit would the Vines have made last year? **(6)**

2 Outline three problems with the commission system operated by the Vines. **(6)**

3 What alternative payment systems might work better, and why? **(8)**

4 What does the above passage suggest about the value of employee involvement and consultation groups? What might be the reasons why many firms make little use of this system? **(10)**

44 A BMW AT TWENTY-THREE

Concepts needed: Mayo, Maslow, Leadership styles

Yin Fan had a wonderful time at the school reunion. It started as soon as she turned up in her BMW. She happily told all the inquirers that it was her company car. 'A BMW at twenty-three!' gasped one. Throughout the evening she was grilled about her career, with many of her former classmates eager to know where she was working and at how high a salary. Several others had made good starts to their working lives, but none as glitteringly as Yin Fan.

When asked for details, Yin Fan explained that her advertising agency job involved planning and buying multi-million pound media campaigns for the agency's clients. She had to liaise with the marketing managers of advertisers such as Cadbury, Heinz and Dixons to find out the target market they were aiming for and then decide which media to use – TV or newspapers? If TV, how much on Channel 3 or Channel 4 or on satellite? How much in each ITV region? And so on. Yin Fan's working life was one of meetings, business lunches and a frantic social life revolving around an advertising agency staffed by young, well-paid people.

Back at her desk the following Monday, Yin Fan found herself enjoying the work more than ever. She smiled at the thought of her school friends' amazement that she had a PA (personal assistant) and a trainee working for her. The day's work revolved around an important negotiation for Cadbury on Channel 4. She met her boss, the Media Director, for twenty minutes to discuss tactics.

Tony was an unusual boss; from the day he hired Yin Fan two years ago, he had hardly ever told her what to do. On that day he gave her the Cadbury and Heinz business to run, and since then had done little more than to offer her the huge Dixons account as well. At first she had been daunted by her total responsibility for decisions involving millions of pounds. She knew that her predecessor had been fired, reputedly because one of the clients had talked about him unenthusiastically to Tony. Yet as the weeks passed she felt liberated by the freedom to make instant decisions. At her previous agency the Media Director had fussed over every aspect of the job, frustrating Yin Fan by interventions that seemed to cause more mistakes than they cured. Occasionally she and Tony talked over work at lunch, but otherwise he focused on his own clients and his Board responsibilities.

So her visit to talk things over with Tony was unusual. She wanted advice because the Sales Manager she would be dealing with at Channel 4 was an old friend of Tony's. With a planned budget of £500,000 for Channel 4, a discount of as little as 10% would represent a lot of money to hand back to Cadbury. So she wanted to establish the right approach to the negotiations.

Despite the pressures of the day, Tony found the time not only to advise Yin Fan, but also to ask her generally about how things were going. She took the opportunity to tell him how she had struck a deal giving Heinz £150,000 of extra, free TV airtime in Scotland, and about a costly mistake on a new business presentation. After 50 minutes she left Tony's office feeling invigorated. By mid-afternoon she had a 16.5% discount rate from Channel 4 and a rather smug smile.

Questions
(35 marks; 60 minutes)

1   Analyse Yin Fan's working life in relation to Maslow's hierarchy of needs.   **(10)**

2   **a**   Describe Tony's leadership style.   **(5)**

   b   In what circumstances might such a style be ineffective?   **(8)**

3   **a**   What is meant by the term 'Hawthorne Effect' and when did it occur in this case?   **(5)**

   b   The motivational importance of the Hawthorne Effect was identified over 60 years ago. Why may it be, then, that many managers still appear to ignore it?   **(7)**

BOOMTIME FOR BANKCHECK

Concepts needed: F.W. Taylor, Herzberg, Delegation and Consultation, Communications.

It had been a marvellous recession for Iain Truscott. His company BankCheck supplied ultraviolet banknote scanners, and demand soared as a wave of forged notes hit Britain. At first BankCheck's 40 employees were delighted at the job security implied by the firm's success. Then they found themselves overstretched as more and more orders needed to be processed. After three months of hectic work, mistakes began to be made with deliveries and invoices, so Iain advertised for more personnel: two sales and two clerical staff, plus three distribution workers. The result was an unwelcome deluge of 600 applicants.

By the time the new recruits started work, demand was already forcing still more appointments to be made. Iain could see this process continuing, so he hired a personnel officer to look after these matters. Yet with every extra appointment Iain was frustrated to find that even more of his time was required to induct the individual into his business and his ways of working. The situation became even worse when he found that the new personnel officer was failing to recruit the right kind of people. BankCheck's success had been built up by experienced, practical workers; yet many of the new recruits were graduates who had bright ideas but were unenthusiastic about applying the procedures that Iain had laid down.

Meanwhile, several of the original staff found jobs with competitor firms that were willing to offer responsible managerial posts to people from BankCheck. To stop this exodus, Iain offered substantial bonus payments to key personnel based on workload (as measured by the number of subordinates the manager was directly responsible for). This worked well at first, but less so as staff numbers rose towards 70.

The situation came to a head at the company's finest hour. Iain had just signed a £2 million contract with the National Dairy Federation to supply a portable banknote scanner to every milkman in the country. The extra work involved in supplying and training each milkman proved too much, and two key managers fell ill. Neither had kept their staff informed of their wider plans, so it was very hard for anyone to take over.

After eight weeks of chaos, in which Iain dashed around the country trying to keep things running, the Dairy Federation warned that if BankCheck could not sort out their administration, the contract would be cancelled and the firm would be sued. Other clients were just as angry, including some very long-standing ones.

Iain knew he must act fast, but felt too drained to think clearly about what to do, so he called in a management consultant.

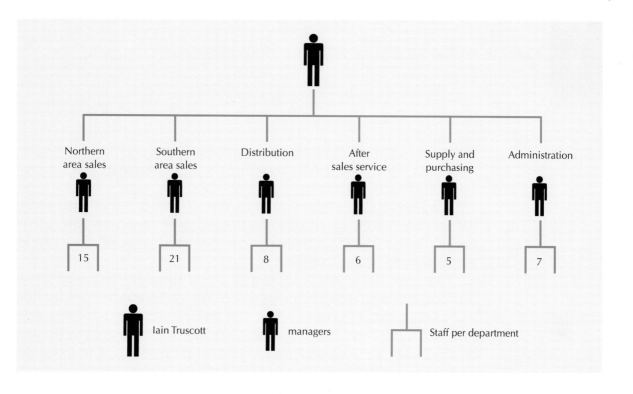

Northern area sales	Southern area sales	Distribution	After sales service	Supply and purchasing	Administration
15	21	8	6	5	7

Iain Truscott   managers   Staff per department

Questions
(40 marks; 60 minutes)

1 a Distinguish between delegation and consultation. **(4)**

   b Outline the causes and effects of poor delegation within BankCheck. **(10)**

2 One factor in BankCheck's difficulties was poor communication.

   a What organisational structures might have been set up to improve the internal communication? **(5)**

   b What difficulties might these structures have presented to such a fast growing small firm? **(5)**

3 a Faced with Iain's situation, discuss the practical advice that might be given by a follower of *either* Professor Herzberg *or* F.W. Taylor. **(10)**

   b What problems might be faced in carrying out this advice? **(6)**

46 THE TRENCH

Concepts needed: Health and safety, Government intervention

'Gary Wilson was very lucky. He suffered a collapsed lung and a broken pelvis, but others have died in similar circumstances…' began the Magistrate as he summed up the evidence he had heard.

It began with Gary's decision to have a year off between A-levels and college. He wanted to earn money quickly so that he could spend the spring in America. As the local builder (Lancashire Houses) offered the highest wages, he started there as a general navvy earning £5 an hour.

Lancashire Houses had been enjoying a local housing boom caused by the arrival of a large Japanese electronics factory. From a two man business, the firm had taken on forty-five employees on three different sites – each building eight houses. The two directors were finding it very hard to keep control over the sites as they had to spend so much time sorting out the problems of financing the £500,000 investment. To get round this problem, they hired site managers for each development and offered each one a £10,000 bonus if they could complete the work by a specified target date. (One week late would mean £8,000, two weeks late £6,000 and so on.)

Gary was shocked from the start at how hard the foreman worked him. In his first week he had shifted mounds of bricks, dug drainage holes, put up hundreds of feet of security wire fencing and cut dozens of metal pipes to length with a fearful metal-cutting saw. Shattered at the end of the week, he looked upon the weekend's driving rain with some optimism, hoping that the site would be too wet to work on Monday. Such illusions were soon dispelled by the foreman's orders, and Gary's day was spent carrying supplies to the bricklayers who were building up the walls in the rain.

The following day a JCB dug an eleven foot trench for laying drains. The foreman called Gary over to help him. Gary saw that water was running into the hole, but the foreman assured him that it was 'as safe as houses'. Both went down into the hole to lay the pipe. Gary was unaware that the correct procedure is to drive strong timbers into the ground at the sides of the hole, to create a wall. The foreman knew, but had not been supplied with the right type of wood, and felt that it was not worth hours of delay for what he considered to be the tiny risk of earth slippage.

Without warning, one of the sides collapsed. The foreman just managed to scramble out, but Gary was trapped. As another side gave way, it looked as though Gary would be buried alive. Miraculously, the wet mud kept just below his neck. After an hour he was freed and taken to an intensive care unit in hospital. He was only fit to be released after three weeks, and then needed two months in a nursing home. The collapsed lung would be a permanent disability.

Lancashire Houses were prosecuted by the Health and Safety Executive under the 1974 Health and Safety at Work Act. By failing to support the trench sides they had committed an offence under the construction regulations. They had also failed to notify the safety inspectors of the start of any of their three construction projects, and had no written safety policy as required by the law. The Burnley Magistrates Court found the company guilty on all charges. The company director in the dock apologised to the court, and explained that since the accident, they had sent their foremen on safety courses. A fine of £2,250 was imposed, plus costs of £56.50. During the hearing it emerged that the company had not had a visit from a factory inspector for three years.

Gary's friends urged him to sue the company for negligence, but when he went to a solicitor he realised that his father earned too much to be able to get legal aid, but far too little to afford the legal costs. The solicitor also made it clear that such cases can take years to come to court, by which time the company might have gone into voluntary liquidation. It was no help to be told by a friend that he should have joined a trade union, which would have taken up his case for him.

Although his accident caused some delays, better weather helped two of the sites to be completed within the bonus deadline. One of the two was the site where Gary's accident took pace.

Source: *Legal reports in 'Health and Safety at Work' magazine.*

Questions

(30 marks; 45 minutes)

1 Statistics show that young people suffer far more accidents at work than any other group. What might be the reasons for this? **(6)**

2 With the benefit of hindsight, what research or checking might Gary have done before taking the job? **(6)**

3 Discuss the underlying causes of this accident. **(10)**

4 What are the arguments against having more factory inspectors and bigger penalties for companies that break safety laws? **(8)**

MANAGEMENT STRUCTURE

Concepts needed: Management hierarchy, Company objectives, Span of control, Labour turnover

The new Chief Executive of British Aircraft Technologies (BAT) was a straightforward man. He thought it was his job to know how all the divisions of the business were doing. 'But how can I', he complained, 'when there are twelve divisions – each answerable to me?' He intended to set a **corporate objective** of cutting costs by 30% over the next three years, but was concerned about his own ability to monitor progress. As the objective was fundamental to BAT's survival in the competitive environment for high technology products, he decided a complete organisational restructuring was needed.

After several months of discussion with divisional senior management, it became clear that eight of the twelve could be merged into four new divisions – each headed by a Chairman. Of the remaining four, the managers in three were implacably opposed to any loss of independence. Yet the involvement of all three in military production suggested the solution that a Chairman be appointed to oversee the three independent divisions. The twelfth division fitted poorly with any of the others, so it was kept separate; it, too, was to be run by a new Chairman.

Within this new hierarchy, the divisional Chairman would be answerable to the Chief Executive, who would in turn be **accountable** to the Board of Directors. The Chief Executive would agree corporate objectives with the Board, then decide divisional goals and budgets in consultation with each Chairman before the start of each year. The Chairman would then have complete autonomy to work within the agreed constraint, and each division would be a **profit centre**.

The new structure proved highly successful. The Civil Aircraft division set its own priority as the reduction of production time, in order to speed up deliveries to customers. This, they reasoned, would increase demand and thereby enable existing capacity to be utilised more effectively.

Within two years the assembly time on their executive jet had been cut from twenty-six weeks to twelve. This was achieved by reorganising the factory layout, automating the more repetitive tasks, and retraining staff to use existing equipment more efficiently. These changes were only implemented after very full consultation with the workforce; indeed some of the most valuable ideas came directly from the shop floor. It was clear that the division would achieve its cost reduction target, and at higher output levels than many had thought possible.

Four of the other divisions adopted more conventional cost-cutting measures, which also looked likely to achieve the 30% cut the Chief Executive demanded.

The Military Products division, though, struggled badly. Its Thames Valley production site for Guided Weapons was losing many high quality, technologically educated staff to local computer firms. Labour turnover was averaging 35% a year on its 2,000 employees. Given that new employees were costing an average of £4,000 to recruit and train, the annual cost was enormous.

The Chairman of the Military Products division argued that the site should be moved to Derby, where the larger pool of skilled labour should ensure longer term employment. The Director of Guided Weapons refused to allow this, however, and reminded the Chairman that he had delegated to him the details of the restructuring. Six months after this, a reorganisation was announced for the Military Products division, in which the post of Director of Guided Weapons became redundant.

Questions

(40 marks; 70 minutes)

1   Explain the meaning of the following (emboldened in the text):

corporate objective

accountable

profit centre. **(6)**

2   What was the Chief Executive's span of control before the reorganisation?
What evidence is there that it was too wide? **(6)**

3   Draw a chart to show the organisational hierarchy after the first restructuring. **(6)**

4   Why is it considered so important for organisations to have a clear structure, with clear lines of authority? **(8)**

5   How might careful consultation help in the reorganisation of the factory layout? **(6)**

6   a   What was the annual cost to BAT of the high labour turnover on the Thames Valley site? **(4)**

b   Explain two other effects of high labour turnover on a firm. **(4)**

48 BRITISH MANAGEMENT TECHNIQUES UNDER FIRE

Concepts needed: Leadership, Industrial democracy, F.W. Taylor, F. Herzberg

A research study into British versus German management style and practices has highlighted many differences. It found that in Britain, attitudes to leadership and consultation showed a more personalised and one-way view which is more suited to a more traditionally authoritarian kind of organisation.

British attitudes to the workforce showed a stronger tendency to emphasise the **'Economic Man' approach** associated with F.W. Taylor. There tended to be more **layers of hierarchy** in Britain and more **differentiated conditions**, e.g. in canteens, rest rooms, and employment contracts. Researchers found that engineers and production people had a lower status in the United Kingdom, and tended to occupy fewer of the top management positions than the marketing and finance professionals. Furthermore, there was less training and education among the workforce in the U.K. than in Germany.

To develop this analysis further, they decided to compare British and German management within the same company – a German manufacturing firm with a large British subsidiary. This would remove certain variables (such as different production processes) and therefore help to focus on factors such as management style, leadership, and consultation.

The company selected was a very forward-thinking one – much concerned with employee job satisfaction. It had already done away with high division of labour assembly lines, and provided exceptionally clean, neat factory conditions. The latter point struck one researcher most forcefully in Britain, 'where standards in factories are so much lower in general than in Germany'.

It emerged that the main contrast was between the British subsidiary and other local British firms, rather than between the British and German branches of the same firm. The company's British workers liked the absence of conveyor belt assembly lines and the payment by salary; one said: 'At other places it's a rat-race because of the piecework.' They also appreciated the more equal treatment: 'Usually office workers are better looked after than us; here the management are pretty decent.'

The comparison with Germany did yield some useful points though:

1   In the German branch, a Works Council had been operational for twenty years, with great success. It provided a regular meeting point between management and elected worker representatives to discuss future plans and any immediate problems. The workforce considered it much more valuable than the contact they have with the boardroom via their two Worker Directors (all German firms have elected Worker Directors – by law).

2 The relationship between Management and Trade Unions seemed much more mature in Germany, as was revealed in this quote from a German manager: 'Here, during the recession, the Unions were very reasonable. The company placed all their accounts and statistics before them – not only the annual accounts… it's no use to employers having dissatisfied workers.'

3 The firm's German managers seemed more aware of the psychology of management and of the need to delegate. The idea of German authoritarianism proved a myth.

Questions
(40 marks; 60 minutes)

1 Explain the meaning of the following (emboldened in the text):

    the 'Economic Man' approach (3)

    layers of hierarchy (3)

    differentiated conditions. (3)

2 What evidence is there that the British managers were more inclined to an authoritarian management style? (8)

3 Discuss the possible effects of engineers and production people having a lower status in the United Kingdom. (5)

4 Professor Herzberg has said that: 'The worst way to pay people is on piece rate…reinforcing behaviour. The best way is a monthly salary.' Consider the likely reasons for this view. (8)

5 Outline three ways in which a firm might benefit from a successful Works Council. Why may this provide more effective consultation than Worker Directors? (10)

49

MRS AHMED'S COUSIN

Concepts needed: Mayo, Piecework, Employment discrimination,
                    Data Protection Act

Mrs Ahmed shrieked when the needle hit her finger. As her cousin helped her to the medical room, she realised that she had nodded off at her workbench. The rushed order for 15,000 pairs of jeans had meant 10-hour days and 6-day weeks for the past month. Mrs Ahmed had not even wanted the extra work, for although the money was needed, a 40-hour week was as much as she could cope with. When she turned the overtime down, the proprietor of Mile End Textiles (MET) had threatened her with dismissal. With no shortage of clothing machinists seeking work locally, she had to accept.

At their thirty-minute lunch break, the other workers asked anxiously about the damaged finger and talked yet again about the harshness of their working lives. Half were on a flat rate of £2.64 per hour, while the others were on piecework. The flat rate represented the wages council minimum, but now that the government was abolishing the councils, there was a chance that the rate would fall rather than rise. The biggest staff grievances were that none received holiday pay and there was no bonus rate for overtime. Mrs Bradfield thought it typical of the manager's meanness, while Mrs Ahmed's cousin pointed out that:

> *'It makes little sense, as it means that we are always
> tired and never have anything to look forward to.'*

As the discussion continued, Mrs Ahmed turned to her cousin and asked her to tell everyone what she had learned about the wage differentials in the factory. This was risky, as her cousin was supposed to keep secret the things she found out in her new post as office assistant. She hesitated, but was soon persuaded to say that:

> *'The men are all on much more than the women. In the warehouse
> they earn £3.50 an hour and the mechanics are on £4.80. It's the
> same in the office, with Dave the book-keeper getting more than
> Sarah, our materials buyer.'*

The all-female machinist section was outraged to hear that the warehousemen were earning so much extra. Making jeans was hard, skilful work, whereas the warehousemen could work at their own pace and the forklift trucks took most of the physical labour out of the job. Several muttered about joining a union, but they all knew that the MET management would never give it recognition.

That afternoon the cousin was summoned to see the proprietor. He said straight away that her conversation had been overheard and that she was being dismissed for breach of trust. She pleaded to have her job back, as it had taken her four years at MET to make the switch to the office. Her regrets were too late.

After ten months of applications, interviews and rejections, it was a radio programme that made Mrs Ahmed wonder whether her cousin had been placed on an employers' blacklist. She persuaded the cousin to write to the local Textile Employers' Federation for a copy of any computerised files held on her. To her surprise the Federation did send information, and it contained a damning comment about 'her disruptive influence'. Clearly, to have any chance of getting another job in the industry she would have to get that phrase removed. In despair, she turned to the Citizen's Advice Bureau.

Questions

(40 marks; 60 minutes)

1 a   On what grounds could the company be taken to court for sex discrimination?   **(5)**

   b   How might the women proceed in this action?   **(5)**

2 How might Mile End Textile's management approach have been viewed by a
   follower of Mayo's Human Relations school?   **(10)**

3 What is the business significance of:

   a   the abolition of wages councils
   b   keeping pay differentials secret
   c   a management not giving union recognition?   **(12)**

4 What advice might the Citizen's Advice Bureau have given the cousin about her
   legal position?   **(8)**

50

FACTORY SAFETY

Concepts needed: Communication, Break-even, Piecerate

'Not another accident! That's the eighth this week, and the day shift haven't had a single one.' As Production Manager of PowerMo Lawnmowers, Mike was responsible not only for safety but also for output, and he knew each production line accident lost him an average of 60 units. He was a great believer in delegation, so he left the Night Shift Manager to get on with things. Though, as Mike admitted to himself, he had not seen much of him lately, so they ought to meet to discuss the situation. The night shift would not be in until five o'clock, so Mike spent the morning digging out figures on the accident rate by shift over the past year. He passed them over to his management trainee for comment, who turned them into the bar chart shown below.

Meanwhile, Mike consulted his six day-shift foremen about the monthly variations in safety. One explained:

> *'Well, you're always going to get peaks before holiday times when you're on piecework, aren't you? The lads are aiming to get a good 20% more in July and December than they do regularly. And, if you work 20% faster on those grinding machines, it's not surprising that you get sloppy.'*

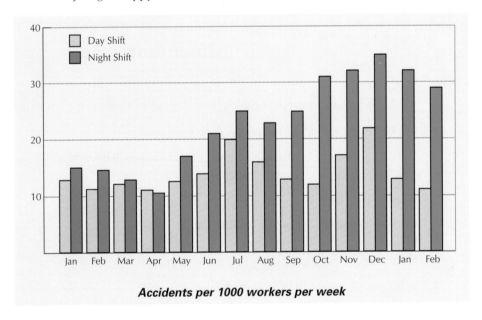

Accidents per 1000 workers per week

All agreed that there seemed no reason for the long-term accident rate to be rising, and that all seemed well for the coming Spring sales peak.

A quick check on the night shift's productivity figures revealed that there had been no improvement since last May, so there was evidently some other cause. Instead of talking to his night shift manager that afternoon, Mike decided to call in unannounced that evening. It occurred to him that he had not actually been there at night since just after the shift manager's appointment last May.

The afternoon's monthly management meeting proved sticky. The sales manager presented a report on customer feedback, which showed dissatisfaction with product quality and with delivery reliability over the past six months. Mike defended his department stoutly, blaming the 'second rate materials and components bought in by purchasing' (whose manager was away that day). Yet he found it harder to fend off the following implied criticism from the financial controller:

> *'I cannot understand how we have let the reject rate rise 50% in the last year. If it's due to faulty components, why are they not checked before wasting labour time on them? This has put our variable costs up to £1.40 per unit instead of the budgeted £1.32, which has cut our contribution per unit by 8 pence to 32 pence. So now our breakeven point has risen to 100,000 units.'*

Mike's evening visit proved more illuminating than he had anticipated. During the day, the factory was a hive of purposeful activity. Now, he observed men shouting out conversation, even jokes, above the mechanical din. They were working on dangerous machinery, and supposed to be producing products to exact specifications, yet concentration levels seemed low. Mike looked in vain for the night shift manager or his foreman, until he found them in the office. He kept calm enough to find out that neither man knew of any problems. Both assumed that the safety, productivity, and wastage figures were quite satisfactory; they had heard nothing to the contrary.

It was the trainee, the following day, who completed the misery of Mike's week. He had heard from a secretary that the shop stewards for the night shift had asked for an urgent meeting with Mike's boss.

Questions

(40 marks; 70 minutes)

1 What indications are there that PowerMo's internal communications are poor? Outline the main problems this could cause the firm. **(10)**

2 Draw a fully labelled break-even chart to show the planned and the actual financial position of the firm. Note that the firm's maximum capacity is 150,000 units. **(10)**

3 Discuss the likely advantages and disadvantages to PowerMo of using a piece rate payment system. **(10)**

4 Use the evidence provided as a basis for discussing the general importance to businesses of monitoring factory safety. **(10)**

51

TEAMWORKING – THEORY AND PRACTICE

Concepts needed: Recruitment, Discrimination

'I'm Ronnie Stannard, very pleased to meet you.'

Ronnie sat down and looked carefully at Yeisho's three-man interview panel. They all looked friendly, but very formal. Earlier that day she had undergone three hours of aptitude and attitude tests; she felt tired, but now had to be at her best.

'Ronnie is, um, unusual. Is it your full Christian name?', asked one of the men in suits. She assured them that it was hers from birth. Later, one asked suspiciously about 'the reference on your form to Fulham Ladies' Football Club'. He needed reassurance that women's football was increasingly widely accepted. Despite these concerns about whether Ronnie would fit in with the other staff members, the interviewers soon decided that she was an ideal recruit. Her astute answers to questions about her commitment, ambitions and attitude to work came across very well. She impressed them with her explanation of how she had become Fulham's coach as well as player. To her great delight she was offered the supervisor job on the spot.

That night she ran the training session for her football team. It was, as usual, a quick-fire mixture of hard exercise, skills training, short five-a-side matches and banter. After 90 minutes all the team were laughing and sweating in equal measure. After a shower they pulled on their Fulham tracksuits and went out for their customary curry.

During the meal, talk turned to their previous coach, Terry. He had been tough on discipline, but the harder he tried to teach them a new skill, the less confident they felt in their own abilities. He made them feel that their only role was to get the ball to the team's star player – and she never passed it to anyone. Their season had been tense and unsuccessful. Ronnie had changed all that. The star had relaxed into being a proper team member, and the exact same players as last year's relegation contenders were now third in the National Women's League.

The following Monday Ronnie started work at Yeisho Electronics. She was to be the supervisor of the finished assembly production cell, though her first week would consist of induction training. She listened with amusement about the company's teamwork philosophy, its morning exercises, the company uniform and its continuous improvement (kaizen) groups. Yet whereas Ronnie looked happier and happier as the week progressed, the other staff on the induction course looked less and less so. When, on the Friday, they had to come in fifteen minutes early for a team briefing and exercises, most had surly faces. Ronnie positively glowed.

The next Monday would be her first day on the production line. She arrived at 7.30 to prepare herself for the 7.45 team briefing session. To her surprise the first worker strolled in at 7.55 and most came in together at precisely 7.59. All Ronnie could do was to insist that they arrive promptly tomorrow and then hurry them onto the production line for the start of the 8.00 shift.

That week proved the most stressful of Ronnie's life. She was being ignored by the men she was supposed to be supervising. Gradually, though, she pieced together what had happened. The previous supervisor had been promoted from the shopfloor and had built up a team spirit based upon contempt for the 'Japanese gimmicks'.

The unit had worked effectively until quality problems emerged. Then an audit of the cell's methods of working revealed how far it was from the Yeisho approach. Foolishly, though, the factory manager had not told the personnel department about the problem before going on holiday. So Ronnie had been totally unprepared for the inevitable hardships of taking over such a team.

Saturday's fixture against Doncaster was a great relief for Ronnie. Her teammates realised that she was tense and, on the coach journey up the M1, dragged the story out of her. They felt that she should dump the problem on the factory manager's lap, but they also worried that people might see the situation as a woman unable to manage a group of men. Over coffee at a service station they agreed that she should:

1   explain the situation to the factory manager on his return from holiday the following Monday;
2   call each person, in turn, off the production line for a private chat about the situation, warning each that without cooperation she would have to issue formal warnings about insubordination;
3   keep the factory manager fully informed at every stage.

Coming to this conclusion was a great weight off Ronnie's mind. She was able to play a full part in the afternoon's 2 – 2 draw and slept more deeply on the coach home than she had done for days.

At 7.40 that Monday Ronnie went to see the factory manager. She was astonished to find two of her production line workers there already. The manager asked her to wait outside 'for a few minutes'. A quarter of an hour later she was called in to be asked how she had managed 'to upset the men so much in such a short time'. Although furious, she controlled her temper enough to put her side of the case and to state her three-point plan. The manager listened coldly to what she had to say, and just said 'leave it with me'.

Ronnie went to the personnel manager who had been on the selection panel and had inducted her. She explained the whole story but he seemed embarrassed to hear it. All he said was: 'Graham's the factory manager and what he says goes, I'm afraid.' She left in a daze, with her mind swirling with thoughts of teamwork and team management. Where should she go from here?

Questions

(40 marks; 70 minutes)

1 Outline the strengths and weaknesses of Yeisho's recruitment and induction procedures.   **(10)**

2 Discuss the degree of similarity between Yeisho's stated personnel management policies and Ronnie's approach to running the football team.   **(10)**

3 Use the text as a starting point to assess why discrimination exists in certain workplaces.   **(10)**

4 What is your assessment of how these events actually ended? In other words, what happened next?   **(10)**

52 PUTTING HERZBERG INTO PRACTICE

Concepts needed: Productivity, Profit, F.Herzberg, Conflict and change

Although Professor Herzberg's researches date back to the late 1950s, it was still unusual in the mid-1970s for British businessmen to have heard of him. So Frazer Park was a rare Managing Director to not only have studied Herzberg, but also to be determined to implement his recommendations. His target was the semi-skilled workers producing his firm's main product: plastic-coated wire bindings. He knew he was taking a risk, because Herzberg's researches into job satisfaction were conducted on white collar and engineering jobs. There had always been dispute, therefore, about whether the theories could be applied to semi-skilled and unskilled factory work.

At the time Frazer Park became Managing Director of Russell Gray Holdings (RGH), the production of the wire bindings (the kind used on calendars and computer manuals) was divided into five tasks (see below). He saw his first task as the combining of these functions into one. In that way, each worker would have a complete unit of work; they could follow an order through from its arrival to its despatch. All the operatives would be trained to check the quality of the wire on arrival from suppliers, and the quality of their own finished products. Any sub-standard goods sent out would be traceable, because every box sent out was to be signed by the worker. This began as a sensible monitoring process, but quite soon clients started to ask for specific operators by name, which provided recognition for achievement.

This reversal of the classic process of division of labour did cause a short-term reduction in output, especially from those workers whose previous, specialised jobs

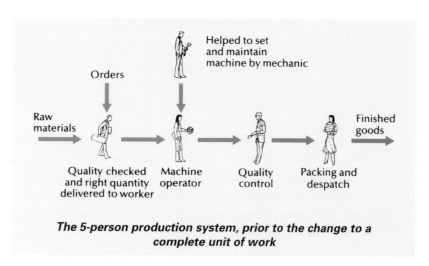

The 5-person production system, prior to the change to a complete unit of work

had higher status than that of machine operator. To counter this, Park knew that he would need to enlist the help of the employees to improve working practices and methods. So problem-solving groups were established. Typically, they would consist of two operators, an engineer, and one person from each of Purchasing and Sales. Problems tackled and solved included strengthening the packaging, designing a new wire-pressing machine, and tackling the problem of late deliveries caused when workers were ill or on holiday. Russell Gray Holdings (RGH) had this system in place long before quality circles became trendy.

When asked about the value of these groups, the Works Manager said:

> 'The more angles and options you can get to make the decision from, the nearer you are to a correct solution…and involving the people in the factory creates interest – a break from the normal routine – a chance to think…One of the biggest problems a manager has is getting people to change their ways of working. Involving people in making decisions helps to overcome resistance to change.'

Having addressed the higher order needs of the workforce, Park tackled the 'hygiene/maintenance' needs. Productivity bonus schemes were phased out, so that factory workers could be put on the same salaried basis as office and managerial staff. The foremen were very apprehensive about this, as they imagined it would be much tougher driving a workforce that no longer had a financial incentive to work hard. In fact, this problem arose with a mere handful of the sixty workers, and most of those chose to leave within a month.

In the longer term, RGH found that moving people from piece rate to time rate helped focus on the need to raise productivity by better machinery or methods, rather than by 'harder work'. Furthermore, Park made it clear that he intended his workforce to be paid at the top end of the local pay ranges, and for a share of any productivity gains to be used to increase real earnings further. These policies helped to bring about an atmosphere in which raising productivity could be viewed as a common aim.

By 1979 Park felt the confidence to remove a standard complaint among industrial workers – the differences in conditions of service between them and 'staff'. So the shopfloor workers were given pension rights and sick pay, while for the first time clocking-in was stopped for all employees (though new white and blue collar staff had to clock in for their first 12 months until they had earned the right to staff status).

As Herzberg's study highlighted, for many employees the major source of dissatisfaction is not related to status or pay, but is due to a feeling of being over-supervised. Frazer Park's own trust in his workforce, and his establishment of enlarged jobs with self-checking, both pointed to the need for a streamlined management structure. So, in consultation with staff, he cut the layers of hierarchy from five to three over a number of years.

This led to a wide span of control, which forced supervisors to delegate more,

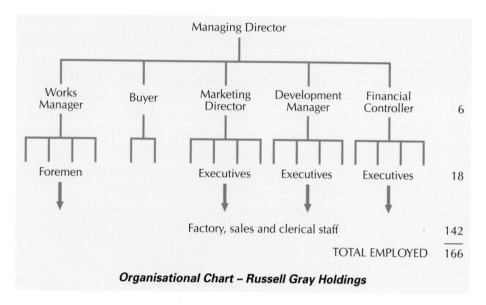

Organisational Chart – Russell Gray Holdings

and check up less on their subordinates. Throughout the organisation, people were expected to take responsibility for their own decisions.

A further benefit of the new management structure was the reduced number of intermediaries between shopfloor and Boardroom. This helped Park to achieve what he felt certain was a key piece in the jigsaw – the achievement of good communications. He wanted the workforce to understand fully not only what was going on currently (and why), but also what was planned for the future. Monthly briefing meetings were established, and a company newsletter was distributed every week.

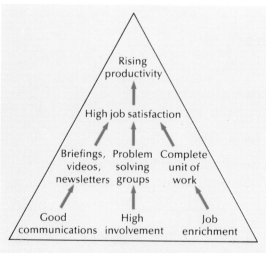

The Russell Gray Method

He felt particularly strongly that staff (even managers) tended to misunderstand the nature of 'profit'. By now, in the early 1980s, RGH's profit was approaching £750,000 per annum on a turnover of £5 million, so there was a lot of scope for employees to feel that someone was getting very rich from their efforts. So Park bought a video camera, and made – each year – a film to explain where the profit had come from and how it was going to be ploughed back into the business. All employees were given an hour off work to see the film and to talk about it.

RGH's style of management proved highly successful. After initial teething problems, product quality, delivery reliability and productivity all rose. Yet higher productivity can represent a threat to jobs, unless rising demand allows output to rise. This could have undermined Park's whole programme, as no-one would discuss labour-saving or cost-cutting measures if they were talking themselves out of a job. In RGH's case, the ending of long-standing patents during the 1970s meant that maintaining market share and output was a real struggle. So a strategy was needed to absorb the extra labour time being generated.

At first, RGH retrained staff to work in-house on processes that had previously been subcontracted. When there were no more jobs that could be done internally, the managers looked for new product opportunities. One such was the Snakey toy (the rings that walk downstairs), which was produced in a variety of bright colours for firms such as Habitat and Hamley's. For the management, Snakey represented a business opportunity; for the workforce it represented an outlet for their extra productivity – in other words, job security.

By 1985, with sales of over £7 million and profits topping £1 million for the first time (a better profit margin than ICI), it appeared that RGH's model management was set for long term success. Then to the complete shock of the workforce, Frazer Park 'resigned'. The reasons for this remain unclear. Probably either RGH's American owner decided that Park was becoming overly absorbed in his design of a perfect employee-centred company, or they demanded that he generate higher short-term profits than he thought wise. Visiting the factory soon afterwards, it was clear that the workforce was deeply sad to lose him. The Personnel Manageress who had helped implement many of his ideas left soon afterwards. The new Managing Director had a tough act to follow.

Source: *from visits to the firm, the name of which has been changed.*

Questions

(50 marks; 90 minutes)

1   a   Identify the features of Frazer Park's policies that fit into Herzberg's two categories: motivators and hygiene factors.   **(8)**

   b   Why might it be a mistake to tackle one but not the other?   **(6)**

2   Why might one expect that a reversal of the process of division of labour would lead to a reduction in output (apart from the status problem mentioned in the text).   **(6)**

3   Discuss the benefits and costs of 'involving people in making decisions'.   **(10)**

4   How might employees misunderstand the nature of 'profit'? Why is it important to management that the term should be understood fully?   **(10)**

5   Why can productivity be a source of conflict between management and workers? How did Frazer Park attempt to turn it into a common aim?   **(10)**

A DAY IN THE LIFE OF TERESA TRAVIS

Concepts needed: Communications, Delegation

Teresa sat down at her desk and switched on the PC. It flashed up two memos, one from the accounts department and another from the Manchester office. As she read them, her assistant came in with coffee and the mail. 'Deal with Manchester please, Anne,' she said, nodding at the screen.

Anne went over to her desk and called up the memo, to puzzle over its contents and a suitable response. As usual, Teresa had handed on a task that Anne knew little about; and if she quizzed her boss about it there was likely to be a sharp retort about 'showing responsibility'. The manager of the Manchester office wanted to know the progress being made on the job for Graylink plc, as the deadline for completion had passed two days ago.

Meanwhile Teresa had rummaged through the post to find a letter from her biggest client. It was a message of congratulation for his satisfaction with the new Sales Director that Teresa had found. She scanned the letter into the internal computer network, to circulate it to her fellow Directors, then composed an elegant reply to the client. Teresa enjoyed great success at 'Park Lane Headhunters', the recruitment agency for senior management personnel, and was not shy about keeping others informed.

Before she had been through the rest of her letters, a telephone call from the Managing Director summoned her to an emergency meeting. A letter had arrived from a long-standing client threatening legal action for negligence over a disastrously unsuccessful appointment. The absence from the meeting of the executive responsible showed the extent of the Managing Director's displeasure. Teresa put forward the view that even though their contracts with clients denied liability for their recommendations, they could not afford the bad publicity generated by a court case. Both of her fellow Directors agreed with this, but the Managing Director eventually said: 'I don't think we can afford to set a precedent. We'll have to brazen it out.'

Back at her desk, Teresa went through the rest of her post, then called up the computer's 'Pending' file. It contained the names and phone numbers of the firms she had decided to contact that week. Part of her job was to press for new clients and therefore extra sources of sales revenue. Teresa decided which companies to try, while Anne phoned to find out the right person to contact and then sent a standard introductory letter. This was later followed up by Teresa phoning to suggest a preliminary meeting, possibly over lunch (depending upon how promising the contact sounded). She decided that she would try three of the numbers that morning.

The first of the contacts was in a meeting, but the second proved promising. Yes, he often needed to appoint senior staff, and indeed newspaper advertising often failed to get the right calibre of applicant, and yes he was free for lunch next Thursday. The third call was to the Personnel Director of a large construction company. It began well, but started to go wrong when the Director referred to: 'The necessity for higher job quality delivery within the Field Installation section and the Attachment Materials Pipeline'.

As Teresa was grappling mentally with this, he asked whether she had experience in finding 'Unix-based Quality System Auditors'. She mumbled an apology and rang off.

It was with some relief that she went off to her lunch appointment with a long-standing client. Nahdia Khan ran a chain of fifteen exclusive, high fashion clothing outlets. Teresa recounted her story of the construction company to hoots of laughter from Nahdia, setting the tone for a relaxing lunch. Over coffee it was interrupted, however, when Teresa's mobile phone rang with an urgent message from the Managing Director, demanding that she return to sort out 'the Manchester problem'.

The afternoon turned quite unpleasant as Teresa blamed Anne for being unable to deal with 'a minor query from Manchester'. The atmosphere worsened when Teresa saw a copy of the fax that her assistant had sent. It made it plain that work on the Graylink account had all but ceased. It was honest but hardly tactful. Teresa phoned the head of the Manchester office to apologise for Anne's 'bizarre' fax, and to assure her that several contacts looked promising. The remainder of the day was spent in a frustrating and fruitless chase for Graylink's new head of finance.

To round off Teresa's day, just as she was about to leave a call came through from the accounts department: 'About that memo…'.

Questions
(35 marks; 60 minutes)

1 Identify the main barriers to effective communication within the case. **(6)**

2 Consider how Teresa could delegate more successfully to Anne. **(6)**

3 How effectively does Park Lane Headhunters use modern, electronic forms of communication? **(6)**

4 Use the case as a prompt to compare the advantages of written and oral communications. **(8)**

5 Research has shown that managers spend over half their working days communicating with others. How might this proportion be reduced without damaging the effectiveness of the organisation? **(9)**

54 THE NEW LASER SCANNING SYSTEM

Concepts needed: F.W. Taylor, Remuneration, Motivation

When the laser scanning system was first mentioned, Suzanne felt the same sense of mild anticipation as the other check-out staff. The management explained that because it would do away with individual item pricing, it would prevent friction with customers over missing or incorrect prices. Furthermore, the fact that it was modern technology might make it easier to get another job in the future.

In the lead up to the changeover, all the staff went on a two day training course. This was interesting and gave Suzanne a chance to get to know her fellow workers far better than ever before. So by the time it was installed, her attitude to the system was very positive. This was strengthened further in the early weeks, when managers came round regularly to ask her how it was going, and when customers chatted about their likes and dislikes of the high-speed service.

The first moment of doubt came when she overheard managers discussing 'IPMs'. The store manager was telling the personnel manager that:

> *'Three of the staff are so far down on their IPMs that they're dragging the store average down. You must sort them out.'*

It soon became clear that IPM stood for Items Per Minute, and that the computerised tills not only checked out groceries, but also checked on staff. When managers realised that information was spreading on the grapevine, they called a meeting to explain how this information was to be used. All the staff were given a copy of the computer print-out from the previous week, as shown below.

Week 4 Summary Of Checkout Operator Productivity (Rear Of Store Operators Only)

Operator	Hours worked	Total items	Average IPM	Operators variance from their average IPM in in best hour	IPM in worst hour
Trudy S.	22	31,680	24	32	17
Simon G.	36	38,880	18	33	13
David W.	14	14,280	17	23	14
Tracy F.	35	52,500	25	30	21
Sonal S.	35	48,300	23	26	20
Suzanne P.	18	31,320	29	38	22
Jane H.	35	40,000	19	23	16
Steve H.	24	31,700	22	34	13
Eileen L.	38	57,000	25	36	16
Mutlu M.	20	25,200	21	27	17
AVERAGE	27.7	37,060	22.3	30	17
U.K. AVERAGE	24.5	36,450	24.8	30	20

The ten check-out staff were told that head office set a minimum IPM target of 22 per head. Any who failed to achieve this would be retrained, moved to other duties, or have fewer requests to work extra hours. Steve asked if there was any way the till could give them a running score of how they were doing, but apparently there was not. At the end of the session, the personnel manager asked Jane, Steve, Simon and David to stay behind.

Suzanne felt pleased to see how well she had been doing, and wondered whether the company might introduce a bonus scheme based upon IPM performance. She did feel disturbed, though, to think that this clever monitoring device had been sprung upon them. What came as a shock, however, was the pressure she found herself under at break time. Steve and Simon (both students at her college) told her bitterly that their performance had been compared directly with hers. Simon finished off by saying:

'What are you doing it for? They're making massive enough profits anyway. You ought to stop crawling and think of your mates.'

Over the following weeks Suzanne tried to slow down her workrate, but she found this surprisingly hard; she preferred to work at her natural, fast pace. Nevertheless, anything was preferable to poisoning her relationships with her work and college friends.

After four weeks, Steve and Simon had pushed their productivity level up to 22, while Suzanne's had slipped back to 25. The store managers held another meeting, though, because they were getting pressure from the Regional Manager to boost the IPM score up from the 22.8 level it had now stabilised at. The Deputy Store Manager showed clear signs of stress as he shouted:

'We've flogged ourselves sorting out all the teething problems with the new system. You don't know the half of it. All you have to do is to work reasonably hard. We're the ones with the hassles – don't make me pass them on to you.'

As Suzanne's productivity slid back up towards the 30 IPM level, she began to realise how much her back ached after a busy Saturday. During a dull Geography lesson the following Monday, she scribbled some numbers down on paper.

Over the following months several of the original staff left. Many complained about back pains; some also said that migraines were ruining their evenings. All felt that the scanning machines had made their job even more repetitive than before. With new, inexperienced staff being recruited, the IPM average for the store worsened. The Deputy Manager began to pressurise the older hands to work more hours; and when Steve slipped back to an IPM of 19 in the week of the mock A-level exams, the same manager bellowed at him. It was all too much, Suzanne handed in her notice that night.

Saturday hours

8.30 – 12.15 am =	3¾ hours
1.00 – 3.15 pm =	2¼ hours
3.30 – 6.00 pm =	2½ hours
	8½ hours

8½ hours × 60 mins = 510 mins

510 × 30 IPM = 15 300 items

15 300 × (say) ½ lb = 7650 lbs

7650 lbs ÷ 1440 lbs

= 5.3 tons a day !!

5.3 tons lifted for wages of £23.80 !

Questions

(40 marks; 70 minutes)

1 Analyse the mistakes, if any, you believe the store management team made. **(8)**

2 How might a follower of F.W. Taylor view this introduction of laser scanning? **(8)**

3 What use might managers with a more people-centred approach have made of the IPM summary table? **(8)**

4 Discuss Suzanne's thought about basing a bonus scheme on IPM performance. **(6)**

5 Apart from monitoring productivity, the computers controlling the scanning checkouts provide daily printouts of the number of sales of each of the 8,000 lines stocked. They also pass this information on to the head office mainframe computer that shows national figures and trends. What use might management make of this information? **(10)**

THE McKLINE DISPUTE

Concepts needed: Theory X and Y. Trade unions. Pendulum arbitration

'72% I can't believe it!'

McKline plc's Chief Executive was reacting to the result of the strike ballot held at its main factory. The ballot paper had asked the workers whether they were willing to take all-out strike action against the company's 'final offer' on pay and conditions. With such a clear majority, there seemed little doubt that all production of McKline railway coaches would be halted from the first of the following month. With a full order book currently, this would mean delivery delays to customers, which would trigger penalty clauses for missing agreed deadlines.

The Chief Executive called his Crisis Management Committee to a meeting that afternoon. He put forward three strategy options:

1   Present a revised offer, aimed at compromise.
2   Denounce the strike and its leaders, making it clear that the firm will not compromise.
3   Denounce the strike and warn that, if it goes ahead, the entire workforce will be dismissed and new, non-union staff be recruited.

With the exception of one of the four members, the committee was visibly shocked as the third option was read out. She, the Strategic Planning Director, nodded then said: 'I think we should take advantage of the situation to de-unionize our whole operation. Customers will understand and shareholders will be delighted.' As she developed her theme further, it was clear that two of the three members were being persuaded to adopt this radical approach.

The fourth committee member was the Production Director and therefore the person responsible for the factory. He waited until the Strategic Planning Director had finished and then said: 'You're assuming that engineers of the standard required for railway carriage construction can be picked up anywhere. I assure you that our workforce have skills, developed over many years, that are unique in this country.'

The Chief Executive murmured, 'I think you're being rather emotional about this,' and then the meeting broke up, to reconvene the next morning.

Meanwhile, the shop stewards were meeting in the Works Convenor's office. All were jubilant at the ballot outcome, for it seemed to them that, after years of meek acceptance, their members were at last willing to take a stand against McKline's tough management. They speculated on the terms of the compromise offer anticipated from the management side. The only note of disharmony came from one shop steward who could not resist pointing out: 'Three years back, most of you were backing a pendulum arbitration, no strike deal. Where would that leave us today?'

For the rest of the day, the Chief Executive and the Works Convenor fielded a series of questions from journalists. The McKline dispute was of interest because it might become the biggest private-sector strike for many years. The factory employed 2,800 people and dominated local business around Darlington.

The next day's morning papers were full of articles on the dispute. The Chief Executive enjoyed the *Telegraph's* condemnation of 'union barons attempting to rekindle the flames of the 1970s'. Less comfortable was a *Financial Times* article suggesting that the management's decision not to proceed with a pendulum arbitration arrangement now looked ill-judged. On the actual dispute itself, it commented: 'The company's pay offer of 5% seems reasonable, given 4% inflation currently. It is ambitious, however, to tie that in with an end to job demarcation and a change to new shift patterns that would double the amount of night and weekend working.'

Following that morning's meeting of the Crisis Committee, the board of directors was informed that this statement would be sent to the Works Convenor and the media:

PRESS RELEASE

November 10th

McKline plc

McKline plc regrets that a campaign of misinformation by union leaders has produced a ballot result that threatens the survival of the company. As only 65% of employees belong to a union, fewer than half of all staff have voted for a strike. Therefore, we call on the union leadership to act democratically and call off the industrial action. Should the strike take place, the Directors of McKline plc will have to protect the rights of the majority of its staff and the welfare of local industry by dismissing those who break their contracts of employment. It will also end the 40-year recognition of trade unions within the firm.

Several of the directors expressed surprise at the severity of the message but accepted the Chief Executive's assurance that the strike would evaporate in the face of such a threat, together with the generous pay offer.

As soon as they received the company's statement, the shop stewards met in a furious, closed session. Meanwhile, as word spread through the factory, workers abandoned their posts to look for union or management officials to clarify the situation. Seeing the press release did little to calm the situation and, for a while, the shop stewards struggled to prevent outbreaks of vandalism. Journalists lucky enough to be around that afternoon received some colourful quotes and some heartfelt stories.

It was plain that the workforce felt that they had been exploited during the previous five years. They believed that the Chief Executive had deliberately used a period of weak demand for railway coaches as an excuse for undermining the pay and status of factory workers, supervisors and even junior managers. A supervisor expressed it as follows: 'First we were told about the value of delayering the management. This was supposed to give us more responsibility. All it did was give us twice the work and twice the hassle. Then came empowerment, which was intended to provide job enrichment. But all I got was more paperwork that did away with jobs in personnel and accounts... Meanwhile, top management pay has moved ahead and the directors have given themselves doubled salaries in just the past three years.'

Over the next few days, little work took place in the Darlington factory or offices. The official strike was still three weeks away but there was little sense of urgency to complete work before then, either from the shopfloor or from the supervisors. Perversely, the threat of mass sackings had united the factory management and workforce as never before. The common enemy was the London head office.

A week later, the Works Convenor held a meeting for all union members at the local football ground. A crowd of 1,600 turned up to hear a succession of shop stewards condemning the management's stance and demanding that the strike go ahead. Only one of the speakers took a different line. He, representing the clerical bargaining unit, said:

> *'We must not be bullied but have to remember that this is the Chief Executive who closed the Crewe plant down within six months of his appointment. McKline's financial position is poor and labour costs are high. My members want us to find a compromise.'*

Some of the older staff nodded their agreement at the word 'compromise' but when the Convenor rounded off the rally by shouting: 'Well, are we coming out on the first?', there were deafening shouts of 'Yes!'

On 28 November the quarterly meeting of the Works Council took place. The agenda was based, as usual, upon factory plans and changes in the future. Discussion soon turned to the strike and it became clear to the staff representatives that the Production Director was very unhappy about the situation. He also let slip some interesting information about the possible effects of the strike:

> *'I don't know where we will store the supplies we're contracted to receive. Our steel suppliers need three months' cancellation notice ... and our customers will penalise us by £500,000 a week for delivery delays.'*

On 29 November a negotiator from ACAS phoned both sides in the dispute, asking if any help was required. Both declined at first but were eventually talked into considering a last-ditch meeting at ACAS headquarters. Neither side believed it would be beneficial to meet but they wanted to avoid the bad publicity that might stem from being seen as uncooperative. So, on the 30th, with 24 hours to go until the start of the strike and the consequent dismissal of the workforce, the meeting began.

APPENDIX A: McKline Plc Company Accounts – Latest Year

Profit & Loss Account		Balance Sheet	
	£m		£m
Revenue	120	Fixed assets	32
Materials	44	Stocks	46
Direct labour	40	Debtors	26
GROSS PROFIT	36	Creditors	(38)
Overheads	29	Net current assets	34
Interest	5	ASSETS EMPLOYED	66
OPERATING PROFIT	2	Loans	40
Tax	0.5	Share capital	10
Dividends	3.5	Reserves	16
RETAINED PROFIT	(2.0)	CAPITAL EMPLOYED	66

Questions
(40 marks; 80 minutes)

1 To what extent would you regard the prevailing management style as conforming to McGregor's Theory X or Theory Y model? **(8)**

2 Discuss whether the *Financial Times* journalist is correct in describing the company's pay offer as 'reasonable'.

3 Explain the meaning of the terms 'delayering' and 'empowerment'. Why may such approaches prove disappointing when put into practice? **(8)**

4 a What is the business term for the actions taken by the ACAS negotiator? **(1)**

 b How might this dispute have progressed if the pendulum arbitration agreement had been signed? **(7)**

5 Consider the case for and against compromise, as suggested by the shop steward of the clerical workers. What stance do you think the trade union should take at the meeting on 30 November? **(10)**

56 A CASE OF ELEMENTARY DECISION TREES

Concepts needed: Decision trees

The scene is the drawing room at 221b Baker Street…

'My dear Holmes, what is it?'

'Watson, I must explain the facts to you. This slump in the stock market since the outbreak of the Boer War has left me penniless. I must seek my fortune.'

'Holmes, that's dreadful … but perhaps this letter from Inspector Lestrade of Scotland Yard can help. He says that Moriarty's evil influence is spreading. An insurance company is offering 100,000 guineas to anyone that can catch him, and 50,000 guineas to anyone that leads the police to him. By Jove, they're even offering 10,000 guineas for genuine information on him, even if the bunglers at Scotland Yard fail to apprehend him.'

'Splendid, dear Watson, for my brother Mycroft has told me that Moriarty has travelled to Switzerland – near the Reichenbach Falls.'

'Then let us travel on the next boat train. It'll be my privilege to pay for us both.'

'Hold on a moment, Watson. If we visit Reichenbach, I would estimate our chances of finding him at no higher than 60%. If we do, we must

decide whether to tackle him or bring in the police. On our own against Moriarty's thugs we have no better than a 40% chance of getting our man. The police have probably got a 60/40 chance of success.'

'Perhaps we should tell the police straight away, and let them go to Switzerland, then, Holmes.'

'Hm…those idlers will take so long getting there that I suspect they've no better than a 3 in 10 chance of finding him and arresting him …. How much do you suppose the expedition will cost us, Watson?'

'About 200 guineas, I'd say, Holmes.'

Holmes drew his favourite Meerschaum pipe down from the mantelpiece, and a decision tree began to form in his mind …

Questions

(20 marks; 30 minutes)

1 Draw the decision tree. (8)

2 Show your calculations in labelling the diagram, and indicate your decision, based on the expected value of each eventuality. (8)

3 Outline the weaknesses of basing decisions entirely upon the calculation of expected values. (4)

PANDA WOK

Concepts needed: Company aims and objectives, Internal and external constraints

Panda Wok was started five years ago by Laura Piper and Chris Spence. It was Laura's idea to create a Chinese restaurant with a difference. Customers fill a bowl with ingredients chosen for themselves from a huge range of carefully sliced meats, fish, prawns and vegetables. After adding the flavourings, sauces and cooking oil, they hand their creation to one of three cooks who stand by a huge griddle in the middle of the restaurant. Within three minutes the food is cooked and the onlooking customers take the freshly cooked food back to their table. People are welcome to repeat the process as often as they like.

From its opening day in a blaze of free pandas and free media publicity, Panda Wok was a great success. Chris had planned on breaking even in the second or third year, but from the first night the restaurant made money. He was content to enjoy the profits, but Laura was determined to make Panda Wok a national name. Using bank borrowings and the business's cash flow, the company expanded at a furious pace. As the diagram shows, new restaurants were opened with increasing speed. As Laura put it: 'We're steadily turning the country black and white.'

Just twelve months after day 1, with annualised sales running at £2 million, Chris managed to sit Laura down to talk things over. He knew that she was working

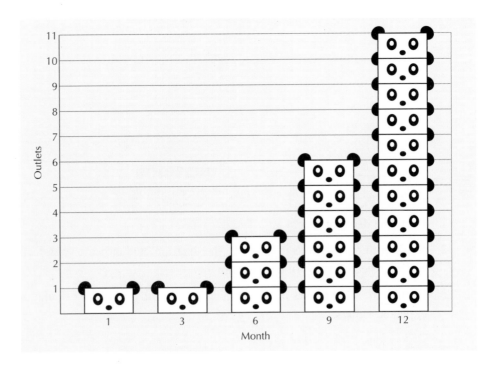

from seven in the morning to eight at night, and then going on to visit a different Panda Wok outlet every day. He half-hoped to see signs of exhaustion on her face, but all he detected was shining enthusiasm: 'I want us to be the first national chain of Chinese restaurants…the Marks and Spencer of catering.'

Chris tried to persuade her that their company was not capable of more expansion: 'Our accounting system can't cope, our bank balance goes ever deeper into the red, and we cannot find the time to look carefully at alternative new sites …we must consolidate…we have no middle management…if we keep on like this our quality control will go and so will our reputation.'

Chris thought he had got through to Laura, but the buzz of satisfied customers at the Brighton outlet that night switched her back to her growth targets.

It took another two months for the first shock to hit the firm. Panda Wok's bank, with little warning, demanded that its £400,000 overdraft be halved within six weeks. This forced a desperate reappraisal. It quickly became clear that the company's contracts to buy new properties made it impossible to cut back spending so quickly. To avoid liquidation, Laura and Chris had to accept a refinancing package which included the bank taking a 40% shareholding in the company. Chris wondered whether this was the time to diversify away from such an income elastic service as a restaurant, but Laura convinced him to keep concentrating on their core skill.

Having survived this phase, Panda Wok returned to its growth path. Its 120 sites were, by now, yielding annual profits of £500,000. Yet this was soon to be dented by a series of difficulties. A direct competitor with better restaurant locations was taking away some trade, while the whole market was affected by a sharp VAT increase on restaurant food. Then came the scandal. The St Albans outlet was prosecuted under the Food Safety Act of 1990 for sloppy hygiene leading to cases of food poisoning. This was picked up by the BBC's Southeast news, and then by the national press. Takings dived. The company almost went under during the following six months, but then began to recover. This time around, Laura was much more cautious. She accepted now that building up the company's quality image was more important than constant expansion.

Questions

(40 marks; 70 minutes)

1 Analyse Panda Wok's company objectives during the timespan covered by the case. **(8)**

2 a Why do firms usually agree their aims and objectives at Board level? **(6)**

   b How might Panda Wok have benefited from this exercise? **(6)**

3 Examine the internal and external constraints faced by Panda Wok. To what extent could they have been foreseen? **(12)**

4 What other constraints might the firm face in future, as the business matures? **(8)**

58 PROBLEMS OF POLLUTION IN A CHEMICAL PLANT

Concepts needed: Company objectives, Trade unions, Social responsibilities, Leadership styles

Chemdex Chemicals is situated on Teesside, in the northeast of England. It employs 1,200 fulltime workers – half the number of five years ago. Yet Chemdex is still the main local employer in an area where male unemployment is 19%. As with other local labour forces, the level of unionisation has fallen; just 41% of the workforce belong to a trade union. Chemdex produces weedkillers, pestkillers and chemical dyes for use in paint. Over recent years, fierce competition from Germany and from ICI has often pushed Chemdex into losses, as is shown by the graph below.

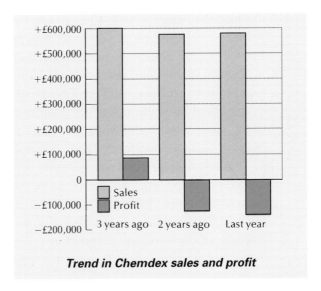

Trend in Chemdex sales and profit

The firm has recently launched a new, highly effective weedkiller (Weedex). Sales are building up rapidly, and the product is soon to be featured on BBC TV's *Gardeners' World*. The firm's management is already talking about the new product as the company's saviour.

Yet many in the factory are worried about the fumes given off in the production process. They frequently escape from the safety valves, leaving a fine blue powder everywhere in the factory, and even on the washing of the local houses. Following furious complaints from its members, the factory workers' union AGU has just held a meeting at which eighteen operators have complained of blinding headaches, and seven say they have fainted when overcome by the air pollution.

AGU's membership also includes the maintenance mechanics, who tell the meeting that they believe the entire Weedex plant has been designed so poorly and constructed so shoddily that leaks are inevitable. The meeting votes that the shop stewards should discuss the situation with the management, and ask for an independent report on the nature of the blue powder.

The union's request that this issue be discussed at the Works' Council is an irritant to a management that is wrapped up in the success of the Weedex launch. Latest forecasts show that in the coming year it should transform a £100,000 loss into a £400,000 profit. That would provide the funds for a desperately needed factory modernisation programme. The Works Manager is aware that the Weedex production equipment is leaky and unstable, but the Managing Director only seems interested in discussing ways of boosting output.

Frustration has led the Works Manager to ask the Chief Scientist at Chemdex to write a report on the chemical, and send a copy to the Managing Director. This has been completed and shows that the blue chemical is copper hydrocyanide. The concluding paragraph reads:

'The quantities found in the atmosphere within the factory represent a serious, if long term, health hazard. As the situation is in direct contravention of the Health and Safety at Work Act, I strongly recommend the immediate adoption of lightweight oxygen masks for all factory workers in contact with Weedex.'

At the Works' Council, the Managing Director starts by saying to the employee representatives that the success of Weedex is vital, and that if its launch is disrupted and thereby falters, the whole weedkilling division will be closed, causing four hundred job losses. He also declares that:

> *'We are not willing to discuss the blue powder at all, as it is
> precisely the ingredient that our competitors would like to identify.'*

At the subsequent union meeting, there are many grumbles about the bullying tactics of the Managing Director, but the threat of redundancies is enough to weaken the workers' resolve. This would probably be where the matter rested were it not for a local journalist's enterprise in talking to local mothers and doctors. The local newspaper's headline 'Children Turning Blue!' is even picked up by the national media. As environmentally conscious supermarket stockists of Weedex start phoning for details, the Managing Director springs into action. The company puts out a press release saying that they are already implementing a 'green strategy' to make production 'even safer'.

Within a week, filtration devices costing £25,000 are fitted that halve the air pollution, and plans are underway for a new, safer production line to be built alongside the existing one.

Questions

(40 marks; 70 minutes)

1 How would you describe the leadership style of the firm's Managing Director? **(6)**

2 a Identify and explain the factors that led Chemdex to its apparent objective of short-term profit maximisation. **(6)**

b What conclusions can you draw from the Chemdex experience about the drawbacks of such an objective for companies in general? **(8)**

3 How strong a position does the AGU appear to be in at the plant? What constraints are affecting it? **(10)**

4 It is sometimes assumed that firms have a relatively simple choice between social responsibility and profit. Discuss the circumstances in which there can be conflicts between competing social responsibilities. **(10)**

59 PANETTERIA ITALIANA

Concepts needed: Company objectives, Constraints, Pricing policy, Profit

Salvatore Falcone arrived in Britain from southern Italy in 1967, with no English and no money. A brother living in South London gave him a job for a while, and then helped to finance the rental of premises that could serve as a small bakery. The brother acted as a sleeping partner, putting in the initial finance, but not getting involved in running the business.

The bakery started in 1969, producing Italian rolls and French bread from a second hand oven. Salvatore did the baking, and his wife Sebastiana served customers – usually 'helped' by their young children. Sales went well, but low profit margins made it hard to pay the overheads. Pricing was constrained by the presence of an established bakery across the road, plus a Tesco, Co-op, Safeway, and Sainsbury within a one-mile radius. Trade began to pick up when, in 1972, the manager at the local Berni Inn inquired about deliveries. They agreed to supply 100 rolls per day. This soon drifted up towards 200. Then, by word of mouth within the organisation, other Berni branches sent orders. Soon, deliveries were needed for up to thirty miles away to over a dozen branches.

Salvatore had an extension built at the back of the shop to cope with the extra mixing machines and ovens needed. He also had to buy two secondhand vans and hire two drivers. Even that was often insufficient, so he had to dash off in his Mini on the three hour round trip to Berni's Windsor and Bracknell restaurants. Such journeys would come on top of his baking hours, from midnight to 10 a.m.

By 1975 the bakery was selling 9,000 rolls a day, all but 1,500 of which were to Berni. Having worked for five years without taking a salary, he was at last able to spend money on his family. In addition, he bought out his brother, and purchased a lease on the shop, financed by a mortgage. Then, with just one week's notice, Berni cancelled the order. A head office buyer had negotiated a cheaper price from a factory baker. This swept away over 50% of Salvatore's turnover. He had to give his drivers their notice, and sell off the vans. Terrible pressure from overwork switched to worries about financial survival.

The Falcones realised that their only option was to squeeze more revenue from the shop itself. More customers were needed, and each would need to spend more. They thought carefully about their product range, and about the market locally. Work was about to start on a housing estate nearby, so they decided to offer a wide range of snack foods. They made filled rolls, French bread sandwiches, and pizzas. Within a few weeks, this was not only attracting the building workers but also the staff and students from a nearby Art College. Within a year, boys from the local secondary school were queuing at lunchtimes; their school canteen had apparently changed for the worse.

PANETTERIA ITALIANA

CALL IN OR PHONE   6 MERTON PARK PARADE,
KINGSTON RD,
WIMBLEDON,
LONDON
SW19 3NT

NAME	INGREDIENTS	PRICE		
		WHOLE	½	¼
PLAIN	TOMATO, CHEESE	1.50	1.10	55p
MARGARITA	TOMATO, CHEESE, OREGANO	1.60	1.10	55p
ONION	TOMATO, CHEESE, ONION	1.75	1.10	55p
ONION & HERBS	TOMATO, CHEESE, ONION, HERBS	1.75	1.10	55p
MUSHROOM	TOMATO, CHEESE, MUSHROOMS	1.90	1.10	55p
MUSHROOM & HERBS	TOMATO, CHEESE, MUSHROOMS, HERBS	1.90	1.10	55p
PEPPER	TOMATO, CHEESE, PEPPER	1.90	1.10	55p
PEPPER & HERBS	TOMATO, CHEESE, PEPPER, HERBS	1.90	1.10	55p
ANCHOVY	TOMATO, CHEESE, ANCHOVY, OLIVES	1.90	1.10	55p
SALAMI	TOMATO, CHEESE, SALAMI	2.20	1.10	65p
SALAMI & MUSHROOM	TOMATO, CHEESE, SALAMI, MUSHROOMS	2.45	1.10	65p
SALAMI & MUSHROOM & HERBS	TOMATO, CHEESE, SALAMI, MUSHROOMS, HERBS	2.45	2.20	65p
PEPPERONI	TOMATO, CHEESE, PEPPERONI	2.20	1.30	65p
PEPPERONI & MUSHROOM	TOMATO, CHEESE, PEPPERONI, MUSHROOMS	2.45	1.30	65p
TUNA	TOMATO, CHEESE, TUNA	2.20	1.30	65p
TUNA & HERBS	TOMATO, CHEESE, TUNA, HERBS	2.20	1.30	65p
TUNA & OLIVE & ANCHOVY	TOMATO, CHEESE, TUNA, ANCHOVY, OLIVES	2.45	1.30	65p
PINEAPPLE	TOMATO, CHEESE, PINEAPPLE	1.75	1.10	55p
PINEAPPLE & HAM	TOMATO, CHEESE, PINEAPPLE, HAM	2.00	1.10	55p

Thought also went into expanding their range of bread. The trend towards healthy eating had made white bread unfashionable, so Salvatore experimented with wholemeal. This proved a frustration, as he could only bake it after he had finished the white, which meant it being ready at 11 o'clock. Partly due to that, and partly because customers were not used to buying brown bread there, he was often left with unsold loaves. That wiped out the profit margin, meaning that his extra working time had been for nothing. Eventually, though, it began to sell consistently enough to make it profitable.

The third element in their product mix had always been to offer a range of imported Italian groceries: salami, mortadella, pasta, cheeses and biscuits. They expanded the range, and bought a slicing machine to speed up their customer service. Eventually four suppliers were used to deliver the produce weekly.

During the second half of the 1980s, these three areas flourished. Further expansion was needed at the back of the shop, but at last this could be financed quite easily. A new, bigger oven was bought for £5,000, plus a £3,500 dough mixer that worked half as fast again as the previous one. The small size of the selling area of the shop became the main problem, with long queues building up each Saturday.

Even so, the economics of the business were based upon ignoring what would have otherwise been the largest cost – labour. When pricing products, Salvatore would calculate the cost of the direct ingredients used, but neither the labour cost nor the overheads. When the product was in competition with others, such as large white loaves – he would also take the prevailing local price level into account. Overall, though, pricing was on a simplified cost-plus basis.

The main element of labour cost being ignored was his own. On a Friday, he began mixing dough at midnight. Batch after batch would then be produced: large white, small white, doughnuts, large French, small French, rolls, large wholemeal, small granary, granary French, then pizzas. Each required 20 minutes of mixing, 5 minutes to cut and shape the dough, 20 minutes to 'rest', and 20-45 minutes of baking; after eleven hours of rapid, non-stop work, he would be ready to help serve the customers. Meanwhile, Sebastiana and one of her daughters would have been serving since 8.30 a.m.

The profits of the business were, by now, based primarily on the higher value added lines such as French bread, filled rolls and pizzas. A £12 bag of flour would produce thirty large loaves, or sixty small, or seventy-five French. Given that they sold for 65 pence, 38 pence and 36 pence respectively, large loaves provided very little contribution towards labour and overhead costs. Fortunately, five hundred French sticks were sold for every hundred large loaves per day.

After twenty years in the business, Salvatore had still not mastered how to avoid wastage, however. Not that he regarded it as wastage, for every day's unsold bread was delivered to a nearby convent. Experience had taught him that each day's sales would depend upon the weather (very poor on rainy days), but there would also be inexplicable, random factors. On paper, it would be more profitable to produce just below the average sales level (as each unsold large loaf 'wasted' over 50 pence). Yet this would mean many customers being disappointed on the days of erratically high demand, so output was kept quite high. The Falcones aimed to not only make money from their business, but also to gain satisfaction from their high reputation for quality of product and service.

For the future, Salvatore planned a trip to Italy to buy a machine for producing fresh pasta. Apparently they were available for £5,000 in Britain, but £2,000 in Milan. His son would take over the baking while he was away. In twenty years husband and wife have never had a holiday together but if Franco makes a good stand-in, even that may be possible in the future. In the longer term, nothing would please Salvatore more than to see his children take over completely.

Questions
(40 marks; 70 minutes)

1 Discuss the Falcones' business objectives. Were they always the same? **(10)**

2 What internal and external constraints affected their business? In what ways were they more able to cope with them than a large firm? **(10)**

3 The main direct cost of producing bread is the flour. Calculate the gross profit margin on large, small, and French loaves based upon the information available. How might Salvatore use this data? **(10)**

4 Consider the strengths and weaknesses of Salvatore's pricing method. **(10)**

60

ECONOMIC CHANGE AS AN EXTERNAL CONSTRAINT

Concepts needed: Inflation, Interest rates, Value of the pound, Gearing

Rawsthorn Clothing had enjoyed three years of high profitability, thanks to a consumer spending boom that guaranteed high output and generous **profit margins**. By the third year it was looking to expand.

From its base in Burnley, the firm had been supplying the womenswear market for eighty years. Now the Directors had decided to diversify into children's clothing, for they thought an opportunity existed for a producer of high quality, classically-styled childrenswear. Despite their recent high profits, it was still necessary for them to borrow a substantial sum to establish a highly efficient, new factory.

This put their gearing up to 40% of capital employed, but the Directors were not concerned because their large retail customers had given enthusiastic verbal support to their scheme. Only the Production Director dissented from the Board's decision, on the grounds that:

'The labour content of a child's garment is only a little lower than that of an adult, yet the price of the finished product is far lower.'

Just five months before the new factory was due to open, however, the economic climate began to worsen. Signs of rising **inflation** had led the Chancellor to push interest rates up quite sharply, and the pound had risen as a result. By opening day, Rawsthorn was starting to detect a reduction in orders throughout its product range. The salesforce made it clear that this was due to three factors:

1   Retailers wanted to cut stock levels to reduce the finance cost;
2   Customers were buying less as rising mortgage rates cut their **disposable incomes**;
3   Those that were still buying tended to buy imported goods that were now more price competitive.

Even more worrying were reports from their overseas agents that Rawsthorn's recent price rises had hit sales more sharply than anticipated.

The poor trading conditions made retailers reluctant to stock Rawsthorn's new childrenswear range. The *Financial Times* monthly Retail Survey had just revealed that most shop managers expected weak consumer demand to persist for at least a year. Shopkeepers felt that its high quality, high price

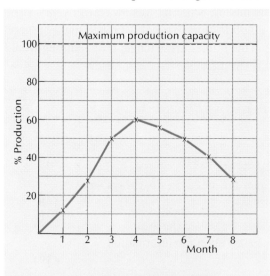

Production of childrenswear

proposition was inappropriate to the current marketplace. Eight months after opening, the children's clothing factory was producing at only 30% of single-shift production capacity, causing heavy losses. Even the womenswear division could do no better than to break even, so the company as a whole was trading in the red.

Questions

(40 marks; 70 minutes)

1 Explain the meaning of the following (emboldened in the text):

   profit margins
   inflation
   disposable income. **(6)**

2 Explain how the salesmen's comments relate to the economic circumstances outlined earlier in the paragraph. **(9)**

3 What was the significance of the reporting of the expectations of the retail trade? In what other ways can expectations affect business realities? **(10)**

4 How would the poor trading position of Rawsthorne be affected by its gearing level? **(6)**

5 Outline three approaches that you believe the Directors could adopt to bring the company out of the red. **(9)**

61

AN ETHICAL DILEMMA

Concepts needed: Profit, Business ethics, Social responsibilities,
Government intervention

It was as if someone had spat in the Marketing Director's face. All round the mahogany boardroom table, the smartly dressed men sat stiffly, too shocked to move or speak. Teresa, the only woman present, gulped as she realised that her naive question had ground the meeting to a halt. She knew they were all highly sensitive on the subject, but it had seemed reasonable to ask:

> *'Did you see the World in Action programme last night?'*

Of course, it had been a particularly ferocious attack on the tobacco industry, complete with stomach-wrenching pictures of smokers' diseased lungs, and legs amputated due to failing blood circulation. The programme had even aimed a barb at the man at the head of the table. It pointed out that the International Tobacco Company's Marketing Director had given public assurances that the firm's advertising was never aimed at young people, yet a leaked internal memo signed by him said:

> *'Motor-racing sponsorship may be hard to justify on*
> *cost efficiency grounds, but it is the only way we can*
> *reach the teenage market.'*

Teresa reflected that in the twenty or so meetings she had attended between International Tobacco Company (I.T. Co.) and her advertising agency, the subject of health – let alone social responsibilities – had never been raised. Yet she had chatted with most of these men on their own over lunch, and knew them all to be caring parents who had thought deeply about the ethical dilemma of being responsible for the advertising of half the country's cigarettes.

One or two felt guilty about their situation, but most had rationalised it away by convincing themselves that their efforts were not persuading people to start smoking, only to get existing smokers to switch from one brand to another. Outside commentators might sneer at this idea, but they comforted themselves that research had never uncovered anyone who attributed their first cigarette to an advertisement.

Fortunately, the spell that had immobilised the meeting was broken by the arrival of tea. After the waitress had left, the advertising agency's Chairman was able to move on to the next item on the agenda: Project Plover. He presented data giving the background to this proposed new product (shown on page 169).

Background Research Data For Project Plover

Recent market share trends for low tar brands		Views of smokers of low tar brands	
Last 6 months	22%	Would switch to lower tar if taste OK	52%
6–12 months ago	20.5%		
12–18 months ago	19%		
18–24 months ago	18%	Would switch for 40% less tar	59%
24–36 months ago	17%		

Source: *Ex-factory sales figures*   Source: *ANR Research*

Teresa sat there tensely as her Chairman ran through the presentation that she had written. She had spent four months on Project Plover (a codename used for security purposes), and dearly wanted the I.T.Co. Marketing Director to approve the £200,000 needed for the final preparations before its launch as a new cigarette brand. Inwardly, she applauded her Chairman's clear explanation of the consumer proposition '40% less tar but no less taste than the leading low tar brand'; and his expert account of the middle-class, female niche that this brand would fill in the market.

When he finished, it was the I.T.Co New Product Development Manager's turn. He explained that Plover was forecast to achieve a 1% share of the 5,000 million* pack annual cigarette market, with a gross profit margin of £120 per thousand packs (i.e. 12 pence per pack). Even with a launch advertising budget of £2.5 million, a handsome contribution should be generated. Nor would this be especially at the expense of other I.T.Co. brands, as their competitors held 75% of the low tar market.

'So, what's your opinion, Bob?' asked the agency Chairman.

'Well…' replied the Marketing Director, 'I'm worried at the longer term implications. We've already led nearly a quarter of the market down to low tar and low nicotine cigarettes. If we now encourage them to smoke even weaker cigarettes, are we not just helping them give up altogether? We have a responsibility to think of the company's future. I think we'd better shelve this project.'

Teresa blinked in amazement at what she had heard, and looked round the table to see who would challenge this statement. No-one did. They moved on to the next Agenda item – Snooker sponsorship.

* Apologies for the huge, but realistic, numbers. United Kingdom cigarette sales amount to 5,000 million packs times 20 per pack i.e. 100,000 million cigarettes per year.

Questions

(40 marks; 70 minutes)

1   Outline the ethical questions raised by the above account.   **(10)**

2   How profitable would Project Plover be to I.T.Co. in its first year?
    What other reasons are there for the company to want to launch this product?   **(10)**

3   Discuss the issues of responsibility that emerge from the text.   **(10)**

4   What arguments might the cigarette industry put forward against a complete
    government ban on all cigarette advertising and promotion? Comment on these
    arguments.   **(10)**

62 THE MEDICINE BUSINESS

Concepts needed: Advertising, Cash flow, Restrictive practices, Remuneration

Mike felt terrific. After three months of looking for his first post, he had been offered a new practice on the edge of Hatfield. It would be the only G.P. surgery for a group of new housing estates in this Hertfordshire town. It seemed a just reward for the five years in university and four years of vocational training that he had just been through.

At the interview, the Chairman of the local Family Practitioner Committee (F.P.C.) had warned him that he would not qualify for the £15,000 government grant for setting up new practices. This was because he had not been qualified for the minimum two year period. Yet Mike felt confident that the Committee and the Department of Health would give him all the help he needed; and anyway, in nine years of training he had never been told about problems in starting up a surgery.

Where to start, though? Mike decided to wait until the F.P.C. had sent the lengthy book that sets out the extremely complex arrangements for – and restrictions on – G.P.s' work and remuneration. For whereas many people assume that G.P.s receive salaries, in fact their pay is based upon a series of fees and allowances.

Within a few weeks of his appointment on 30th December 1988, Mike felt he understood enough to get started. The only capital he had was £2,000, so he had to rent premises. As the new estates had nothing suitable, he hired two Portakabins which could be joined to provide areas for a surgery, a waiting room, a reception, and the necessary washing facilities. These were placed on the edge of council land that was still being built on. The F.P.C. would pay the monthly £736 rent, but three months in arrears. In the future, a proper Health Centre was scheduled to be built nearby; Mike would then operate from there.

As he became more aware of the fees, allowances and expenses provided for G.P.s (see **Appendix A**) Mike was struck by how heavily geared they were to existing, large practices. For not only did he require a minimum of 1,000 patients to obtain the full allowance, but also all payments would be received well in arrears. G.P.s receive their earnings quarterly, based upon the number of patients on their list, plus the fees incurred, during the previous three months. As these quarterly cheques apply to the patients on the doctor's list at the start of the quarter, if Mike took patients on in February he would receive no payment for serving them until after 30th June.

However, lateness in payment was only part of the problem. The other was that of getting patients at all. For at that time doctors were not allowed to advertise (this changed in 1990). New practitioners could announce their opening in the local paper, but no more. This had long been agreed between the N.H.S. and the doctors' representatives, because the profession was said to doubt the ethics of attempting to persuade people to switch doctors as they would brands of soap powder.

Despite these difficulties, Mike managed to open the Manor House surgery on 20th February 1989. His bank manager had provided a £10,000 overdraft facility, but by decorating and furnishing the Portakabins himself, he had not yet used more than £3,000 of it. The biggest financial outlay was for medical supplies and dressings, on which £2,400 was spent.

Having started the practice, he now needed to generate enough money to pay himself a living wage, and to pay the wages of a receptionist/clerk/book-keeper. The F.P.C. would pay 70% of one employee's salary, but again it would only be paid in arrears. To boost awareness of his practice, Mike decided to get a friend to encourage the local newspaper to write an article about him. When this appeared, other G.P.s in the area complained about his 'soliciting' custom, and he received a stern rebuke from the F.P.C. The same occurred when – some months later – a vicar's wife wrote a piece in the parish magazine praising the quality of care provided by 'this splendid new doctor'.

Mike had always realised, though, that word of mouth would be his most valuable form of publicity. With that in view, he set up various clinics providing preventative medicine for which no NHS fees were available (and were therefore not available at many of the other practices locally). Despite being on call 24 hours a day, seven days a week, he also made a point of sounding sympathetic to night-time calls at home.

Slowly the medicine worked. By 1st April there were 170 patients on his list; by 1st August this had grown to 550. There looked to be the prospect of 1,000 by the end of 1989. Yet Mike's only income in the eight months since he had been appointed had been £903. In July his Building Society mortgage went unpaid, and by August the practice overdraft stood at £8,000. For many months to come the costs that resulted from treating more patients would outweigh the revenues based upon the number of patients three months before. It was clear that careful accounting and a friendly bank manager would be the only way of surviving for several months.

Mike felt an acute sense of grievance against a system that made it so hard to set up a new surgery for any but the well-off. He had many criticisms of the Conservatives' funding of the N.H.S., but applauded their decision to allow advertising in future; he would certainly run informative advertisements in the local paper. Yet he also acknowledged the advantages of his position. Instead of joining an established practice where he would be the junior partner, he was able to make all the decisions for himself. Indeed if all went well he would be able to build up a patient list of around 3,000 – which would provide him with a substantial income.

He could not help thinking, though, that after nine years' study to become a G.P. he should not really be expected to teach himself to be a businessman as well.

Sources: *The doctor concerned, and from the magazine Medeconomics. (The name of the town has been changed.)*

APPENDIX A

In 1989, General Practitioners worked to the following package of fees and allowances:

Fees and allowances 1989

BASIC ALLOWANCE	£11,100 p.a.
(doctors with fewer than 1,000 patients receive £11.10 per patient)	
CAPITATION FEES	
(under 65 years old)	£8.95 each
(65–74 years old)	£11.60 each
(over 75 years old)	£14.25 each
NIGHT VISITS	
(first 1 or 2)	£20.25 each
(next 3-5)	£10.13 each
(over 6)	£2.02 each
Vaccinations	£4.45 each

N.B. There were many other specific fees for relatively unusual treatments – too many to list.

(The Department of Health believed that, in 1989, these fees would provide a doctor with the average number of patients [2,000] with an income of £31,105 plus expenses of £14,656 per annum.)

Questions

(40 marks; 70 minutes)

1 Based upon the information available, what business concepts might it be useful to include within doctors' vocational training? **(6)**

2 What annual income could a doctor with 500 patients (all under 65) expect if 5% of them were vaccinated per year, and if that doctor was called out to a patient on thirty-six separate nights? **(6)**

3 a The doctors' representatives were concerned about the persuasive powers of advertising, while Mike would regard its use as informative. Discuss the significance of this. **(6)**

   b What would restrict doctors from using advertising in a misleading way? **(6)**

4 What evidence is there in the case study that the G.P. system is full of restrictive practices? Why may that matter? **(8)**

5 Consider the advantages and disadvantages of scrapping the fee and allowance system, and paying doctors on a salary basis. **(8)**

Concepts needed: Cash flow, Economic policy, Government intervention

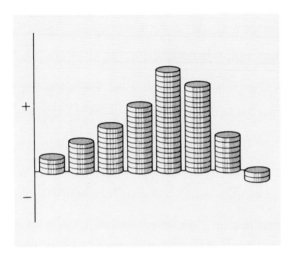

'Nothing's gone right since Labour got in,' said Mr. Martin bitterly. Protex Limited had been very successful in the years prior to the election. Booming consumer demand for home security systems had enabled the firm to increase sales 50% by volume (100% by value) in the previous four years. This had made it appear economic to automate their production methods, as the costs of the new, high technology equipment could be spread over many units of output. Furthermore, the labour-saving aspects of the equipment not only helped to keep direct costs low, but also helped Protex to cope with the coincidental fall in the number of young people within the workforce.

The Finance Director had been the only one to question whether it was wise to borrow substantial sums to finance a mechanisation programme that would be unprofitable if demand fell. The other Directors made it clear that they were confident that the fifteen years of continuous growth in the home security market was not likely to stop. Indeed, the Marketing Director had pointed out that the market had grown from £360 to £840 million over the previous four years. As the Board members took their seats at the start of the meeting, Mr. Martin (the Managing Director) muttered:

> 'Within two days they'd pushed interest rates up to protect the pound. Then came that first budget, with its ending of mortgage tax relief above the standard rate – that did for our top-priced, high margin range...'

The Marketing Director took the story up:

> 'Even worse was the decision to make every burglar alarm fitting firm apply for an operating licence. Half of them left the industry – they couldn't be bothered to go through the red tape to get their certificate; and of course those fitters were our customers.'

The Finance Director couldn't help wondering if there were other reasons they left the industry, but he said nothing. He wanted to get people onto the main item on the agenda – the cash flow crisis. He reminded everyone that they faced their poorest revenue period (December–February) with an overdraft just £20,000 below the limit set by the bank.

He presented the following figures:

Winter Quarter Cash Budget

Forecast revenues;	£540,000
Gross profit margin:	30%
Salaries and overheads:	£220,000
Interest payments:	£82,000

After they had discussed ways in which the cash shortfall could be funded, conversation returned to the change in the political context of their business operation. The Production Controller warned that a new environmental pollution law would soon force them to invest in £80,000 of filtration equipment, ending their discharges of industrial paints and dyes into the river. Mr. Martin exclaimed 'The Socialists want to put us all out of business! How can we compete with the Japanese with the millstones they place round our necks?'

As they were leaving the boardroom, the Finance Director mentioned to Mr. Martin that he had been glancing, that morning, at the Report and Accounts of Securimax (Protex's main United Kingdom rival).

'How are they doing?' asked Martin.

'Very well,' came the reply.

Questions

(40 marks; 70 minutes)

1 Examine the factors that seem to have led to the marked decline in Protex's cash flow position since the election. **(10)**

2 To what extent should the government be blamed for the problems Protex is grappling with? Or was Protex management responsible for errors of judgement? **(10)**

3 On the basis of their forecasts, how much more funding are they going to need in the coming quarter? How might they attempt to finance this shortfall? **(10)**

4 Businesses can attempt to influence the type and the policies of government in various ways. How do they do so and why? **(10)**

64

THE EMPLOYEE BUY-OUT AND THE MILLIONAIRE MECHANIC

Concepts needed: Business organisations, Privatisation, Leadership styles

A minor clause in the Conservative Party's 1979 election manifesto promised that the National Freight Corporation (NFC) would be sold off to the private sector. NFC, the parcels, removals, and road transport business, had a dismal record during the 1970s under state ownership. Despite major brand names such as BRS and Pickfords, it often made losses, and had shed 15,000 jobs between 1973 and 1979.

The new Government planned to privatise it in 1980, but the severity of the recession meant that the sale would be uneconomic. A group of senior executives, led by Chief Executive Peter Thompson, then proposed an employee buy-out. A vigorous campaign was started to persuade employees of the advantages of owning shares in the business in which they worked and interest free loans were made available through the company to help them take a stake in the business. As a result, over 10,000 of the 22,000 workforce invested an average of £600 in the buy-out in 1982. The government, delighted to be able to fulfil its election pledge, agreed to sell for £7 million. The employees, their families and NFC pensioners held 82.5% of the equity, with each share bought for £1.

In its first year as a private sector business, a profit of £11.8 million was achieved on a £493 million turnover – a huge turnaround from the losses made previously. As the table shows, this was just the start of rapid progress.

Following privatisation, NFC found that customers had more confidence that they would receive a better service; employee ownership became a selling point. One advertisement showed a picture of four drivers with the caption:

> 'They behave as if they own the company – because they do'

Internally, the change of ownership required a change in management style. Managers had to be prepared to be accountable to the people who worked for them. The annual shareholders meeting – so often a rubber stamping exercise in large public companies – gave knowledgeable employees the chance to quiz Directors on company plans and practices. The Managing Director of NFC's Distribution Division found that:

> 'If you are prepared to put yourself in a room with 50 or 60 drivers and discuss a problem it tests your mettle. There have been many times when I have come out of something like that losing fifty-nil. But you very quickly learn that if you can handle that situation it is a very effective way of getting through to people.'

	1983/4	1984/5	1985/86	1986/87	1987/88	1988/89
	£ million	£ million	£ million	£ million	£ million	£ million
Turnover	565.8	679.9	751.4	911.4	1,255	1,494
Pre-tax profit	16.1	27.2	37.0	47.4	67.1	90.2

Despite the encouragement of a more open style of management, the employee buy-out was no workers' cooperative. It kept a conventional management hierarchy, with full authority given to line managers. The whole organisation was split into profit centres, and managers were given financial incentives to meet or beat the targets. Nor did it look automatically at promotion from the shop floor; sixty-five graduates were recruited per year for management training schemes.

Where NFC enjoyed a great advantage, though, was in the feeling of teamwork injected by the common share ownership. This was reinforced by the mechanism by which shares could be traded. As the company wanted shares to be held only by employees, their families and NFC pensioners, it set up an internal marketplace, enabling shares to be bought and sold four times a year. This method ensured that the value of the shares (determined by profitability) was a constant source of discussion among the workforce. It therefore maximised the chance that employees would behave at all times as if cost minimisation and revenue maximisation was their personal concern. Such a goal is rarely achieved in organisations of 30,000 employees (as NFC was by 1988).

Yet despite the evidence of the success of the employee buy-out, NFC decided at the end of the 1980s to get a stock exchange listing. For only in this way would larger shareholders feel sure of being able to sell at the time they wished to (on retirement, for instance). The very success of the business made this almost inevitable, as the internal market share price had risen to 185 pence by late 1988. So the purchaser of £1,000 worth of shares in 1982 would want £74,000 for them*; but how many other workers could afford that?

In February 1989 NFC obtained a stock market listing. At the same time it held a Rights Issue at 130 pence to raise £47 million to finance further expansion. Employees were encouraged strongly to take up their rights; the firm even offered to lend them the money. For Sir Peter Thompson remained determined to keep up the level of employee share involvement for as long as possible. He believed that there is a big difference in attitude between worker-shareholders who have only a small minority of shares between them (as in the case of Sainsbury's or British Gas), and those that have the majority, controlling stake.

On the first day of trading, the share price topped £2.50. A mechanic was reputed to have holdings worth over £2 million, as he had mortgaged his house in 1982 to buy £20,000 of stock (he was keeping silent, so the story was unconfirmed).

As the era was ending of NFC as Britain's biggest employee-owned organisation, *The Times* reflected on the lessons to be learned. It concluded:

1 'Buy-outs are better than bail-outs'.

* adjusted for scrip issues and share subdivisions.

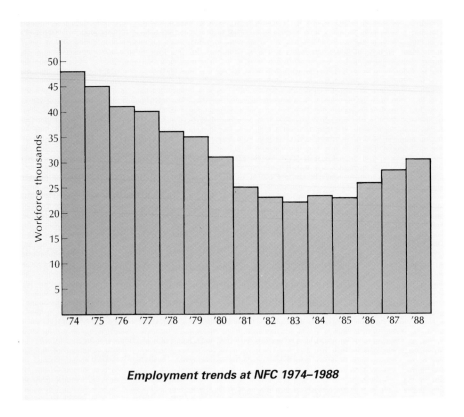

Employment trends at NFC 1974–1988

2 'Privatisation can work in the public interest ... when employees and managers alike are given a stake in the business and when the organisation is forced to be competitive. ... Mrs. Thatcher's policies take almost no account of this. As a result the government is creating a small number of management-run monopolies.'

3 'The Conservatives are wrong to think that fear is the best incentive: fear of takeover for management and fear of unemployment for the workers. In NFC's case cooperative effort has been highly effective in securing consent to necessary change.'

Sources: *Extel; The Financial Times; McCarthy's Financial Services; The Times*

Questions

(50 marks; 90 minutes)

1 Outline which of NFC's successful management policies could have been implemented under state ownership, and which could not. **(10)**

2 Consider the differences between NFC's structure and that of a workers' cooperative. What further benefits might the latter provide? **(8)**

3 a Show why the purchaser of £1,000 worth of shares in 1982 would have wanted £74,000 for them in late 1988. **(4)**

   b If the owner had held on, she/he would have been entitled to the 7 pence dividend per share planned for 1989. What income would have been provided in 1989? And what % yield would it represent for a new investor paying £2 per share? **(6)**

4 As employees can now sell their shares to outsiders on the Stock Exchange, the company will probably become a normal plc during the 1990s, i.e. with most shares held by institutional investors. In what ways might this be a disadvantage to NFC's continued progress? **(10)**

5 Discuss the validity and importance of *The Times'* second and third conclusions on the NFC case. **(12)**

THE OIL CRISIS

Concepts needed: Inflation, Company objectives, Shortage of resources

Looking back, it was hard to believe that no-one in the firm had seen the warning signs. The Chairman of Shell reminded everyone recently that he had made a public statement as far back as 1989 that there would be an oil supply shortage by the mid-1990s. Datona Plastics was not the only firm to be caught unprepared for the doubling of oil prices within the last eight months yet few other firms were in such an awkward position.

Datona made high-grade plastic mouldings, such as car control panels, car seats, and the casings for computer keyboards and monitors. Half its output went to the motor industry, and much of the rest to consumer appliance and electronics businesses. These markets had been booming while oil and petrol prices and general inflation were low, but had been hard hit during recent months. Rising prices had hit people's real incomes; many responded by postponing the replacement of items such as cars, carpets, and home computers.

Datona's special problem was that not only were its sales slumping, but also its costs were spiralling upwards. The plastic pellets that it bought from BP and ESSO were direct products of oil refining, and had therefore doubled in price. As shown below, this had brought about a big change in the composition of the firm's costs, as well as increasing their per unit total.

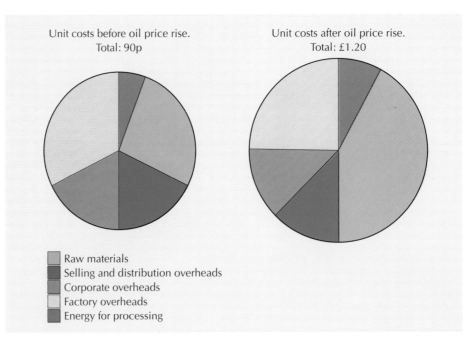

Unit costs before oil price rise.
Total: 90p

Unit costs after oil price rise.
Total: £1.20

■ Raw materials
■ Selling and distribution overheads
■ Corporate overheads
□ Factory overheads
■ Energy for processing

Whereas its car assembly customers could look for suppliers of substitute materials such as leather seats or wood casings (which would add value to the products anyway), Datona was only equipped to handle plastics. Just twelve months ago a leading City journalist had showered praise on the firm's 'sharply focused, clear-sighted management ... wisely refusing all temptation to diversify away from its area of distinctive competence'. Then its share price had been 285 pence – up from the 80 pence of four years before. Now it stood at 160 pence, and even that was partly because the market had not yet appreciated just how hard it had been hit by the oil price rise. As *The Sunday Times* had pointed out the previous week, several of Datona's Directors had sold large portions of their shareholdings over recent months.

During the early weeks of the decline in demand, the managers had decided to continue to produce at normal output levels; they believed that the manufacturers were just trimming back stock levels, and would therefore push demand back up within a week or so. By the time it was clear that this was a misreading of the marketplace Datona had excessive stock levels and a troublesome cash flow position. Ever since, they had been trying to cut stocks back to their normal level of six weeks' worth of sales. However, the Personnel Director's reluctance to put staff on short-time working, plus ever-falling demand, had prevented them from succeeding.

Another twist to the tale had emerged recently. With inflation over the past six months at an annual rate of 14%, the workforce was pushing for a 15% pay rise. The unions rejected outright the firm's case that the *annual* Retail Prices Index stood at 9%, but only 6% could be afforded. A strike appeared a very real possibility.

So the monthly Board meeting took place in very tense circumstances. Opinions split between two positions: one group agreed with the Financial Director's analysis that as there was a danger of making an operating loss of £4.2 million over the coming six months, one of the firm's three factories must be closed down and sold off; the others sided with the Marketing Director who worried that the oil price might slip back if the OPEC cartel members were to break ranks, leaving Datona unable to meet reviving demand from its two remaining plants.

The firm's choice of strategy was to hinge, therefore, on the Directors' hunch about future actions by governments and markets over which they had no control or even influence. As discussion began to get heated, the Chairman asked the Financial Director whether the situation posed a significant threat to the firm's survival. All were stunned at the reply:

> *'If we continue with the current level of overheads, any further slippage in demand will push us into the hands of the Receiver within the year. Even at current levels of demand our operating losses combined with our poor cash flow will set us back five years. I believe it is our responsibility to our shareholders and the majority of our workforce to cut back without delay.'*

The Marketing Director stayed silent as the others slid over to the Financial Director's side. She reflected that in good times the marketing department dominates, but in times of crisis power lies with the purse strings.

Questions

(50 marks; 90 minutes)

1 State the term given to:

   a household items such as cars, carpets and home computers

   b inflation sparked off by rising input prices

   c share dealing based upon knowledge not yet available publicly. **(6)**

2 **a** Explain why, in Datona's circumstances, it proved unwise to refuse 'all temptation to diversify'? **(8)**

   b The journalist's opinion was based upon the many cases of unsuccessful diversification. Why do firms struggle so often when they move away from their area of distinctive competence? **(8)**

3 Comment upon the negotiating positions adopted by labour and management within Datona's collective bargaining process. Would you see the Financial Director's policy of cutbacks as part of that process? **(10)**

4 Explain the meaning of the Marketing Director's statement about the oil price. Why would this worry the marketing department especially? **(10)**

5 If the oil price sticks at its higher level, what strategies might Datona consider for the longer term? **(8)**

66 THE BHOPAL TRAGEDY

Concepts needed: Communications, Multinationals, Laissez-faire v. intervention, Social responsibilities

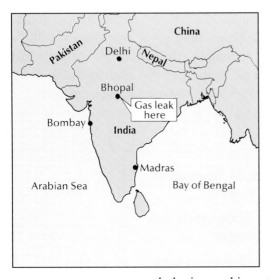

On Monday 3rd December 1984, a poisonous cloud of methyl isocyanate gas escaped from a storage tank at a pesticide plant in Bhopal, India. The factory was owned by one of the largest chemical producers in the world – the US firm Union Carbide. Eye witnesses reported a mushroom cloud that escaped from the factory and descended on the town. The main effects of the gas were to cause serious damage to eyesight and to blood circulation by implanting cyanide into the blood's oxygen. Within days 1,200 people died and at least 10,000 were very seriously affected. It was the world's worst recorded industrial accident.

A major problem for the doctors was lack of knowledge of how to treat the chemical's effects. A pathologist working at Bhopal's main hospital said bitterly: 'Why hasn't Union Carbide come forward to tell us about the gas that's leaked and how to treat it? Is it not their moral duty? They have not come forward.' Doctors were disturbed by unexpected problems such as one child who died suddenly, two hours after having shown no previous ill effects. They were also swamped by the scale of the damage – more than 100,000 people needed treatment out of a total population of 800,000. Worst affected were those living in the slums that had built up around the factory.

The factory's owners emphasised immediately that the incident was 'unprecedented', and that the storage tank was equipped with sophisticated safety systems. However, Indian politicians asked whether safety standards in Third World nations were less strict than in the home countries of parent companies. They also criticised western firms for selling India low technology plants that they then failed to keep up to date. Within a day of the accident, Union Carbide halted production of methyl isocyanate (MIC) at its United States plant, while awaiting the findings of an investigation into the causes of the disaster.

By Monday 10th December, the death toll had risen to 2,000 and Union Carbide was being sued for $12,500 million by American lawyers representing families affected. The lawyers argued, as did the Indian government, that Bhopal victims should receive the same, high compensation levels that American families would get. Union Carbide rejected this claim, and offered $1 million of humanitarian aid.

Soon it emerged that the company had no emergency procedures arranged with the local community. One of the plant's managers said:

> *'We did not know that such a small amount of gas had the capacity to destroy human lives to this extent. We thought our safety controls were adequate, so we did not do any community education.'*

Even harder for the firm to explain away was that although the factory had only started producing five years before, it was not equipped with the computer controls used in the older US plant. So, for example, if gas leaked from a Bhopal storage tank, an employee had to spot it and then break the glass of a box that controlled a safety system; in the United States, a computer would do this instantly and automatically. It also became clear that the Bhopal factory's safety record was very poor. Several gas leaks had occurred before, including one fatal incident. After that fatality, factory trade union officials had (in 1982) put posters up throughout Bhopal which said:

> **'Warning – Save Yourselves From Death.**
>
> **The Lives Of Thousands Are In Danger.**
>
> **The Factory Is Making Gas But Does Not Use Safety Measures.'**

The union officials now complained that their warnings had not been taken seriously enough by the press, the company or the State government. The press rejected that charge, however, stressing that they had written many critical articles including one headed:

> *'Bhopal on the brink of a volcano.'*

The press turned to the responsibility of the Indian government. Why had safety inspectors been so lax and, above all, why had a shanty town been allowed to build

up right next to the factory? It later became clear that the relevant authorities lacked the experience of this kind of western technology to recognise the dangers involved. So, since they were happy to have jobs brought to a poor area, they left it up to Union Carbide.

American journalists were repeatedly surprised that the company's US spokesmen know nothing of these points. Then one Carbide official admitted that communications with their Indian operation had virtually broken down. Nevertheless, Union Carbide's Chairman (Warren Anderson) continued to speak with pride about his company. He rejected suggestions that facilities at Bhopal were outdated and said the chemical industry's safety record was a 'wonder of the world'.

The short term effects of the tragedy upon the company appeared to be significant. The share price dropped sharply as investors worried about the firm's ability to pay the billions of dollars of compensation that were anticipated. The credit rating agency Standard and Poors lowered Carbide's credit rating, making it more expensive for them to borrow money. But by 17th January 1985, Mr. Anderson was confident that 'the Bhopal tragedy would have little effect on the company's ability to conduct business'. He also felt that the firm was adequately protected with insurance and had managed its cash flow well enough to 'put us in pretty good shape financially'.

By August the US MIC plant was in full operation and Carbide's shares had recovered to their pre-Bhopal level. For whereas the awful publicity of recent months would have hit the sales of a producer of consumer goods with a clear corporate identity, Carbide's products were bulk chemicals bought by other companies. So the sales turnover from their wide range of chemical products was barely affected.

On 20th March 1985, Mr. Anderson presented the results of his company's inquiry into the tragedy. Its original cause was water getting into the underground tank of MIC, which sparked off a chain reaction. This would not have caused danger had not a refrigeration unit been inoperable for six months, and a gas escape safety flare been 'undergoing maintenance'.

What made world headlines, though, was the Chairman's innuendo that sabotage may have been responsible. This became the company's main defence over coming years, even though it failed to convince the Indian Government. He also made it clear that he held the local (mainly Indian) management responsible for the alleged safety deficiencies. He said 'Non compliance with safety procedures is a local issue'. By implication, he went on to blame the Indian government's policy of insisting that a high proportion of local management should be from the local community. Later that year, on 8th September, Carbide created a new post of Vice President in charge of community and employee health, safety and environment. His task was to co-ordinate the setting of corporate standards, and ensuring their effective implementation.

In the early months of 1985, bereaved or injured families were led to expect prompt settlement of generous compensation. Yet it took eighteen months for Union Carbide to defeat the victims' attempt even to get the case tried in America. This was the crucial victory for the firm, as Carbide would have had to pay out more than the US firm the Manville Corporation, which had been instructed to pay $2.5 billion to 60,000 American victims of asbestos disease. Only in February 1989 was payment made to the victims in a 'full and final' settlement. Carbide's shares jumped $2 as the Indian Supreme Court awarded $470 million in compensation.

As *The Guardian* commented 'The stock market registered its financial verdict on the gruesome tragedy'. The newspaper also reported that the death toll had risen to over 3,000 and that over 55,000 people remain chronically ill from lung disease, and permanent eye and stomach disorders. Union Carbide, with record 1988 profits of $720 million, made it clear to financial analysts that they would not be affected by the settlement, as they had already set aside more than $470 million from previous years' profits. For Union Carbide, the Bhopal tragedy was over.

Sources: *The Financial Times, The Guardian* and *The Times*

Questions

(50 marks; 90 minutes)

1 Examine the problems of communication revealed in the text. **(10)**

2 Discuss the difficulties of multinationals operating in Third World countries, from the point of view of the company and of the host government. **(10)**

3 Calculate the average dollar payment to the Bhopal victims compared with the asbestos sufferers. Why may the courts have decided on such different levels of compensation? **(10)**

4 How might a free marketeer or laissez-faire thinker justify their views in the face of a disaster as this? **(10)**

5 Which different groups can be said to have responsibility for accidents like that at Bhopal? Why do such groups seem so poor at living up to those responsibilities? **(10)**

A PRESSURE GROUP TRIUMPH

Concepts needed: Pressure groups, Restrictive practices, Pricing strategy, Takeovers

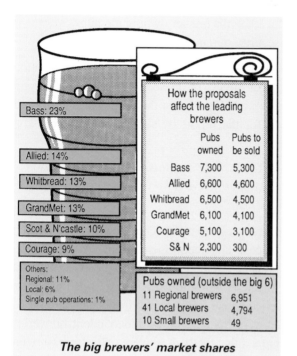

How the proposals affect the leading brewers		
	Pubs owned	Pubs to be sold
Bass	7,300	5,300
Allied	6,600	4,600
Whitbread	6,500	4,500
GrandMet	6,100	4,100
Courage	5,100	3,100
S& N	2,300	300

Pubs owned (outside the big 6)	
11 Regional brewers	6,951
41 Local brewers	4,794
10 Small brewers	49

Big brewers' market shares:
- Bass: 23%
- Allied: 14%
- Whitbread: 13%
- GrandMet: 13%
- Scot & N'castle: 10%
- Courage: 9%
- Others: Regional: 11% Local: 6% Single pub operations: 1%

The big brewers' market shares

During the 1980s, the government prided itself on its challenges to cosy monopoly practices. It took on trade unions, the opticians, direct labour organisations of local councils, and many nationalised industries – and won. Then, in 1989, it took on the breweries, long known to be one of the country's most powerful lobbyists.

The Monopolies and Mergers Commission (MMC) had been asked by the Office of Fair Trading to look into Britain's unique system of 'tied' houses. The system was one of vertical integration, in which breweries controlled many of their outlets (pubs and off-licences). Apart from brewery-owned pubs, tenant landlords were tied into selling just one supplier's beer, spirits and soft drinks. Even apparently 'free' houses were being tied by brewers offering low interest rate loans in return for exclusive selling rights. The MMC estimated that more than 87% of pubs were brewery-controlled.

The March 1989 report described the £16 billion industry as a 'complex monopoly' in which it found 'hostility to would-be competitors and distortions of trade' wherever it looked. The brewers were also judged to have used their monopoly power to impose unjustified price increases. Since 1979 the price of a pint of bitter (excluding VAT and excise duties) had risen by 15% more than inflation generally, as measured by the Retail Prices Index. The Commission was also critical of the 10 pence price premium charged for lager, for which it found no good reason. Indeed, some brewers had lower production costs for lager than for other beers.

According to the MMC, this overcharging was due to the ability of the big firms to keep out the many small, local brewers. Monopoly power was concentrated among the 'Big 6' (see diagram); together they held 82% of the market. Individual market shares appeared quite low, but should be thought of as national averages, hiding the true regional pattern. In much of Norfolk, for instance, Grand Metropolitan held over 40% of the market share; the same was true of Allied (Tetley's) in Yorkshire and Courage in Kent.

The MMC's recommended solution proved more sweeping than the industry

had expected;

1 A ceiling of 2,000 pubs per brewer. This would only affect the 'Big 6', forcing Bass, for instance, to sell off 5,300.
2 A ban on any more loans made in return for sales of a particular brewer's beer.
3 Every publican to have the right to buy a 'guest beer', not produced by the brewer owning the pub.
4 Greater security of tenure for tenant landlords.

To enormous approval from the Consumers' Association and from Fleet Street, Trade Secretary Lord Young said that he was 'minded' to accept the proposals. He showed his backing for the report by stating publicly, on 21st March, that:

> *'The MMC conclude that this complex monopoly restricts competition at all levels, against the public interest.'*

The 'Big 6', through the employers' pressure group The Brewers Society, then set about demolishing the MMC's case and recommendations. A massive £6 million advertising campaign was launched. It held out the grim prospect of quaint countryside locals being sold off, if the Commission was successful. Journalists and MPs were bombarded with worried letters from small brewers, all claiming to be acting independently of the Brewers Society. Other independent breweries welcomed the MMC report, and claimed that the 'Big 6' were putting pressure on the smaller firms. The President of the tenant landlords' group went even further. He declared that breweries were threatening to sack landlords who failed to support the fight against the MMC.

Even more significant was the pressure the brewers managed to put on Lord Young from the government's own back benches. By early May, fifty Conservative MPs had signed a Commons motion congratulating 'this highly competitive industry' on its huge investment in improvements to pubs. The powerful Conservative backbench 1922 Committee summoned Lord Young to quiz him on his plans. Given the anti-monopoly stance of so many Tories, it was unclear why such support was being given to the brewers. Labour Party claims that the Tories were looking after their paymasters were countered by Conservatives who stressed that they were simply passing on the concerns of their constituents. Soon afterwards, newspapers began writing stories about Department of Trade meetings with the brewers, and about probable concessions.

On 10th July, Lord Young published his plan for dealing with the beer market. It represented a remarkable climb-down from what he had been 'minded' to accept just four months before. The *Financial Times* commented that 'the beerage has won hands down'. Under Young's compromise plan:

1 Brewers would not have to sell off any pubs, but half of those above the 2,000 level would have to become free houses; owned by the brewery but (in theory) free to buy from any supplier.

2 All tied and tenanted pubs must sell at least one cask-conditioned ('real ale') guest beer.

3 A review of the licensing system which restricted the opening of new pubs to those for which a local 'need' could be demonstrated (the brewers used this to limit competition).

The value of brewery shares jumped up in response to this heavy dilution of the original proposals. Opposition MPs claimed that Lord Young had caved in to the brewers and their strong political lobby. With cruel timing, several brewers announced price rises of up to 8 pence a pint the following day. This gave Young's opponents more ammunition to fire at him. It is not known if this brush with the power of the brewery vested interests contributed to Lord Young's resignation from the government a month later.

Sources: *The Financial Times; The Independent; The Publican; The Times*

Questions
(40 marks; 70 minutes)

1 Theory would suggest that vertical integration is a sound business objective. Why, then, was the MMC complaining about it?   **(10)**

2 Outline the strengths and weaknesses for the consumer in Lord Young's later proposals compared with the original MMC ones.   **(10)**

3 What factors might lie behind the brewers' 10 pence price premium for draught lager over draught bitter?   **(10)**

4 Many MPs are sponsored by, or are 'consultants' to, outside bodies such as trade unions, employers, or public relations agencies. What specific help might these MPs provide for their clients? What other methods could an organisation use to put pressure upon government decision makers?   **(10)**

68 HANSON – ASSET STRIPPING OR BUSINESS BUILDING?

Concepts needed: Take-overs, Profit centres, Corporate governance, Company accounts, Gearing

> '*It is not a pyramid or a matrix. The management system is a solar system, with everyone circling around the sun in the middle, James Hanson*',

said a former Hanson Trust director. Another director found one day that Hanson had poached his assistant. He wrote Hanson a polite note suggesting that he might have been consulted. 'The last thing I need is snotty little notes from you,' came the reply. This from the Chairman of one of Britain's top ten companies.

The arrogance revealed above can be put down to the astonishing success of the Chairman concerned. For James Hanson, together with his business partner Gordon White, had been responsible for transforming a company with a market value of £300,000 into a much-feared £10 billion giant (and they became Lord Hanson and Lord White in the process). In 1965 they had gained control of a tiny company which they built up and renamed Hanson Trust. During the 1970s Hanson and White made a series of takeover bids for ever larger industrial firms in Britain and America. This gave the company a base upon which they built spectacularly in the 1980s.

In 1981, Hanson Trust paid £95 million for Ever Ready, a company with profits that were sagging in the face of severe competition from Duracell. £41 million was quickly recouped by selling off Ever Ready's overseas businesses. Its Research and Development department was sold off to Duracell and 60% of its UK workforce were laid off. By the end of the decade, the rump of the business was making £40 million profit per year.

Following a series of purchases of retail and construction businesses, Hanson made a huge leap forward with its 1985 bid for Imperial Tobacco. After a fierce **takeover battle**, Hanson emerged the victor at a price of £2.6 billion. Imperial held brands such as John Player, Embassy, Courage Brewery and Golden Wonder within two years Hanson had sold off every part of Imperial other than its tobacco interests, and raised £2.4 billion in the process. Within four years, Players and Embassy – bought in effect for £200 million – generated £200 million of profit per annum. So Hanson was making a 100% return per year on its investment.

This was achieved by far more than just financial juggling. Hanson's long-term success was rooted in its management methods. The takeover of Imperial illustrated this. On acquiring the business, a Hanson director went in to supervise the installation of Hanson accounting systems and financial controls. Later, a second head office team took over, learning the tobacco business and deciding how best to restructure it. This team wound down Imperial's head office, cut its nine layers of management hierarchy to four and rationalised its salesforce and production plants. Having made these changes, the team then withdrew to allow Imperial

Tobacco's newly appointed chief executive to run the business.

The Hanson approach has always been to allow extreme decentralisation within rigid financial disciplines. The chief executive of each division agrees tough financial targets at the start of each year and must meet them. Failure to do so threatens, at best, the arrival of a head office team of accountants or, at worst, the departure of the chief executive. All capital expenditures above £500 require head office approval, since the control of cash outflows has always been a key to Hanson's financial management. Subsidiaries must supply head office with detailed information on capital spending, cash flow and their ratios of profit to working capital. Apart from that they run themselves.

The other aspect of Hanson's reputation was a hard-headedness with shareholders' money. For although key managers received substantial bonus incentives to reward success, corporate luxuries were frowned upon. Before Hanson, Players' middle managers could enjoy a restaurant away from the factory canteen, at which sherry and wine would be served. Senior staff would travel worldwide to support the John Player Special grand prix racing car – a form of sponsorship costing millions of pounds a year. Hanson swept these indulgences away, to the delight of shareholders.

In 1985 the *Financial Times* noted that Hanson needed to bid for bigger and bigger companies in order to keep itself growing. For although it was good at cost-cutting within the firms it took over, there was little evidence that Hanson could make businesses grow. With tongue in cheek it pointed out that this might end up with Hanson bidding for ICI.

On May 14th 1991 a mystery buyer paid £240 million for a 2.5% stake in ICI, Britain's largest manufacturing company. When, a day later, Hanson confirmed that it was the purchaser, the ICI share price shot up. Analysts suggested that a bid worth £11 billion would be needed to win ICI. Hanson, with cash holdings of £7.4 billion, could afford to do that without sending its gearing through the roof.

Instead of making a bid, Lord Hanson proposed a full-scale merger. He suggested that ICI could benefit from his tighter budgetary and financial controls, while Hanson could benefit from ICI's international marketing expertise. The ICI Board rejected the proposal outright and actively prepared its defences against the anticipated bid.

How ICI divisions ranked, by turnover

Division	World rank	World leader
Agrochemicals/seed	2nd	Ciba-Geigy
Explosives	1st	ICI
Industrial chemicals	10th	*
Paints	1st	ICI
Pharmaceuticals	18th	Merck

* This is such a diverse field that it is not possible to identify a single market leader. Shell is the world leader in petrochemicals and plastics.

Surprisingly for a firm with the courteous reputation of ICI, a major thrust of its defence proved to be a vigorous attack on Hanson's methods. It hired expert accountants and analysts to put Hanson's record and accounts under the microscope. Four themes emerged:

1   Short-termism. ICI suggested that Hanson could only buy and sell businesses, not build them, leading to skimping on Research and Development spending. Its figures showed that whereas ICI spent £679 million on R&D in 1990, from sales of £12.9 billion, Hanson spent only £34 million out of £7.2 billion of sales.

2   **Corporate governance.** ICI attacked Hanson's business morality, which it blamed on the lack of strong, independent directors on Hanson's Board.

Hanson's secrets start to unfold

The Observer, 23/6/91

3   Strategy. Hanson take-over victims had always been producers of stable, low technology products such as bricks or cigarettes. These required low investment spending and had predictable sales that could form the basis of the financial targets used to run the subsidiaries. So why was Hanson thinking of buying a producer of advanced chemicals, plastics and pharmaceuticals, a company with huge Research and Development needs?

4   Succession. With Lords Hanson and White both over 70, who would become the future leaders of the business?

With so many questions being asked about Hanson plc, its share price sagged, signalling that investors were not willing to back its bid for ICI. Hanson had to defend itself by offering to make a series of changes to its Board membership and accounting policies. It tried to fight back by contrasting ICI's bureaucratic structure with its own decentralised methods; but ICI's tactics had been so successful that no Hanson bid emerged. On May 8th 1992, Hanson quietly sold its ICI shares at a small profit.

Hanson plc Company Accounts at September 30th (simplified version)

Profit and loss account	1991 £m	1990 £m
Sales turnover	7,691	7,153
Costs and overheads	6,372	5,868
Operating profit	1,319	1,285
Taxation	284	314
Profit after tax	1,035	971

Balance sheet	1991 £m	1990 £m
Fixed assets	6,628	5,761
Stocks	992	984
Debtors	1,192	1,126
Cash at bank	7,771	6,883
Creditors	(4,751)	(4,226)
Assets employed	11,832	10,528
Loans and provisions	8,507	7,694
Share capital	2,355	2,354
Reserves	970	480
Capital employed	11,832	10,528

Sources: *The Financial Times, Hanson plc Report and Accounts 1992; The Sunday Times; The Times.*

Questions

(50 marks; 100 minutes)

1 Explain what is meant by the following terms (emboldened in the text):
   takeover battle
   corporate governance. **(4)**

2 Discuss the picture that emerges in this case study of Lord Hanson's management style. **(8)**

3 Decentralisation with the aid of tight budgetary control is a commonly used management method. What are its strengths and weaknesses? **(8)**

4 a If Hanson had bid £11 billion for ICI in May, using £7 billion of cash and borrowing the remainder, what would its gearing level have been by September 30th 1991? Compare that with the actual balance sheet gearing figure. **(6)**

   b Why may Hanson's gearing position have restricted its actions? **(4)**

5 Based upon the evidence available to you, how valid do ICI's criticisms of Hanson plc's short-termism and strategy seem to have been (themes 1 and 3 in this case study)? **(10)**

6 Identify the shareholders who may feel concerned about the way in which large companies are governed? For what reasons may they be concerned? **(10)**

69 THE WINTER OF DISCONTENT

Concepts needed: Trade unions, Inflation, Monetary policy, Direct controls, External constraints

The Labour Party took power in February 1974 after the Conservatives had failed to cope with the bargaining power of leading trade unions such as the mineworkers (NUM) and the engineers (AUEW). The Tories had also been responsible for a consumer spending boom generated by a high money supply/low interest rate policy. So the Labour Prime Ministers Wilson and (from 1977) Callaghan, had a constant struggle to cope with the inflationary legacy. A struggle made worse by the expectation of working-class Labour voters that 'their' government would reward them with higher living standards, just as the Tories had done for the better-off.

As inflation spiralled upwards in late 1974 and early 1975, it became commonplace to forecast that Britain was heading for **hyperinflation.** The government responded by agreeing upon a statutory prices and incomes policy with the main unions. The maximum weekly rise allowed to any employee was to be £4 plus 5%. The flat rate element was to ensure that lower-paid workers would do better relatively than the better paid. Also part of the scheme was the establishment of the Price Commission, to which all firms would have to apply for permission to increase their prices. It received legal powers to scrutinise the accounts of any firm to make sure that such increases were justified by cost factors. Opinion polls showed that these measures had wide public support.

Given the success of the government's **direct controls** at cutting inflation (see graph), it made sense to follow through with Phase 2 and Phase 3 incomes policies in 1976/7 and 1977/8. However, these were voluntary, and were imposed more strictly by the government on its employees than by private sector firms. The resentment felt increasingly by state employees also built up among many groups of private sector manual workers. They suspected (with good reason) that company managers were able to get round the pay restrictions by awarding themselves company cars, or changing job titles in order to get 'promotion'.

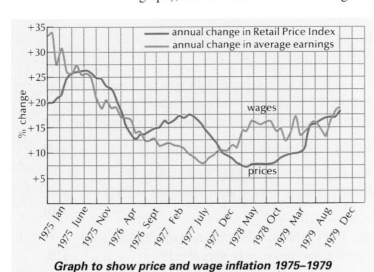

Graph to show price and wage inflation 1975–1979

HEY DIDDLE DIDDLE...

Early in 1978, Chancellor Healey announced that Phase 4 of the incomes policy would be for a 5% increase in basic pay. The Trade Union Congress (TUC) made clear that they wished to return to free collective bargaining, with no state intervention. Nevertheless, the union leaders still supported Labour's notion of a social contract, in which wage moderation would be rewarded by increased government spending to create more jobs. This harmony between the political and union leaderships made it seem possible that Phase 4 would stick. So although Labour enjoyed a 4% opinion poll lead in August, Prime Minister Callaghan announced in September that instead of calling an Autumn election (as most expected), he would wait until 1979.

What became known as the 'winter of discontent' began with a lengthy pay strike at Ford's that Autumn. The concessions won by the Ford strikers seemed to have an effect upon the expectations of many other groups. It started in earnest in early January 1979, when lorry drivers and oil tanker drivers came out on unofficial strike over a 25% pay claim. Within a few days, petrol stations were running out of petrol, and those remaining open had queues of up to a hundred cars. In Manchester, a garage charging double the normal price was finding plenty of takers.

Meanwhile the lorry drivers were using **secondary action** to picket docks and depots, and there were clear signs of stock shortages of food and industrial components. To cap it all, the public sector unions called 1.5 million workers out for a 'day of action' on Monday 22nd January, to herald the start of an all-out campaign for a minimum weekly wage of seventy pounds.

During the week in which this industrial storm had blown up, the Prime Minister had been away in the Caribbean. On his return, he announced complacently: 'I see no chaos'; a misjudgement that he was not allowed to forget in the election later that year.

By 16th January – a week after Callaghan's return – the lorry drivers' strike had been declared official by the Transport and General Workers' Union, and was biting. Despite a voluntary agreement with the government not to conduct secondary action, it was being used widely at docks and depots. There was also clear evidence that strikers and pickets were ignoring their union's recommendation to allow through essential food supplies. Tesco's managing director reported that:

> *'All our depots are now being picketed...we are absolutely helpless.'*

Opposition leader Mrs. Thatcher urged Callaghan to legislate an end to the unions' legal protection from being sued by firms suffering from secondary action; he refused.

During that same week a train strike disrupted commuters and post alike, and workers at both British Airways and British Airports Authority were threatening strike action. With British Leyland and British Steel having to halt production due to shortages of components, the crisis was deepening. By the 19th, around 200,000 workers were laid off due to supply shortages, and certain packaged foods were unavailable. Evidence of anarchy seemed to be everywhere. At Cadbury's Bourneville factory, three hundred women attacked and broke up a picket line of fifteen striking lorry drivers. Elsewhere a lorry was forced off the road by flying pickets, who then attacked the 'scab' driver.

The government's response was to offer to relax its 5% pay ceiling for lower paid and public sector employees. In addition, it announced a tightening of the powers of the Price Commission in an attempt to discourage employers from conceding wage demands. For it was made clear that large pay settlements would have to be paid out of profit margins, not from price rises. The Prime Minister also called in the TGWU leader Moss Evans to warn him that if he could not control his pickets, troops would be called in to safeguard food supplies.

A 'day of action' by 1.5 million public sector workers, the biggest strike since 1926, took place on 22nd January. In London, the 2,300 ambulance men had warned in advance that they would not even provide emergency cover. *The Daily Telegraph* reported that the ambulancemen's spokesman had said:

> *'If it means lives lost, that is how it must be. This time we are*
> *determined that the capital will take notice of what we are saying.'*

In fact the ambulance men relented, but the wide publicity given to the above statement left the impression that union leaders and members had lost their sense of proportion. The press coverage following the day's strike emphasised this by highlighting that gravediggers went on strike: 'BODIES GO UNBURIED'. Three days later *The Daily Telegraph* had these two headlines on its front page:

AMBULANCEMEN LEFT SICK MAN IN SNOW

BODIES LEFT IN WARD BY PORTERS

Although neither story lived up to its billing, there was no doubt that some people in caring jobs were applying union methods of blacking goods and stopping work in a disturbingly harsh manner. Early in February the Archbishop of Canterbury called for a change of heart from 'strikers with no pity' – but disruption to hospital services continued. The unions involved always stressed that the overwhelming majority of their members behaved with dignity and compassion, but that was not the public's impression.

On 29th January, with the lorry strike in its fourth week, the Transport union won an arbitration award that was just £1 below its claim for £65. This success egged the public sector workers on further, and street cleaning and rubbish collections were halted in many areas. Memories of piles of rubbish in the streets were added to those of petrol queues and unburied bodies in the folklore of the 'winter of discontent'.

Only in March was the government able to head off the strikers by announcing the formation of a Pay Comparability commission. This was empowered to award whatever level of pay rise was necessary to bring public sector workers' pay up to the level of the private sector. This was a major victory for the public sector unions. Yet the way they had achieved this 'victory' was to make it inevitable that Mrs. Thatcher would be elected with a mandate to weaken union power. That duly occurred on 4th May, 1979.

Sources: *The Daily Telegraph; The Financial Times; HMSO.*

APPENDIX A: *Employment vacancies – 1976/80 (monthly averages in thousands)*

Quarter	1976	1977	1978	1979	1980
Jan–March	97	138	170	220	179
Apr–June	121	162	214	264	172
July–Sept	131	159	220	252	121
Oct–Dec	138	160	230	226	98

Source: *Annual Abstract HMSO*

Questions

(60 marks; 100 minutes)

1   Explain the meaning of the following terms (emboldened in the text):

　　hyperinflation
　　direct controls
　　secondary action **(6)**

2   How would a high money supply/low interest rate policy leave an inflationary legacy? **(6)**

3   Use the text to identify what you think were the key mistakes made by the Callaghan government in 1978–79. **(8)**

4   **a**   Use the graph and the figures in Appendix A to discuss the economic background to the 'winter of discontent'. **(8)**

　　b   How important were these economic factors compared with the other causes? **(8)**

5   An important feature of the disputes was that most were started or magnified by unofficial action.

　　a   How does this differ from official action? **(2)**

　　b   Why do you suppose this explosion of unofficial action occurred? **(6)**

6   Since 1978–79, both sides in a strike have tried hard to win the propaganda/image battle. Why is this considered so important? **(8)**

7   If a business expected a high level of industrial action within the economy, how might it respond? **(8)**

THE 3 IN 1 WASHING MACHINE

Concepts needed: Break-even, Cash flow, Advertising, Product life cycle

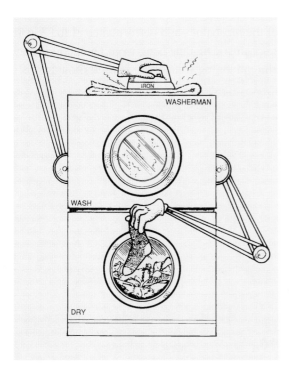

It was Jane's idea that had started it. She had been so fed up with her Mum's moaning that she snapped: 'You won't be happy till there's a machine that washes, dries, and irons all the clothes automatically.' When her boyfriend heard about it, he started messing about with electronics; ten months later the 'Washerman' 3 in 1 washing machine was a full, working prototype.

Now came the big decision; should they sell the idea to a big company, or try to manufacture it themselves? All Tim was sure of was that he should patent the idea as soon as possible.

They decided to visit a bank manager for advice. Before going, they tried to work out what kind of sums were involved. Much of the costs would come from bought-in components, so they felt fairly certain of the following estimates:

components	£280 per unit
materials	£60 per unit
factory labour	£10 per unit

(they had argued about whether labour is a fixed or a variable cost, but Jane's view prevailed – that as they intended to pay their workers per unit produced, they must treat factory labour as a variable cost).

They were less certain of the fixed costs, and so decided to work on both optimistic and pessimistic figures.

rent and rates	£6,000–12,000 per month
staff salaries	£14,000–24,000 per month
other overheads	£10,000–14,000 per month

After further arguing, they agreed that they could charge £500 per machine, and should sell their total output of 300 machines per month. Armed with this information, they went to the bank.

The manager worked out the best and worst profit position based upon their information, and frowned. He then said:

'You really need to do a lot more work before I can help. Have you thought about the likely length of life cycle of the Washerman? After all, your forecast of overheads assumes that the machinery you buy will have useful life of five years. But what if the product fades away after three? And what about a cash flow forecast? Surely you realise the importance of that.'

By the end of the meeting, though, the bank manager was becoming increasingly impressed with Tim's explanation of the mechanics and performance of the 3 in 1. So Jane and Tim went away feeling optimistic that the bank would help, once they had given their financial and marketing planning some more careful thought.

Questions

(30 marks; 45 minutes)

1 a What is meant by the term patent? (2)

 b If they wished to stop anyone else from using the brand name 'Washerman', what should they obtain? (1)

2 What profit could be expected (both optimistic and pessimistic) if the forecasts made are correct? (5)

3 State three ways in which a break-even chart could be of use to them? (3)

4 Discuss the factors that would influence their decisions on an advertising strategy to ensure consumer acceptance of the 3 in 1? (8)

5 On the assumption that the product works well, how might Jane and Tim set about forecasting the probable length of the life cycle of the 3 in 1? (Try to come up with specific ideas, i.e. just 'market research' will not do.) (7)

6 Outline two reasons why a cash flow forecast would be of value in this situation. (4)

71 A SMALL BUSINESS START-UP

Concepts needed: Distribution, Market research, Cash flow forecast, Break-even

'He'll never give it to us,' said Michael glumly. Jane agreed that 17-year-olds could hardly expect to get a £1,000 bank loan, but she was determined to try. They sat nervously in the bank manager's waiting room, avoiding looking at each other.

Since leaving school, they had both put so much work into their business plan that it was impossible to believe they might have to abandon it. Both had worked to save £750 in a year, so £1,000 from the bank would give them the £2,500 they needed as start-up capital.

From their homes in Surbiton they planned on serving the wealthy homes of Weybridge and Esher with a 'Dewfresh Flower Delivery', door-to-door service. Mike knew the routines of the Covent Garden wholesale market, and realised that he could buy boxes of Grade one daffodils for £20 per 100 bunches, which could be sold to customers for 90 pence per bunch.

They had worked out their fixed costs at £1,000 per month, and had conducted a survey of one hundred adults in Esher and Weybridge. From this they estimated that they would get 2,000 orders per month, with an average value of £5 per order. As the variable costs should only amount to £2 per order, this seemed promising.

As part of their preparations for their visit to the bank, Jane had worked out a cash flow forecast. This showed that they would have used up all the £2,500 by month two, but profits should bring money in after then. Jane's main worry was that customers would want to receive some credit.

Then a door opened and they were ushered in...

Questions
(40 marks; 60 minutes)

1 Develop two reasons why Mike and Jane might be better off obtaining supplies from a wholesale market, instead of directly from the flower producers. **(6)**

2 Explain three reasons why their market research survey might prove inaccurate. **(6)**

3 Why was Jane worried about customers wanting to receive credit? **(4)**

4 Draw a break-even chart based on the figures given above. Assume that the highest number of orders they could cope with is 2,500 per month. Plot fixed costs, total costs, and total revenue. **(9)**

5 Assuming orders do start at a rate of 2,000 per month, outline three reasons why they may decline in following months. **(6)**

6 If disappointing sales cause only 1,000 orders per month, what profit or loss will they make? (Show your workings.) **(4)**

7 How might they promote their new service, to ensure that people in their target market get to hear about it? **(5)**

FORD'S MODEL T – THE BIRTH OF MODERN INDUSTRY

Concepts needed: Scientific management, Demand, Division of labour

At the turn of the century, production of cars was mainly done by skilled workers who crafted the car with the aid of quite simple machinery. Henry Ford's small car factory followed this pattern, until demand for his newest model (the Model T) forced him to look for ways of speeding up output. Ford's twelve to fifteen young engineers were given the freedom to test the performance of new machine tools against their existing methods. If they could prove the superiority of their new system, the factory layout would be changed in whichever way would allow output to be expanded most rapidly. They soon found that the easiest way to increase output per worker was by getting parts moving automatically from one production stage to another. At first this was done with downward sloping chutes, then later with conveyor belts. When cost-saving measures were introduced, Ford passed these on as price cuts to his customers. As demand increased further, they found it possible to subdivide different units of work into smaller and smaller operations. At first, unskilled workers were used to produce these parts repeatedly; then the engineers set about devising machinery that would simplify the work even further.

By 1910, Ford's success had enabled him to afford to construct a massive new factory at Highland Park. By 1913, many of the main components were being constructed on assembly lines. In late 1913, experiments were carried out on a moving line for the car chassis. This proved highly successful. By June 1914, a chain-driven line (as is still used in many car factories) had cut assembly time from 12 hours to 93 minutes. Within a year, Ford had introduced moving assembly lines throughout the plant.

Yet the ever-increasing mechanisation of the plant made it a progressively more unpleasant place to work. The constant pressure to keep up with the pace of the line, plus the appalling noise and dust levels, resulted in Ford's labour turnover reaching 380%. A 13% pay rise (to $2.34 per day) had no impact on the problem, so in January 1914 Ford created world headlines by adopting the unprecedentedly high figure of $5 per day (more than many Americans and British earned per week).

The five-dollar-a-day wage ensured that **Fordism** became widely discussed and admired by managements, workers and consumers throughout Europe; and Ford became a folk hero in America. He had shown that mass production could enable high wages to be paid, yet consumer prices cut (see Appendix A). The fact that Ford offered no choice of colour or model design was not seen as a disadvantage at a time when people were thrilled to be able to afford their first car. At their height, Ford's Highland Park and the new, massive River Rouge plants produced two million Model T's in one year – giving Ford 50% of the US car market in the early 1920s. It was only later in that decade that customers began to switch to the wider range of models provided by General Motors. Model T production ended in 1927, by which time Ford had produced over fifteen million.

APPENDIX A: Model T pricing and sales 1909–1916

Year	Retail Price	Sales
1909	$950	12,292
1910	$780	19,293
1911	$690	40,402
1912	$600	78,611
1913	$550	182,809
1914	$490	260,720
1915	$440	355,276
1916	$360	577,036

Questions

(30 marks; 45 minutes)

1 Explain your understanding of the term Fordism (emboldened in the text) **(3)**

2 a Draw a demand schedule that plots price against quantity for Ford's Model T. **(9)**

  b Outline three factors that might have been operating to distort the relationship between price and demand during this period. **(6)**

3 What terms are usually used to convey the meaning:

  a Output per worker **(2)**

  b Subdividing different units of work into smaller and smaller operations. **(2)**

4 What evidence does the passage contain of the influence of F.W. Taylor's views on 'Scientific Management'? **(8)**

Concepts needed: Company objectives, Marketing strategy, Value of the pound, Stocks, Break-even

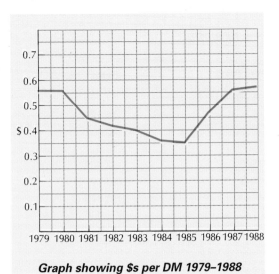

Graph showing $s per DM 1979–1988

The first half of the 1980s were marvellous for the German Porsche Company. A booming US economy was matched by the vast salary increases in the City of London, as the 'Big Bang' generated an upsurge in the demand for City dealers and analysts. The newly acquired wealth on both sides of the Atlantic found an outlet in the most flamboyant status symbol of its time – the Porsche sports car. The strength of the dollar made it possible for Porsche to sell in the United States at very profitable prices. As the United States president Ronald Reagan boasted about the 'mighty dollar', it seemed reasonable to assume that this would continue.

In the early 1980s, the Porsche family had appointed an extrovert German-born American (Peter Schutz) as Chairman. His strategy was a marketing-led one, of developing products and distribution networks that would enable sales to grow rapidly among the new, younger rich. America was booming, so it became the focus of his efforts. A new car, the 924, was designed that would bring the young buyer into the Porsche price range whilst they were not very high up the corporate ladder. Schutz believed that the qualities of their cars would ensure that as they rose in seniority, these people would trade up to the more expensive models. The 924 was priced at £12,000 – far below most Porsches, and comparable with BMWs and Audis. Its profit margins were lower than their other models, but the 924 sold very well in the United States, assisted by the strength of the dollar. By 1985/86, 65% of Porsche sales were in America, and extra factory capacity had been built to cope with record sales volumes.

Then, in 1987, everything turned sour. The dollar had been falling sharply against the Deutschmark, forcing all the German carmakers to increase their prices in the United States. This came at a time when traditional buyers of £30,000 Porsches were becoming dissatisfied with the image portrayed by the young drivers of models that looked similar, yet cost less than half the price. Worse still, in October 1987 came an unexpected and dramatic stock market crash. The sharp falls in share prices led to much lower levels of activity on the stock market, and a more sober approach to spending. Lower salary levels plus the new sense of cautiousness led to reduced demand for sports cars in general and Porsche in particular.

As capacity utilisation dropped and profits disappeared, the supervisory board

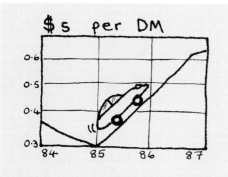

replaced Schutz with Mr. Branitzki, their former finance director. What followed were swingeing cost and labour cuts, three day weeks in most of their factories, a rapid reassessment of its model and marketing policy, and sharp reductions in output; from 51,000 cars in 1986/87 to 31,000 in 1987/88. This proved sufficient to cut stocks from their pre-cash level of 15,000 cars to just 6,000. Rumours abounded of the firm collapsing under the weight of its problems, and of the chances of the family selling out to a wealthier rival.

By 1989, though, the firm had adjusted to a new, lower demand plateau by slashing its break-even output level. The 924 model was dropped, thereby increasing the average selling price by 10,000 Deutschmarks. New, high performance models were introduced that were tailored for the European market – helping to cut the US share of Porsche sales to 45% of the total. As well as streamlining and improving its product range, the company reconsidered its dealer network in Europe and America, putting the emphasis on specialisation rather than numbers.

Mr. Branitzki was concerned not only to restore the company's exclusive image, but also to prepare for the growing competition from Japanese sports cars in America. In 1988/89, the company spent 24% of its turnover on capital investment, training, and research and development – a considerable act of faith given that profits represented just 1% of sales revenue. By mid 1989, it was clear that Porsche had pulled through, with sales and profits rising once more.

Sources: *The Financial Times; HMSO UN Monthly Statistics Tables*

Questions

(40 marks; 70 minutes)

1   Discuss the wisdom of Schutz's marketing strategy. **(10)**

2   What was the importance for Porsche of the rise in the value of the Deutschmark from 1986 onwards? Why was it especially important for the 924 model? **(10)**

3   From the data given, what was the reduction in demand for Porsche cars in 1987/88? Explain the reasons for the cost-cutting measures the firm took, and how they would help to cut its break-even output level. **(10)**

4   Use the information above as the starting point for considering what influences the objectives a firm sets itself. **(10)**

74 THE PRINCE AND THE TURNSTILE

Concepts needed: Direct and indirect costs, Depreciation, Profit

When made redundant, 25 year old Jim Tilley was left with £5,000 and a fierce determination to be his own boss. As a fanatical supporter of Blyth Spartans Football Club, he had become used to helping out by maintaining and repairing their turnstiles. Now he would set up Tilley Turnstile Services and try to make a living out of his hobby.

His first step was to get 1,000 brochures printed that explained the two main services: repair and maintenance. These he mailed out to the professional and leading amateur football clubs, plus other venues such as cricket clubs and racecourses. The week after completing the mailing was the worst of his life. He had no responses at all.

Then a letter arrived from Kilmarnock inviting him to come up and give a quote for a pre-season overhaul of their sixteen turnstiles. He was up in Scotland within three hours; by the end of the afternoon he had the contract. For £400 the club had its turnstiles made good and on arriving home three days later, Jim worked out that he had made £200 as pay/profit.

The next four weeks were crazily busy, as club after club invited Jim to work for them. He priced each job along the same lines as his first, working out all the direct costs, then adding 100%. With money flowing in, he bought a van and rented a factory unit, on an industrial estate.

Then in late August the phones went dead as the pre-season work dried up. Eventually jobs came through from clubs that needed repair work to broken turnstiles, but the turnover was pretty low. Jim realised that he needed longer term work to fill in the gaps. He decided to move into the manufacture of turnstiles for new sports stadia or the replacement market.

First, however, he would need extra finance. Discussions with his local banks got nowhere, but a television programme led him to contact the Prince's Youth Business Trust. Jim was allocated an advisor who helped him construct a business plan as the basis for a loan application. The Trust itself lent £4,000 on a low interest rate and this commitment encouraged Barclays to lend the same amount.

Most of the £8,000 of new capital went into the machinery needed to make the turnstile structure. Jim planned to subcontract the production of many of the components, but he wanted full production control over the most critical parts. The Prince's Trust advisor helped to set up a software package to enable Jim to calculate the following data on unit production costs.

	Production Run			
	1	2–4	5–9	10+
Bought in components	£485	£455	£360	£320
Raw materials	£145	£125	£90	£80
Labour	£330	£330	£450	£480
Other direct costs	£100	£90	£80	£70

The advisor queried the rise in unit labour costs for 5+ units, but accepted the explanation that Jim would have to employ extra workers. These he expected to be less efficient than himself due to their lack of product familiarity and their lesser incentive to make the business successful.

The decision was made to price the turnstiles at 50% above total direct costs. Jim reasoned that his £2,000 per month of ongoing overheads had to be covered by the existing repair and maintenance business, so there was no point in counting them twice. The only specific turnstile overhead was £200 per month of interest and depreciation on the new machinery.

A new mailing to the same list of clubs plus a press feature in *Sports Management* magazine led to two orders. One, from the Greenacre Cricket Club, was for four turnstiles and the other for twelve turnstiles from Ayr racecourse. Fortunately the delivery dates were staggered, with Greenacre wanting the turnstiles installed within three months and Ayr within six months.

Even though the four turnstiles were Jim's first ever production run, the Greenacre job went remarkably smoothly. The only hiccup was over cash flow, as his suppliers demanded early payment whereas the Cricket Club proved to be very slow payers. Although Barclays helped by providing a £5,000 overdraft, the charges and interest costs involved took £500 off the profit on the job.

For the Ayr contract, Jim knew he would have to hire a welder and a fitter. This proved very time-consuming, as 40 people responded to the small advertisement he placed in the local paper. Even after two days of interviews he did not feel confident that he had picked the right people. The job had to be started, though, so it seemed silly to waste any more time. Two men were hired on the understanding that the job would cease when the contract was completed.

On the day they started, both workers were keen to learn about the job. By the end of their first week, however, Jim kept noticing how different they were. The fitter worked enthusiastically, helping in all sorts of ways as well as getting on with his work. Some of his suggestions for increasing efficiency were very astute. The welder, however, took frequent breaks and was never willing to do anything other than weld. The quality of the work was fine, but his attitude was infuriating.

As the weeks went by, Jim became ever more aware that the job was slipping behind schedule. Then vandalism at Cardiff F.C. forced Jim to spend a week in Wales. On his return, the fitter was spitting with rage at the welder's laziness and offhand manner. Jim was torn between the desire to sack the welder and the knowledge of the time it would take to replace him. He stumbled on without making a decision, living with conflict in his workplace until the Ayr job was finally completed, five weeks late.

The Ayr officials were so upset by the delay that they refused to pay in full; they deducted 5% from the bill as compensation. Jim squawked, but was too desperate to get paid to argue. The delay had pushed up his costs and sent him up to the overdraft ceiling. For a fortnight he was unsure of survival, but eventually the payment came that solved the cash shortage.

After that experience, Jim was far more careful with his recruitment procedure, always employing the same fitter whenever possible. In the second year, work flowed in more consistently, giving rise to the possibility of making a permanent appointment. Tilley Turnstile Services was on its way.

APPENDIX A: Extracts from the business plan

Sales Turnover to Date		Forecast Monthly Turnover (excluding turnstile manufacture)
July	£1,400	October – June (average) £4,500
August	£15,000	
September	£3,100	

Questions
(40 marks; 70 minutes)

1 Outline Jim's main strengths and weaknesses as a manager of a small firm.   **(8)**

2 Calculate the salary/profit Jim could expect to receive in his first year of trading. State clearly any assumptions you have made.   **(10)**

3 **a** What might explain the differing attitudes to work of the fitter and the welder?   **(6)**

   b How might Jim have handled the situation better?   **(6)**

4 Organisations such as the Prince's Trust exist to help small firms start up and develop. Use this case as the starting point to consider the main problems faced by new small firms.   **(10)**

75 THE SURVIVAL GAME

Concepts needed: *Location, Marketing mix, Profit, Franchising*

The Survival Game was first played in June 1981 in the woods of New Hampshire, USA. Two teams – each armed with paint pellet guns – attempt to infiltrate the other's base camp, capture their flag and return it to their own base. It proved to be a huge success and by 1988 it had become a $150 million industry.

Survival Game U.K. Limited was formed in 1984 to establish this new sport in Britain. Its owners identified two markets: weekend leisure for sporty types and a weekday business market training course in teamwork. In 1985 the company achieved 2,500 customers. Word of mouth plus television coverage pushed demand up rapidly to 60,000 players by 1988. This sales explosion was accommodated by Survival Game U.K. setting up three of its own sites plus twenty-one franchised outlets. Each site covers over twenty acres of partly wooded terrain, and is usually rented from a large landowner or local authority.

Allan Burrows is an enthusiastic Survival Game player, whose £15,000 redundancy payout has tempted him to become the twenty-second franchisee. He has been having to make a 100-mile round trip to travel to the Norwich site, and so sees potential in developing one in Ipswich. A phone call to the firm's London offices reveals the following information:

1 Franchise fee – £10,000 for an eight year contract to manage the sole Survival Game U.K. site in Suffolk. Included would be all the equipment needed to start, including 50 'Splatmaster' pistols and 12,000 Splatballs (filled with washable orange paint).

2 Training and promotion – full training is given to all franchisees, not only in the running of the game but also in accounting and publicity techniques.

3 Back-up services – including supplies, national marketing and public relations.

4 Financial Projection (assuming 40 players for 75 days in the year, i.e. 3,000 customers) – as follows:

Sales revenue

	Game fee	£48,000
	Paint pellets	£30,000
	Other revenue	£10,000
	Total sales:	£88,000

Cost of sales

	Paint pellets	£20,000
	Other costs	£5,000
	Total direct costs	£25,000

Overheads

	Site rent	£3,750
	Wages	£6,500
	Other overheads	£19,750
	Total overheads	£30,000
	Pre-tax profit	£33,000

Allan was impressed, and decided to contact a local landowner to see if a suitable site could be rented per day. There proved to be a thirty acre wooded site available at a daily rate of £80. He also wanted to consider catering facilities before committing himself. Allan knew that he and his friends found food the only disappointment about their trips to Norwich. After a morning's action one wanted a substantial and enjoyable meal. So Allan negotiated with a local caterer to provide a hearty, barbecued meal for £8 per head. He felt he should charge his customers no more than £5 for this, so he had to build this loss into his profit projections. Apart from the fact that he realised that high local labour costs would add 50% to the wage bill, Allan was happy about the rest of Survival Game U.K.'s forecasts.

A fellow game-player sounded a note of caution, however. He said that Survival Game magazine had been carrying advertisements offering a complete set of 'Splatmaster' guns and equipment for just £1,200. As he said: 'Anyone could start up in this business now'. Furthermore he knew the editor of the magazine, and had learned that its circulation had levelled off after its sharp rise in recent years. Allan phoned Survival Game U.K. about these points and was reassured to hear that they attributed the magazine's sales hiccup to its editorial weaknesses, not to flat demand for the game itself. In fact Survival Game U.K.'s managing director said that:

'In the first six months of this year there have been 10% more game players than in the same period last year. So business is booming.'

Questions

(40 marks; 70 minutes)

1 Allan appears to be willing to accept the first site he finds. What factors should he consider when deciding on the location of his Survival site? **(10)**

2 How might Allan's marketing to the weekend leisure market differ from that towards the business market? **(10)**

3 Calculate the annual pre-tax profit Allan could expect if he went ahead with the Survival Game U.K. operation. How could he try to increase this level of profitability? **(10)**

4 Discuss the factors Allan should consider in deciding whether to buy the Survival Game U.K. franchise, or set up an independent Survival outlet. **(10)**

THE FARLEY'S SALMONELLA CRISIS

Concepts needed: *Balance sheets, Ratios, Market share, Branding, Social responsibility*

In November 1985, it was announced that Boots the Chemist was interested in buying Farley's Health Products for a rumoured £40 million. This was a substantial premium over the value of Farley's **tangible assets**, but reflected the worth Boots placed on a 100-year-old, major brand name. Negotiations proceeded with Farley's owners – the giant drug company Glaxo.

Then, just two days before Christmas, a public warning was given that parents should stop giving their babies Farley's babymilk products as they had been identified statistically as being **correlated** with an outbreak of salmonella poisoning. Thirty-one babies under one year of age had been diagnosed as having salmonella since November 1st; one had died. Although originally linked to Farley's only in theory (because careful investigation had shown that a very high proportion had consumed Farley's products) physical checks then revealed the source of the organism within the factory. Nevertheless, this connection could not be taken as legal proof that any particular baby's suffering was caused directly by a Farley's product.

All the firm's babymilk products were withdrawn from shops throughout the world. The shock value of a story about poisoned babies ensured that both Farley's and Glaxo had to endure a great deal of bad publicity. Most supposed that consumer mistrust would prevent Farley's from ever returning to the babymilk market. Not that this would mean the end of the Farley's name, for despite an initial slump in sales of Farley's rusks, the firm soon succeeded in persuading consumers that the separate cereals factory was unaffected and totally safe. This important task of reassurance was helped by the separation of the safe Plymouth cereals factory from the Cumbrian factory.

In early January, Glaxo announced the voluntary liquidation of Farley's. The Holding Company emphasised that this was not in order to duck any claims from customers, nor to escape from the operating losses being incurred. It was just to enable them to split the business in two – to make it easier to sell the cereals side as a going concern, and to **liquidate the assets** of the milk division. For it was quite clear that Glaxo wanted to be rid of the Farley's embarrassment as soon as possible.

Farley's Health Products Limited had £3.25 million Shareholder's Funds. This was swamped by the estimated £9 million loss from withdrawing and destroying stocks. This seemed a remarkably high figure given annual babymilk sales of £20 million. However, the product's long shelf life plus the **low stock turnovers** of its chemist stockists throughout the world, meant a high stock value to be bought back.

Farley's problems came as a windfall to its competitors in the babymilk market, as Farley's had previously held a 24% share. The market leaders (SMA) announced that 'Our output has doubled since Christmas. We have worked every day since to fill the gap'. For although SMA took 41% of the 1985 market, its sales opportunity was magnified by the fact that Farley's not only stopped producing, but also withdrew stocks from the distribution pipeline. Also useful for SMA was that their Hampshire factory could increase deliveries more quickly than the rival Cow & Gate and Milupa (supplying from Ireland and France respectively). Clearly the sales bonanza for SMA would only be short term, though they could hope to get their fair share of the 24% hole in the market.

To the surprise of many, Boots bought the whole Farley's business for £18 million in March. The Cumbria factory reopened in April, but closed a week later due to a recurrence of salmonella. It was Boots' turn to suffer damaging publicity. Only in September 1986 did Boots manage to relaunch Farley's babymilk brands – giving a clear hint to the retail trade that their objective was to recapture the 24% market share.

Given the severity of the test to their customers' brand loyalty, it was to be expected that the achievement of this objective would take many years. Yet in April 1989 a Boots spokesman announced that the failure to achieve better than a 15% share of the babymilk market made it necessary to close one of Farley's production sites. So the Plymouth factory was to be closed with the loss of two hundred jobs, and baby cereal production switched to Cumbria. The resulting improvement in capacity utilisation would restore Farley's profitability.

Sources: *The Financial Times 1985/86; The Guardian 1989.*

Questions
(40 marks; 70 minutes)

1   Explain the meaning of the following (emboldened in the text):

      tangible assets
      correlated
      liquidate the assets
      low stock turnover.   **(12)**

2   Recently, many companies have started including an estimate of the value of their brand names on their balance sheets. Discuss this practice in the light of this case study.   **(8)**

3   Explain why 'the sales bonanza for SMA would only be short term'. Estimate what SMA's fair share of the medium term market would be in the period before Farley's returned.   **(10)**

4   Comment upon the reasons for, and implications of, Boots' decision to close its successful cereals factory at Plymouth.   **(10)**

77 THE BLACK HAIRDRESSERS

Concepts needed: Critical path analysis, Profit, Break-even

It was a Business Studies project that made Kim think seriously about opening the hairdressers. She had always enjoyed fixing friends' hair, but knew that hairdressing trainees were badly paid, so saw no sense in thinking further about such a career. Then came the project.

She had set herself the objective of identifying where and how to open a profitable new hairdressers in Sparkbrook (Birmingham).

A survey among fifty fellow students revealed that 40% went to hairdressers regularly, but few were satisfied with the standard and atmosphere of the salons. She noticed that several had scrawled on the questionnaire comments like: 'All hopeless with Afro-Caribbean styles' which was a view she agreed with heartily. So Kim began to research the prospects for a black hairdressers.

She knew enough about marketing to understand the pros and cons of segmenting the market in this way. If there were no rivals, she would have a good chance of dominating the niche, with all the profit potential that implied. However, if her clients were mainly young (as seemed almost inevitable), she might end up **segmenting a segment**, and thereby have a large share of such a tiny market that overheads would be impossible to cover (see diagram).

The gap Kim has identified

Segmentation of the market for hairdressing for adults

A trip to the library told her that 40,000 over-16s lived in her part of Sparkbrook, of which 25% were believed to be of Caribbean origin (and 50% were women). Kim then roped three friends into spending a day interviewing people in the nearby High Street. They approached 140 black women, and managed to get 80 interviews. Kim felt sure that they supported her strategy, and that with 60% saying they would definitely try a new, black salon, she had a potential base of 3,000 customers. Kim was then able to forecast her revenue, on the assumption that half the potential customers would come once every three months, and spend an average of £15 per visit.

Now, a year after getting her A-levels, her lifetime savings of £8,000 were to be sunk into the business (along with £4,000 from her parents and the same from the bank). She knew the site she wanted, but needed to make sure that her limited capital would cover not only the start-up period, but also the early months in case custom proved slow to develop. Her bank manager advised her to set 40% of her funds aside for working capital, i.e. for the day to day running of the business. Given her tight cash constraint, Kim decided to plan the start-up period with great care. She realised that the shorter she could make that period, the less time she would suffer **cash flow difficulties**.

These were the stages she knew she must go through:

A   obtaining the site; this would take 2 weeks and would have to be completed before any other activity could begin;

B   designing the layout, decor and equipment (3 weeks);

C   rebuilding and redecorating (6 weeks);

D   buying the equipment ready for installation as soon as C is completed (1 week);

E   installation of equipment (1 week);

F   hiring staff; this would take about 4 weeks, but could be started after the site was obtained;

G   training staff; this would take 3 weeks and could only begin once the equipment had been installed;

H   advertising when the salon is to open (2 weeks);

I   run a one week half price opening offer.

Adding these up came to 23 weeks, which seemed worryingly long, so Kim drew a **network** diagram to show how to schedule these events to enable completion to take the least possible time.

With just one week until opening time, Kim had just £3,500 left in the bank. Would this be enough to tide her over the half price week? She had calculated that her weekly overheads would be £900, but her £2 variable cost per customer would only generate £5.50 contribution this week.

Fortunately Kim pulled through the early problems and soon had a thriving ethnic hairdressers. Word-of-mouth proved her main advertising medium, and pulled people in from far enough afield to counteract the worries about segmenting the market excessively.

Questions

(40 marks; 60 minutes)

1 Explain the meaning of the following phrases (emboldened in the text):

    segmenting a segment
    cash flow difficulties
    a network   (9)

2 Show how the figure of 3,000 potential customers was calculated.   (4)

3 a Draw the network required by Kim, labelled to include the earliest start times and latest finish times of each activity. Indicate the critical path.   (12)

   b In what ways could this diagram help Kim?   (6)

4 On the basis of her forecasts, what weekly profit could Kim expect after the launch week was over (assume four weeks per month). How many customers would be required per week to break even?   (9)

78 **BODY SHOP INTERNATIONAL**

Concepts needed: Franchising, Ratios, Social responsibilities

When Anita Roddick launched her first Body Shop in a small street in Brighton in 1976, she devised a publicity stunt: a phone call to the local paper protesting at alleged attempts by neighbouring funeral parlours to block the shop and its name. That flair for publicity was to remain a theme throughout the following, dazzling years of growth.

Anita and her husband Gordon had hit upon a real commercial rarity – a trendy concept with staying power. Although 1976 was long before 'green' issues became prominent, there were already notable movements against animal experimentation, and towards healthy, natural products. The Roddicks' success was to encapsulate this into a genuine niche in the retail market – a shop providing a range of natural cosmetics and toiletries that had not been tested on animals, and that came in refillable containers. Bright window displays and prominent locations ensured high sales without advertising. As the biggest costs in the production of most cosmetics were the packaging and the advertising, Body Shop was able to charge relatively low prices, yet enjoy very high profit margins.

With the Brighton shop proving an instant success, the Roddicks decided to expand by the then unusual means of franchising. This would allow their brand name to become established quickly, thereby making sure that customers thought of Body Shop as the originator of this idea.

By 1981, twenty-two outlets had been established in Britain, and seventeen overseas. Company profits of just £31,000 reflected the experimentation that was still taking place under the Body Shop banner. To a great extent, Anita and Gordon were still teaching themselves how to handle a successful business. Finding suppliers to make their ever-widening range of products, screening franchise applicants, and organising distribution had all to be **delegated to new, salaried managers**. It also took them some time to realise just how high they could push the prices of their unique, highly fashionable products.

With the early 1980s seeing a rapid rise in the firm's fortunes, Gordon felt that the company was ready for a stock market listing. As its short life-history made it unsuitable for a full stock market launch, its shares were offered for sale on the Unlisted Securities Market (USM) in April 1984. Gordon has since said that:

> *'We were attracted by the advantages of a high profile, especially because of our High Street image. It also improved our credibility.*

We became contenders for prime retailing positions with people who would have shown us the door a year before.'

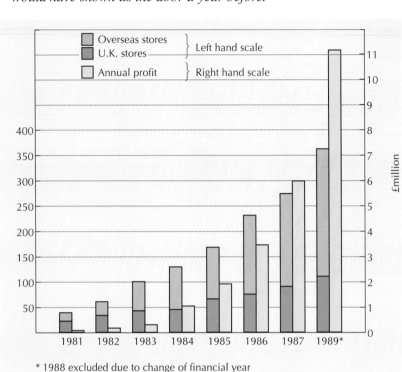

* 1988 excluded due to change of financial year

Diagram of Body Shop outlets and profit

Deciding what price to charge for shares in a unique company is always difficult. Body Shop's stockbrokers decided on a price of 95 pence – valuing the company at 25 times its forecast earnings (profit) for 1984. This seemed high, as most retail shares stood at a Price/Earnings ratio of 12. Yet the firm's growth record and potential ensured that investors clamoured for the stock. The share price doubled in the first week of trading, and within eighteen months had risen above 800 pence. As the Roddicks had sold less than a quarter of the shares in the company, their remaining holdings were worth over £50 million by the end of 1985. Early in 1986, Body Shop International plc left the USM and became fully listed on the stock market.

The company's continued growth moved increasingly towards overseas markets. By 1986, Body Shop was Britain's biggest retail exporter by far. The once esteemed Mothercare chain had suffered badly in its attempt to break into the United States; even Marks and Spencer had achieved little in its years of dabbling in France, Canada and Belgium. Body Shop's **unique niche** made it far better able to succeed. Yet the Roddicks also showed great sense in waiting until their formula had worked in other countries before tackling the huge US market in 1988.

One aspect of the formula that they began to rethink, though, was their early practice of granting franchisees monopoly rights to a city or area. This gave the franchisee the choice of how many outlets to open, plus freedom from competition. In 1989 they went against this by buying out some of their own franchisees. The Edinburgh franchise was bought for £1.3 million, giving its holder a capital gain of perhaps 1300%. Then the company that owned the monopoly rights to all outlets in Leeds, Liverpool, and Manchester was bought for £4.5 million. This firm had been making a £925,000 annual profit on net assets of £350,000.

More importantly, the end of the 1980s saw a shift in the public and political mood that gave the business yet more impetus. In 1988, the **growing environmentalism** forced Mrs. Thatcher to make a speech that set the Conservatives' claim to be seen as the 'green' party. In 1989, the real Green Party had great success at the polls. At the heart of this trend was Anita Roddick, who had (in May 1987) signed a two year agreement with the pressure group Friends Of The Earth. She agreed to display environmentalist publicity in Body Shop windows, and to encourage franchisees to campaign locally on pollution issues.

As concern mounted about the impact upon the ozone layer of the destruction of the Brazilian rainforests, Anita Roddick was to be seen not only talking about it, but also acting. Under the slogan 'trade not aid' she set about creating a range of rainforest-based cosmetics, such as a cleansing cream based upon Brazil nut oil. Creating a demand for raw materials from the forests would, she hoped, give the Brazilian government and landowners an incentive to keep the forests intact.

Within Britain, the Roddicks' social zeal found outlet in the establishment of a soap factory in Easterhouse, Glasgow. Its origins were in a visit made by Anita in 1988. A community leader pointed out that while her company was helping less developed countries, it was ignoring 'Britain's own Third World': the inner cities. As Body Shop needed extra supplies of soap, it was decided to set up a factory in Easterhouse rather than in the affluent area surrounding the firm's Sussex headquarters. It opened in April 1989 with 29 employees. Body Shop received widespread publicity for going, in Mrs. Roddick's words, 'where angels fear to tread'. A sceptical reporter from *The Financial Times* found locals who were irritated by 'her patronising attitude'; but none could doubt that the company had a magical way of combining social and environmental initiatives with self-publicity and therefore profitability.

By 1989, the Roddicks' family holdings in Body Shop were worth more than £200 million. Those who had bought shares in 1984 had seen their investment rise tenfold in five years. Staff and franchisees were encouraged to share in the Roddicks' nutritional and environmental concerns, and received a high standard of training at Body Shop's purpose-built centre. Customers received attractive, effective and environmentally-friendly products that they felt good about buying and using. In these early years of its life, Body Shop seemed to achieve the ideal mix of commercial success and social responsibility.

Sources: *Body Shop Prospectus and Annual Reports; The Financial Times; The Guardian; The Investors' Chronicle.*

APPENDIX A: *Body Shop International – Financial record (1983-89)*

	1983	1984	1985	1986	1987	*1989
					All figures in £000s	
Sales turnover	2,143	4,910	9,362	17,394	28,476	73,007
Pre-tax profit	202	1,044	1,929	3,451	5,998	15,243
Shareholders funds	374	812	1,683	3,445	6,587	23,477
Capital employed	450	1,132	1,941	3,692	6,865	24,236

* 1989 is the 17 months to 28th February, as the financial year was changed.

Questions
(60 marks; 100 minutes)

1 Outline the business significance of the following phrases (emboldened in the text):

delegated to new, salaried managers	**(4)**
unique niche	**(3)**
growing environmentalism	**(3)** **(10)**

2 To what extent was Anita Roddick's flair for publicity the key to the success of the business? **(10)**

3 The text mentions that franchising helped the Body Shop name to become established quickly. What other benefits would you expect it to have received from franchising instead of opening shops itself? **(10)**

4 Why might investors be prepared to pay for a share on a Price/Earnings (P/E) ratio of 25, when there are other reputable firms valued at a P/E of 12? What would have been the P/E ratio of Body Shop at the end of their first week of trading in 1984? **(10)**

5 What evidence is there that Body Shop was operating on 'very high' profit margins, and that these enabled them to generate exceptional rates of return on capital/assets employed? **(10)**

6 Why don't all firms achieve a good 'mix of commercial success and social responsibility'? **(10)**

79

FAT SAM'S FRANCHISE

Concepts needed: Break-even, Contribution, Profit, Marketing model, Franchising

Fat Sam's Pasta Joint was a highly successful restaurant in Soho, London. It offered

'All the pasta you can eat for £2.95'.

This good value was combined with lively, bright design and atmosphere to make Fat Sam's a hugely popular place for young people. Fat Sam's owners realised that the same concept could work in many other locations, but they did not have sufficient capital to develop a large chain of restaurants themselves. So they appointed a Franchise Manager, who was set the objective of developing Fat Sam's into a hundred-strong chain.

The new manager decided on the following terms for anyone who wished to become a franchisee:

1   A £5,000 fee to be paid on signing a 5-year Franchise Agreement;
2   Fat Sam's to be paid 8% of the franchisee's sales turnover (including 3% to be used for advertising).

In return, Fat Sam's would provide assistance on siting, interior design and shop fittings, menu and provision supplies, and financial management advice. A franchisee would hardly need a chef, as all sauces could be supplied directly by Fat Sam's.

Although the company advertised their franchises in the magazine 'Franchise World', the first person to apply was a waitress working in the Soho branch. Gill had no business experience, but she was sure she understood how to create the fun atmosphere needed for success, and was willing to take out a £100,000 second mortgage on her house to fulfil a lifetime dream of being her own boss.

She already knew that Fat Sam's took an average of £7 revenue per customer, with variable costs per head of £1.80 for food and 50 pence for drink. Even a novice entrepreneur could appreciate that a mark-up of over 200% presented a promising prospect.

Within a week, the Franchise Agreement had been approved by Gill's solicitor and was signed. She was sure that a good site existed in the centre of the town nearest her house (Colchester) and as it had no competing pasta restaurant, Fat Sam's agreed with her choice. Fat Sam's calculated that the site would take five months to be fully decorated, fitted and therefore become operational. The start-up costs were estimated at £100,000 (including the franchise fee).

Within a few weeks, Gill was becoming increasingly worried by the dithering of the Franchise Manager who was supposed to be helping her. Progress was slow, and many of the interior fittings were being supplied at what Gill thought were outrageous prices. Yet as the suppliers were the only ones who could supply her with fittings in the correct Fat Sam's colours and designs, she was stuck. After seven months, her money had run out, and the opening was still not in sight. She borrowed £25,000 more from her family, and two months later the outlet was finished.

Having spent out all £125,000 she was desperate to start trading, in order to bring in some cash. It came like a thunderbolt to hear from the Franchise Manager that he had still not managed to obtain the licence needed to serve alcoholic drinks, but she could not wait. Fat Sam's Pasta Joint opened in Woking without any advertising, and with signs up apologising for the fact that only the soft drinks on the menu could be served. In such circumstances, it was quite pleasing that 800 customers were served in the first week – only 200 down on her forecast. Of course, the extra start-up expenditure meant higher interest charges on her borrowings, so her fixed costs were higher than originally planned, at £2,898 per week.

Sadly, the poor start meant that Gill's restaurant was rarely full, which undermined the bustling atmosphere she knew she needed. So not even the arrival of the drinks licence (one month after starting) stopped a relentless decline in the Woking outlet's revenue. A friend worked out the following chart to show her how her customer base was moving towards the break-even level.

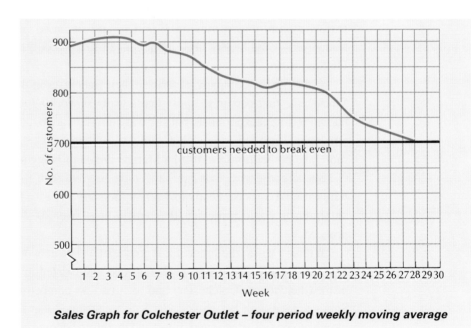

Sales Graph for Colchester Outlet – four period weekly moving average

Forty weeks after she started trading, Gill's bank manager persuaded her to give up. Her bitterness towards Fat Sam's and their Franchise Manager turned into rage as she was forced to sell her house. The price it fetched was enough to repay all her debts, but she was left homeless and virtually penniless.

(The above account is true in every detail, though the name of the firm has been changed for legal reasons.)

Questions
(40 marks; 70 minutes)

1 What does the text demonstrate about the weakness of taking out a franchise when starting your own business? **(10)**

2 Before the delays occurred, Gill had budgeted for weekly fixed costs of £2,500 and an average of 1,000 customers per week. Assuming a 50 week year:

   a What profit would she have made in the first year?

   b How long would it have taken her to repay her £100,000 loan? **(10)**

3 Much business studies theory revolves around the idea of scientific decision making. What does this mean, and how might the adoption of a framework such as the Marketing Model have helped Gill avoid the difficulties she encountered? **(10)**

4 a How does the sales chart on page 222 differ from a break-even chart? Discuss its comparative advantages and disadvantages.

   b Prove that the break-even number of customers is 700. **(10)**

80

MARLBORO AND MARKET POWER

Concepts needed: Company objectives, Marketing strategy, Price elasticity, Profit, Social responsibilities

Within seconds of the announcement, its shares had plunged in value by $13.5 billion, and those of its rivals by even more. The whole US stock market suffered its biggest one-day fall for over a year. Within days newspapers were questioning the billion dollar value placed upon brands throughout the world. The cause was the decision by Philip Morris, the world's most profitable cigarette company, to slash the price of the world's most valuable brand – Marlboro cigarettes. The American media soon dubbed April 2nd 1993 as 'Marlboro Friday'.

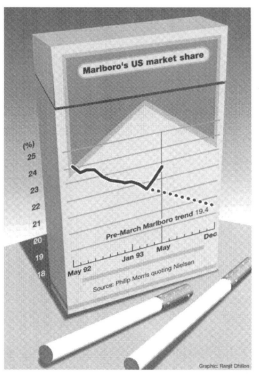

The price cut of a full 20% applied only to the American market, but since Marlboro accounted for over 100 billion of the 500 billion cigarettes sold per year in the US, the profit implications were huge. Philip Morris acted to try to reverse the erosion of Marlboro's US market share, from 25.8% in 1991 to 24.5% in 1992. Recession-hit consumers were switching to cheaper branded cigarettes and to own-label varieties with no brand image. Discount cigarettes had grown from a 7% market share in 1985 to 19% by 1990 and up to 36% in 1992. Philip Morris, the industry's price leader with its best-selling Marlboro brand, felt it had to respond. As a Wall Street analyst put it:

> 'This is not a new price war. It's the latest blast in a price war which has already been going on. Philip Morris has come down with both feet on the market. It's going to destroy the discount brands.'
>
> (Roy Burry, Kidder Peabody, *Financial Times* April 5th 1993).

William Campbell, the tobacco president of Philip Morris laid himself open to potentially fierce criticism for a decision that was expected to cut 1993 and 1994 profits by over $2 billion dollars per annum. The image-building of the brand had been so successful that by the 1980s Marlboro outsold its nearest rival more than four times. With annual marketing spending of over $100 million in the US, Marlboro had been able to impose a series of price increases that rival brands had to follow. Otherwise their image might have become devalued.

Leading brands in 1991 (by volume)

Marlboro	25.8%
Winston	7.5%
Salem	5.4%
Newport	4.7%

Source: Tobacco Reporter/Euromonitor

Between 1980 and 1991, the price of 20 Marlboro trebled while prices generally (and government taxes) only doubled. This created an opportunity for the companies whose minor brands had been squeezed by the Marlboro marketing machine. For although Philip Morris had pushed the price of the main brands up to $2.20 by early 1993, the economics of cigarette production pointed to lower rather than higher prices. Raw tobacco prices were falling in real terms, and modern machinery could produce 15,000 cigarettes per minute – more than twice the speed and productivity of a decade before. It was now possible to manufacture and distribute a pack of 20 cigarettes for 30 cents. Even with 40 cents of tax and a retail mark up of 20% a profit could be made by selling at one half of Marlboro's price.

As Philip Morris pushed prices up, small producers were able to offer supermarket chains an own-label product that could sell below the **psychological price barrier** of $1 per pack. As discount sales shot ahead during the 1980s, the large manufacturers moved into the cut-price market. The second largest manufacturer, RJ Reynolds, made a key move in 1987 when it set up the Forsyth Tobacco Company to make a $1 house brand of cigarettes for the huge K-Mart store chain. The cigarettes were made at the same factories that produced the $2.20 Winston and Salem brands. RJ Reynolds hoped that the use of the invented company name 'Forsyth' would minimise the **cannibalisation** of their own brands. Its success, however, merely forced Philip Morris to pursue the same discount market.

By early 1993, the cigarette market had split into three price segments. The established brands at $2.20, second ranking brands at $1.50, and discount or own label products at $0.99. When it cut the price of Marlboro, Philip Morris also tried to merge the two bottom segments into one. Philip Morris pushed the prices of its mid-range brands down to around $1.30, and raised its cheapest products up towards that same figure. The tobacco giant wanted to change the market's structure as indicated below.

Price segments pre-April 1993		Segments post-April 1993
$2.20	Established brands	
$1.80		Established brands
$1.40	Second-rank brands	
$1.20		Second-rank and discount products
$1.00	Discount products	

Within a month RJ Reynolds announced that it was following Marlboro's lead. It cut the price of its Winston brand. By September it was forecasting that its 1993 US tobacco operating profits would be 43% lower than the previous year – a fall of $900 million.

Philip Morris, meanwhile, was putting a brave face on its announcement of a 53% fall in US tobacco profits for the three months to June. It declared that its price cut had been successful, reversing an eight month decline in Marlboro's market share. From a low of 21.5% in March, Marlboro's share was said to have risen to 24% in July. This would do little to restore the brand's short-term profitability, but that was not the point of the strategy. William Campbell was attempting to regain the initiative in the American cigarette market, to ensure the long term success of Marlboro and Philip Morris.

Although the Marlboro move made sense strategically, it led analysts to question the **brand valuations** that many companies were placing on their balance sheets. If the world's most valuable brand could not hold its desired price premium, could it be that consumers had learned to see beyond the packaging and the image to the product inside? In which case should companies such as Guinness drop the brand valuations from their balance sheets?

Whereas the financial analysts were worried, marketing professionals showed less concern. They felt consumers were still fully prepared to pay a price premium for a reputable brand, but that Marlboro had pushed that premium too far. Their only doubt was that Philip Morris may have overreacted to a problem made worse by recession. If the market share of discount brands stabilised at 35–40% of the market, Marlboro could still have traded very profitably at $2.20. No-one doubted, however, that Marlboro's action was one of the boldest decisions in marketing history.

Sources: The *Financial Times, The Independent, Wall Street Journal.*

Questions

(40 marks; 80 minutes)

1 Explain the meaning of the terms (emboldened in the text):

       psychological price barrier
       cannibalisation
       brand valuation. **(9)**

2 What appeared to be the price elasticity of Marlboro cigarettes in 1993? **(5)**

3 **a** What profit could a manufacturer make per pack from a discount brand selling at 99 cents? **(4)**

   b What would be its annual profit if it achieved a 1% market share? **(4)**

4 To what extent was Marlboro Friday the result of a change in Philip Morris's corporate objectives? **(10)**

5 American doctors worried that the Marlboro price cut might lead to an increase in the demand for cigarettes and therefore the health problems caused by smoking. Should the managers of Philip Morris concern themselves about this, or is this purely a matter for the government's health department? **(8)**

81

PEPE JEANS – FROM RAGS TO RICHES

Concepts needed: Indexing, Business organisations, Sources of finance

The business began in 1973 when the 22-year-old Nitin Shah was trading in jeans from market stalls in London's King's Road and Portobello Road. In March 1974 he joined with two brothers to form Pepe Limited. They switched from merely selling clothing to having it designed to their specifications, and then began wholesaling those products to other retailers. By 1980, the Pepe brand name was becoming well known, and rapid development of the **management structure** was needed to keep pace.

Problems of adjusting to this expansion, plus the onset of recession led to large losses in 1980 and 1981. A major problem was that of controlling and managing the 95% of production that came from the Far East. As 90% came from Hong Kong alone, the Shah brothers appointed an independent buying agent there. The stabilisation of supplies that resulted from this gave Pepe the confidence to expand once more. They launched a new brand of extra strong jeans, 'Hard Core', and formed Pepe USA in 1984.

Throughout this early period, raising finance had been a problem, as the Shahs had no assets of their own that could be held as security by the banks. Setting up the first market stall had required £350, but no High Street bank had been willing to lend Nitin the money. The same happened in 1975, when £3,000 was needed to open up their first shop. The Shahs were fortunate in having family contacts with a small banking operation called Meghraj and Sons – who were willing to lend without security. Pepe has stayed with Meghraj ever since.

The success of their US operation meant an extremely heavy demand for **working capital** during 1984 and 1985. For opening up new distribution outlets always means offering generous credit to customers. This meant Pepe had to find the cash to pay for goods to be produced and delivered well before getting paid. In 1984-5, Pepe's customers were given an average of over four months to pay, which tied up £7 million of the firm's money. The Shahs' **cash flow forecasts** had anticipated this huge demand for cash, so they discussed their need for extra capital with their bankers during 1984. Banks were unwilling to lend such large sums purely on the basis of forward orders; as with its first £350, Pepe did not have sufficient property assets to act as collateral.

So the Shahs looked to the City for equity (share) capital. Pepe did not have a long enough track-record to get a listing on the full stock market, but the opening up of the Unlisted Securities Market (USM) in the early 1980s had provided an alternative. The USM was designed to provide capital for small, often high risk companies. Pepe was fortunate that it needed this equity finance at a time when the

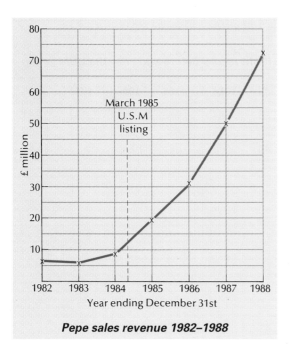

Pepe sales revenue 1982–1988

stock market was booming: the October 1987 slump in share prices made it much harder to raise share capital during 1988 and 1989.

The share offer took place in March 1985. Five and a half million shares (23% of Pepe's share capital) were sold for 100 pence (valuing each brother's stake at over £6 million). £300,000 of costs in City fees and advertising of the **prospectus** left £5.2 million – all of which was put into the business. The success of the share issue not only strengthened Pepe's balance sheet, it also gave banks more confidence in the firm – so it became easier to borrow from then on. The graph shows how the USM listing helped Pepe's sales push ahead to the £100 million mark by the end of the 1980s.

So how did a small business build up from £350 to nearly £100,000,000 of sales against the might of firms like Levi's? The Shahs believe that flexibility was the key. Within the denim jeans trade, not only the cut but also the wash (colour shades) is heavily influenced by fashion; and the fashion may vary in different regions or countries. The Shahs pride themselves on being very close to their market place, so they pick up changing tastes quickly. That marketing skill has been turned into a business advantage by organising their supply and distribution so that Pepe can respond rapidly to the new styles the (mainly young) customers want. When the Levi's 501 ('laundrette') commercial became a cult, Pepe were quick to respond with supplies of fly-button jeans at a time when Levi's could not keep up with the demand they had created. So they benefited from Levi's advertising.

As with any rapidly growing firm, the challenge is to maintain the benefits of being small even when your expansion forces you to develop new layers of management. As Pepe has grown in size, specialists have been appointed in key areas such as Marketing, Personnel and Finance, and the management structure has grown accordingly. However the original family philosophy still persists. The stock market listing reinforced this philosophy by giving key executives a share stake in the business to help reinforce their commitment. In the jeans market, though, success in the past is no guarantee of it in the future. So Pepe will have to keep their flexibility, or else get dragged into a big brand battle with Levi's – which the Shahs have always realised they must try to avoid.

The other main pitfall for dynamic firms is being taken over; the Shahs took care to prevent this by keeping majority share control within the family. The full stock exchange frowns upon families or individuals selling a minority of shares, and thereby raising capital without sharing control. The USM did not share this concern; this was fortunate for the listing enabled the former market stall traders to build up an asset worth over £20 million each by 1989.

Sources: *The Financial Times; Pepe's launch prospectus and annual reports*

APPENDIX A: Pepe's Turnover and Profit record before and after the USM listing

	1982	1983	1984	1985	1986	1987	1988
Turnover (£000s)	6,159	5,883	8,984	19,906	31,113	50,242	72,241
Pre-tax profit (£000s)	226	358	915	2,633	4,208	5,905	8,408
Earnings per share (pence)	1.3p	1.4p	2.7p	7.8p	10.4p	16.0p	22.8p

Questions
(50 marks; 90 minutes)

1   Explain the meaning of the following terms (emboldened in the text):

management structure
working capital
cash flow forecast
prospectus   **(8)**

2   **a**   Using 1982 as the base year, construct an index of Pepe's sales turnover and
profit figures, then draw both lines on a single graph.   **(10)**

   b   What conclusions can you draw from this use of the data?   **(4)**

3   Examine the problems Pepe faced as a consequence of being a rapidly growing
small firm. What solutions were found?   **(8)**

4   Discuss the pros and cons of a stock market listing for firms such as Pepe.
What factors should potential share buyers consider before committing their capital? **(10)**

5   These days, banks promote themselves as advisers and supporters of small firms.
Yet they still require collateral before providing bank loans. Is this as it should be?   **(10)**

82

SOLARTILE – A MINI-MULTINATIONAL

Concepts needed: Raising finance, Multinationals, Profit

James was the Engineering Director of a heating company when the idea hit him. Why not make roof tiles with a solar panel coating, so that energy saving in the home becomes easy to install? Then, whenever new houses are built or householders are replacing their roof, people could choose an energy-saving alternative. James experimented in his workshed at home, and eventually devised the solar tiles, plus an energy collection and storage system that could easily be plumbed into a hot water or central heating tank. Then he patented the idea, and registered SolarTile as a trademark.

Raising the finance to establish production was not too difficult, because his engineering contacts enabled him to identify suppliers of every single component. Therefore his only requirement was for a small assembly plant which could be rented inexpensively. Thirty thousand pounds of his own money plus a £15,000 bank loan was enough to provide the working capital he needed.

The key figure in the start-up, however, was probably James's wife Nicola. She proved to have a flair for PR (public relations). She sent stylish packaged SolarTiles to the producers of TV programmes such as *Tomorrow's World* and *TV-AM*, and generated a remarkable amount of free publicity. Production had just been geared up to meet the resulting high demand when the Saudi Arabian Revolution sparked off the third oil crisis. With the trebling oil and gas prices, James's innovation was suddenly pushed into the international spotlight. Demand from Germany, Holland, and Austria was only outweighed by that from America and Canada.

From the start the business had been highly profitable, so reserves of £60,000 had been built up – half of which was in cash. James felt he needed £100,000, however, to increase production capacity up to the level of demand, so he turned to a Merchant Bank for venture capital. He negotiated a finance package of £55,000 of loan capital and £15,000 of share capital. Giving up one third of his control of the firm was a blow, but he was very keen to seize the market opportunity.

Should they expand output in the United Kingdom, though, or establish production overseas? Reasons of management control suggested staying at home, but transport costs made a multinational structure attractive. An average-sized U.K. house cost the customer £6,000 to roof using the SolarTile method. This comprised

£3,000 materials, £1,000 of assembly and overheads, £250 of delivery costs, £1,000 of installation cost, with the remainder being profit. A few phone calls to freight companies revealed that each complete system would cost £400 to transport to Chicago (a logical site bordering Canada and the United States).

James was also aware that although he could control production more easily in the United Kingdom, successful marketing, distribution, and installation of the systems would need good local management. When he made his profit calculations, he reasoned that increasing capacity in America or Britain would create similar extra factory overheads, and was therefore not a key factor.

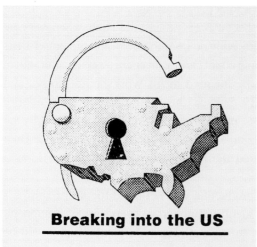

Breaking into the US

A £20,000 market research analysis of the potential North American market convinced James that he would not be able to pass the extra £400 transport cost on to the customers. Therefore he decided to set up an assembly plant in Chicago. He knew that even if local component suppliers could not be found, shipping the (mainly small) components from the United Kingdom would not be very expensive.

For the next four weeks, James interviewed potential managers, and was delighted to recruit an impressive 35-year-old as Managing Director. To ensure his loyalty and commitment, the Managing Director was given a 10% stake in SolarTile US Inc., as well as an $80,000 salary. Together, they worked out revenue and cost forecasts based on the research prediction of 2,000 sales a month. Within eight weeks, the Managing Director had identified a suitable site, and appointed a production and a sales manager. Just ten weeks later, the first complete system came off the US assembly line.

To minimise costs, and to make it easier to set up quickly in the United States, many of the high value, low bulk components were ordered from SolarTile's British suppliers. This enabled lower unit prices to be negotiated, which helped James's profit margins in the United Kingdom. With two of the components, he found that the higher output levels made it cost efficient to buy automated machinery to produce them within their U.K. factory so they carried out the production themselves.

After six months, the US operation began to break even, and its fat order book made high profits look inevitable. Yet four months later, when visiting the Chicago plant, James was shocked to see the chaotic factory organisation. It emerged that the production manager had proved weak and disorganised, but that firing him three weeks before had revealed his popularity among his workforce – twelve out of the fifteen workers had walked out. By the time the staffing problem was ironed out, SolarTile US Inc. had lost $250,000.

The British parent was nearly dragged under by the drain on its financial resources but, having survived, went on to become highly profitable. The decision to set up in the United States rather than export from the United Kingdom was fully vindicated when, two years later, America decided to place a 15% tariff on all manufactured exports from Europe. Other assembly sites were also set up in Germany and Singapore.

A new accountant showed James how he could take advantage of his multinational organisation to minimise his company's tax bills. The tax rate on company profits in Germany is much higher than in America, so SolarTile U.K. began charging higher component prices to Deutsche SolarTile and lower ones to SolarTile U.S. Inc. In that way, the higher costs being absorbed by the German subsidiary ensured lower (apparent) profits. The accountant was able, in this way, to transfer £200,000 of SolarTile's profit from Germany to the United States, and thereby paid the 20% US tax rate instead of Germany's 40% rate. James was a bit worried at the legality of this financial juggling, but the accountant assured him: 'It's a common tax avoidance practice ... called transfer pricing. It's perfectly legal.'

Questions
(50 marks; 90 minutes)

1   What were the main elements in James's success in financing SolarTile in its early years? **(10)**

2   At the time he was deciding whether or not to establish production in the United States, what would James have forecast to be the effect on profit of transporting complete systems from the United Kingdom? Show your workings clearly. Consider the assumption James made about factory overheads. How might this assumption have affected the accuracy of the profit estimates? **(10)**

3   Outline the main benefits SolarTile gained from its multinational expansion. To what types of business might such advantages not apply? **(10)**

4   Should transfer pricing be 'perfectly legal'? Why is it more likely that a group of countries (such as the European Union) would ban this practice than that any individual country would? **(10)**

5   Entrepreneurs need a good idea, the ability to get the best out of others, and a lot of luck. Discuss this statement in the light of the SolarTile example. **(10)**

83 CHOCOLATE SOLDIERS – THE ROWNTREE TAKEOVER

Concepts needed: Takeovers, Opportunity cost, European single market, Brand names

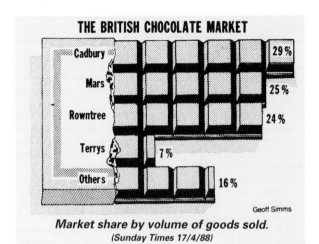

THE BRITISH CHOCOLATE MARKET

Cadbury 29%
Mars 25%
Rowntree 24%
Terrys 7%
Others 16%

Geoff Simms

Market share by volume of goods sold.
(Sunday Times 17/4/88)

At 8.30 a.m. on 13th April 1988, the Swiss chocolate group Suchard launched a '**dawn raid**' on the shares of Rowntree. In a thirty-five minute buying spree they bought £160 million of Rowntree's shares in the London stock market – 14.9% of the British firm's share capital. This was achieved by offering shareholders 630 pence for shares worth 475 pence the previous day. Suchard made it clear that their objective was to build a 25% stake in Rowntree; few doubted that it would soon be used to launch a full take-over bid.

Rowntree's Chairman said: 'Suchard may need Rowntree, but Rowntree does not need Suchard.' Although he was clearly shocked at the threat to the York firm's 130-year history, the Chairman seemed confident that he could fight off a competitor of a similar size to Rowntree itself. As he proclaimed:

> '*Rowntree, the largest confectionery business in the United Kingdom, has one of the best **portfolios** of brand names in the world... Kit Kat, Smarties, and After Eight have taken years of investment.*'

Two weeks passed before the real hammer blow – a full take-over bid at 890 pence cash from the huge Nestlé group (the world's biggest food company). This valued Rowntree at £2.1 billion.

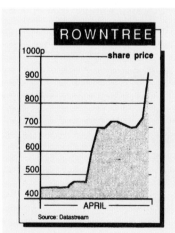

ROWNTREE

1000p
share price
900
800
700
600
500
400
APRIL
Source: Datastream

The Swiss giant made it clear that in the run up to 1992, it was not willing to allow Suchard to gain such a strong position in the European chocolate market. A City analyst maintained that:

> '*Nestlé cannot afford to allow Rowntree to fall to Suchard. Rowntree is a dead duck.*'

The latter view came from examination of Nestlé's balance sheet. This showed that the Swiss multinational had bank deposits worth £2.7 billion. So it could swallow Rowntree from, in effect, its petty cash. With sales and profits more than 500% higher than either Rowntree or Suchard, Nestlé could not be stopped in the marketplace. So action switched to the only other forum for determining the outcome – the government and its Monopolies and Mergers Commission.

For Rowntree's management there appeared to be 3 possible ways of persuading the government to intervene:

1 On the grounds that merger would be anti-competitive, given Nestlé's substantial share of the European chocolate market.

2 That as Swiss laws enabled its companies to protect themselves from being taken over, it would be unfair to allow a Swiss predator to buy up a British firm.

3 That Rowntree's unusual position of being a major British company based in the North meant that keeping it independent was important for regional policy.

Rowntree's problem with the first possibility can be seen in the table below. Neither Nestlé's 3% nor Suchard's 2% of the U.K. chocolate market would add sufficient to Rowntree's market share even to match that of Cadbury's. Many politicians suggested that with the onset of the single European market in 1992, the proper consideration should be European market shares, but the British government rejected this view.

European chocolate confectionery market shares

	UK	Austria	Belgium	France	Italy	Netherlands	Switzerland	W. Germany	Total
				(% by sales value)					
Mars	24	4	6	11	1	23	9	22	17
Suchard	2	73	82	13	–	–	17	15	13
Rowntree	26	–	2	17	–	13	–	3	11
Ferrero	2	–	5	6	34	–	–	16	10
Cadbury	30	–	–	8	–	–	–	–	9
Nestlé	3	5	3	10	5	–	17	8	9

Source: *Henderson Crosthwaite (Financial Times 27/4/88)*

Rowntree's chose to present an upbeat image as a caring employer, a solidly northern firm, and the developer of world markets for such British products as After Eights and the Lion Bar. The latter became an important part of Rowntree's defence. For, despite its weak performance in Britain, the Lion bar had become a notable success in the rest of Europe. Rowntree's management was keen to get across the notion that the sleepy Swiss producers of solid chocolate bars were desperate to buy a firm with proven skills in the marketing of the growing chocolate 'count-lines' sector (single, hand-held bars such as Mars, Flake, and Lion).

The battle of the brand names

Rowntree	Nestlé	Suchard
Kit Kat	Nescafé	Toblerone
Quality Street	Carnation	Milka
Aero	Crosse & Blackwell	Cote D'Or
Black Magic	Findus	
Rolo	L'Oreal	
After Eight	Chambourcy	
Smarties	Libby's	
Yorkie	Milky Bar	

Suchard's Chairman was quite open about the attractions of Rowntrees:

> 'Rowntree is an excellent company with a fascinating range of brands. Brands are the most important thing.'

Behind the scenes, Rowntree carried out extensive lobbying of M.P.s, Ministers, and the employers' organisation, the Confederation of British Industry (the C.B.I.). Public Relations schemes were devised to promote the idea: 'Hands Off Rowntree'. In early May the C.B.I. recommended that the takeover be referred by the government to the Monopolies and Mergers Commission. That would ensure the suspension of the bid for many months while its likely impact was investigated. This source of pressure on the government was silenced, however, when the C.B.I. gave in to Nestlé's public threat to cancel its membership.

The Rowntree unions were also active in supporting the existing management. For the Rowntree family had established at the turn of the century a pattern of **paternalism** that led to the early introduction of a shorter working week, a pension scheme, and good working conditions. Recent managements had tended to maintain these traditions, so the workforce were especially loyal to the company.

By mid May, over two hundred M.P.s had signed motions of support for Rowntree. They were thwarted, though, by the government's desire to be seen to be welcoming to foreign firms, in the hope of attracting investment into extra production here. On 25th May, Lord Young announced that the Department of Trade would not be recommending that the bid be investigated. Although the Labour Party's Bryan Gould described this as a 'betrayal of British industry', many commentators accepted the government's stance that:

> 'Intervention by public authorities in lawful commercial transactions should be kept to a minimum since... decisions of private decision makers in competitive markets result in the most desirable outcomes for the economy as a whole.'

The following day Suchard challenged Nestlé with a £2.32 billion counter-bid at 950 pence a share. This may well have been no more than a ploy to push Nestlé into paying more for Rowntree shares. For Suchard already held over a £100 million profit on the shares they had bought for 630 pence just six weeks before. It convinced Rowntree's largest union that the end was near, however, for on 1st June its Executive urged the management to end their opposition to the bids, and to start negotiating with both of the Swiss firms. The union believed it essential that the new owners should view their Rowntree division with favour, not hostility.

The battle ended, as expected, with a knock-out blow by Nestlé. On 23rd June Nestlé offered 1075 pence (£2.55 billion), which Suchard accepted was more than it could afford. Having accumulated a 29.9% stake in Rowntree, Suchard could sell its shares to Nestlé at a profit of more than £200 million. Nestlé announced that they had given assurances that York would continue to be the centre of Rowntree activity, and that the firm's employment policy and practices would be respected. Nevertheless, the Swiss would not give any job guarantees to Rowntree's 13,000 U.K. workers. Within a few days Nestlé had won the acceptance of the Rowntree Board and shareholders.

Following Nestlé's success, two issues continue to be hotly debated:

1 Is it right to allow successful, profitable, well-managed firms like Rowntree to be taken over unless the bidder can demonstrate some clear social or economic benefit?

2 Do company accounts give sufficient weight to the enormous value of the 'goodwill' represented by the value of brand names? For one of the reasons that Rowntree was 'a dead duck' was because the Swiss rivals were able to offer Rowntree shareholders such a large premium over the pre-bid value of the shares.

Sources: *The Financial Times; The Guardian; The Independent; The Observer; The Sunday Times*

Questions

(75 marks; 2 hours)

1 Explain the meaning of the following words (emboldened in the text):

   dawn raid
   portfolio
   paternalism (9)

2 On 13th April, many shareholders sold out to Suchard at 630 pence per share. What percentage profit had they made overnight? What was the opportunity cost of their decision? (8)

3 Use the table of figures on European market shares to discuss the attractions of Rowntree for the two Swiss firms. (10)

4 Why may the establishment of the single European market in 1992 have influenced the bidders' desire to buy Rowntree? (10)

5 Nestlé was in a position to fund the purchase of Rowntree with cash. How else might one finance the takeover of another firm? Outline the implications of these alternative methods. (12)

6 Rowntree management and unions carried out a united, extensive programme of pressure group activity. Why may it have been unsuccessful in this case? (6)

7 Nestlé paid over £1.5 billion more than the value of Rowntree's physical assets in order to acquire its brands. Why are brand names so valuable? (10)

8 Examine the implications for firms generally of one of the two issues that remained unanswered after the takeover was completed. (10)

MONEY FROM THE TAP

Concepts needed: Decision trees, Contribution, Profit

After three years of highly profitable growth, decisions were needed on the future of Dalesmere. Its sole product was Dalesmere Natural Mineral Water, which it had marketed as the first home-delivery, 'luxury' water. It had been sold at a price premium over the market leader (Perrier), and on a shamelessly snobbish message:

'The exclusive product for exclusive people'

Extensive direct mail advertising in the Southeast, plus sampling stands at London's commuter railway stations proved a successful way of getting custom. The idea of door to door delivery in glass bottles that Dalesmere would collect and recycle, fitted well with the 'green' mood of the times. Most important of all, however, were the circumstances of the year in which Dalesmere happened to be launched. Not only was the summer exceptionally hot, but also there were countless stories in the media about the poor quality of British drinking water.

Now, with £500,000 on bank deposit, Dalesmere could afford to consider its next move carefully. A management consultancy had been commissioned to conduct a S.W.O.T. analysis, summarised below.

Dalesmere S.W.O.T. Analysis
Summary of Main Findings and Conclusions

Strengths:
1 Exclusive image, especially among the 20,000 regular users.
2 Reputation for reliable service, and an environmentally sound product. (Hence the high repeat purchase average of 10 bottles 25 times per annum.)
3 High profitability due to very high margins (*price 79 pence minus bottling and distribution cost 19 pence*).
4 90% of custom in the Southeast.

Weaknesses:
1 High promotional cost of getting new customers (currently £50 per head).
2 Sales declining.
3 Poor image among non-customers.

Opportunities:
1 To use the exclusive image among users, plus the distribution network to market other upmarket products.
2 To invest £500,000 in corporate television advertising in the Southeast, to improve the image among non-users.

Threats:
1 Competition in the home delivery market from three cheaper rivals, plus the recent announcement of milkman delivery of Perrier.
2 That improvements to water quality, led by the European Union, may cut demand for bottled waters generally.

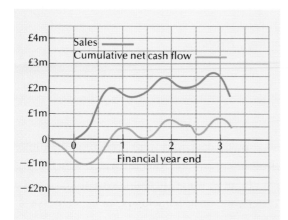

Within the main body of the report, possible approaches to the new product strategy were set out. Dalesmere's distinctive competence lay in its management of its upmarket customer list and its established delivery service. So the new products should be ones that wealthy people would find inconvenient to obtain or to carry home. Group discussion among regular customers examined the rival attractions of offering a delivery service in:

a whole hams and farmhouse cheeses;

b a range of Dalesmere soft drinks and juices;

c a range of organic wines and beers.

Both **a** and **c** were very well received, though it emerged that most were likely to purchase **a** on special occasions only. So option **c** became the favourite.

The choice facing Dalesmere was clarified to either proceeding with the television advertising, or with the 'line extension' – organic wines and beers. Their advertising agency estimated that the £500,000 campaign should boost sales by one of the following possibilities (depending upon the response of their competitors):

■ a 0.2 probability of a 40% rise in customers and sales

■ 0.5 probability of a 20% rise in customers and sales

■ 0.3 probability of a 10% rise in customers and sales

The management consultants estimated that the organic wines and beers would cost £500,000 to set up, and would have a 60% chance of providing sales of £2,000,000 at a profit margin of 40%; plus a 40% chance of half that sales level, though at the same margin.

The management consultants decided to prepare a decision tree based upon this information, and use it as the basis of a final strategy meeting with the Dalesmere directors.

Questions

(40 marks; 70 minutes)

1 What conclusions can you draw from the graph shown? **(6)**

2 Construct the management consultants' tree diagram. **(5)**

3 Calculate the expected values of each decision based upon forecast contribution over the first year; show them and the decisions they point to on your diagram. **(12)**

4 How useful a device is a decision tree in circumstances such as this? **(5)**

5 Taking into account all the information available, explain which of the options you would choose, and why. **(12)**

85 GOOD MANAGEMENT PRACTICE IN RETAILING

Concepts needed: Balance sheet, Ratios, Scientific decisions, Pay-back, Economies of scale

Marie started in the shop at nine years old, helping to fill shelves and occasionally serving customers. Later, she helped her mother deal with the buying side and with the accounts. So by the time she was twenty, her knowledge of the grocery trade was good enough for her parents to feel happy to hand the business over. Marie arranged a mortgage on the shop flat and premises, to provide the capital to buy them a Devon cottage, and then, one day, found herself on her own.

She had taken over a medium-sized, independent grocery shop of 2,000 square feet. Its weekly sales turnover was £24,000 at a gross profit margin of 15 per cent. This was sufficient to cover the £1,000 wage bill and £1,800 of other fixed costs, yet still leave a healthy profit. Marie had no intention, however, of allowing the business to just tick over. She wanted to prove that she could build it up into the biggest independent grocery chain in Derbyshire. To do this would require either a programme of store openings, or buying out rival owners. Whichever way she eventually chose, she knew that the starting point was the raising of finance.

Having already undertaken a large mortgage on the shop, she had neither the **collateral** nor the capital structure to borrow any more. For the business's shareholders funds were outweighed 2-1 by borrowings. She had no wish to bring new shareholders in, so the only option was to generate capital from the business itself. Could she squeeze cash out of her assets? Not from the premises or van; and as she offered no credit to customers, there was no kitty of **debtors**. So stocks were the only asset that might have some potential. Yet her parents had boasted when they handed the shop over that stock was being turned over fortnightly, so it was hard to imagine that much wastage existed there. If stock reductions had limited potential, that left profits as the sole remaining source.

Marie decided to undertake a detailed analysis of the **profitability** of the different sections of the store, to find out what to do next. She spent three weeks measuring up the shop and sifting through the stock books to produce the breakdown shown on the following page.

Before rushing to draw conclusions from this analysis, Marie decided to spend a fortnight chatting to customers about their usage of, and attitudes towards, the shop. They emphasised that convenience was the key – best achieved by offering a wide enough range of goods to ensure that they would not have to travel the nine miles to the nearest large supermarket.

Then she embarked on her new strategy. Fresh foods would be expanded by installing in-store bakery equipment. This would not only give more space over to a section that appeared to deserve it, but would also make the store smell inviting

Weekly Turnover and Profit Analysis

Product	Turnover £	Gross profit £	% of total gross profit	% of sq. ft.
Fresh food	2,800	580	16.5	14.0
Frozen food	1,500	200	5.5	4.5
Other food	6,500	820	22.5	33.0
Confectionery	3,800	810	22.5	8.5
Tobacco	2,400	200	5.5	4.0
Household items	3,500	590	16.5	23.0
Alcoholic drink	3,500	400	11.0	13.0
Total	24,000	3,600	100.0	100.0

and wholesome. Confectionery would be expanded by means of a high quality Pick-and-Mix counter, and by increasing the range of children's lines. It would be supplemented by installing two new counters that would each – she felt – attract more passing trade (and therefore confectionery impulse purchasing): newspapers, magazines and a video library. All these items would, between them, require 500 square feet of floor space. One hundred could come from converting a small office, while the remainder would have to come from the other departments.

The conversion cost £12,000 but soon proved a great success. Turnover rose to £30,000 per week and margins expanded to 17%. This meant a pay-back period of eight weeks – an astonishingly short time – and a greatly improved profit level thereafter. Marie followed this up by extending the video library into full children's and pop music ranges. For the first time, she advertised this development in the local paper, and featured an 'Opening Day Offer – 50p For Any Title'. Just as she hoped, video and confectionery sales grew still higher, reaching £35,000 a week. At this level of trading, £250 of extra staff costs were necessary, but weekly profit was still buoyant at £2,900 per week.

Within six months, the firm's bank balance was high enough to enable Marie to obtain a second outlet. Several weeks of careful looking revealed two interesting opportunities. One was shop premises in a new private housing estate on the outskirts of Mansfield. The other was a thriving grocers and delicatessen in the town centre of Chesterfield. The latter was much nearer to her original shop, so ease of transport and delivery persuaded her to concentrate on it. For she was certain that the next step in improving the profitability of her first store lay in direct purchasing from the manufacturer.

This would entail dropping the business's long association with Spar, but buying direct would boost margins by three per cent. The minimum delivery size imposed by the manufacturers would mean that all deliveries would go to the one site, and would then have to be shuttled from one to the other by a full-time delivery driver. It would also make it likely that higher average stock levels would have to be held. So Marie planned to install a computerised stock control system – efficient enough to counteract the upward pressure on stock levels. She realised that all these apparently high costs would be covered comfortably by the 3% margin improvement on her forecast revenue of £50,000 per week.

In the event, her purchase of the Chesterfield branch provided Marie with another benefit. The store manageress had many useful ideas on improving customer service, such as training staff to keep an eye on the checkouts and to open up an extra till if there was ever more than one customer waiting.

Five years later it was the manageress who was the Personnel Director of Derbyshire Supermarkets, a chain of fourteen stores employing over four hundred people. Marie, the Managing Director of the county's largest independent grocery chain, was starting to set her sights on national horizons.

Questions

(60 marks; 90 minutes)

1 Explain the meaning of the following terms (emboldened in the text):

      collateral

      debtors

      profitability **(6)**

2 **a** Prior to the expansion, what were the firm's approximate gearing and stock turnover ratios? **(6)**

  b Outline why Marie felt that she had to finance expansion primarily from profit? **(6)**

3 To what extent did Marie's management approach fit a scientific decision making model? **(10)**

4 Demonstrate that:

  a The pay back period was eight weeks.

  b 'Weekly profit was still buoyant at £2,900 per week.' **(10)**

5 Discuss which departments the desired floor space should be taken from. **(10)**

6 Outline the main benefits Marie's business seemed to derive from its horizontal expansion. What pitfalls might it meet as it expands still further? **(12)**

WEDGWOOD'S FIGHT FOR SURVIVAL

Concepts needed: *Company objectives, Value of the pound, Inflation,*
Quality circles, Takeovers

Wedgwood had been a famous name in pottery for two hundred years before going public in 1967. Partly due to the extra capital from the stock exchange listing, and partly due to new management, Wedgwood grew rapidly. By the end of the 1970s it was one of Britain's top 200 companies, employing 11,000 people and exporting over half its output.

Then came the savage trading conditions of the early 1980s. High interest rates pushed costs up, for they had borrowed heavily to fund the next stage of their expansion programme. Even more damaging was the sharp rise in the value of the pound at a time when U.K. inflation was higher than in most western countries. Worst of all, though, was the impact of recession on consumer psychology. Troubled by the threat of unemployment, people cut back their spending on luxury durables, preferring to build up their savings. Wedgwood found themselves in a giddy downward spiral of falling revenue, rising costs, and heavy trading losses.

In the face of this threat to their survival, the management conducted an urgent review of costs. Wedgwood's strengths had always been their name; their wide range of products (enabling purchasers to feel they were buying an exclusive article); and the high quality, hand-crafted finish to the pottery. Both the last two factors led to the firm's production being highly labour intensive. Wages and salaries accounted for almost half Wedgwood's total costs. So cost reductions inevitably meant staff cutbacks, which in turn meant cutting down their range of product lines. With fewer lines, a higher degree of mechanisation became economic. With higher productivity, a sharp cutback in the labour force need not lead to a similar reduction in output.

Wedgwood benefited from the good relationship built up with its trade unions over the years. Management explained the company's economic position, and persuaded the unions that large scale redundancies were necessary for the preservation of jobs for the majority. Between 1979 and 1983 four thousand jobs were lost, many through non-replacement of staff leaving, but over one thousand by means of compulsory redundancy. Several factories were closed down and the sites sold off.

With its overheads cut back, Wedgwood was able to operate profitably in the flat trading conditions of 1982/83. Having survived the recession, the company's personnel and production management determined to embark on a programme of employee involvement. The catalysts were management's realisation that future success would depend upon the skills and flexibility of their workforce, and the widespread publicity about quality circles. Wedgwood experimented with this technique, finding that although workers were very wary at first, after about twelve months they began to pay dividends.

Male employees were particularly resistant, for they had borne the brunt of the redundancies and were suspicious that productivity improvements would mean more job cuts. So whereas the women workers began to enjoy their greater say in the running of their sections, the men seemed more inclined to stick to a traditional management-worker division of responsibilities. Senior management accepted this, feeling certain that the men would adapt once they had seen evidence that this new, employee-centred policy was a genuine, long term commitment from the top.

Towards the end of 1983 sales began to pick up, especially in export markets. This trend continued until by 1985 sales were booming. The firm was quite unable to meet the demand from the United States in particular. Production managers bemoaned the short-sightedness that had led senior management in the early 1980s to mistake a cyclical slump for a long term deterioration in the firm's position. Now 4,000 workers had left the industry, and their factories had been pulled down. Nevertheless Wedgwood responded logically to this new prosperity by investing in more highly mechanised production processes, and in Computer Aided Design (CAD) systems. Accordingly, both the design and the production processes were speeded up, enabling a higher output to be achieved from the same factory floor space.

With an ever-improving management-worker relationship, a high rate of investment in both equipment and training, and with booming demand for its products, the future looked bright.

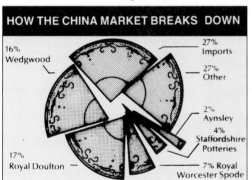

HOW THE CHINA MARKET BREAKS DOWN

16% Wedgwood
17% Royal Doulton
27% Imports
27% Other
2% Aynsley
4% Staffordshire Potteries
7% Royal Worcester Spode

In April 1986, London International – the British conglomerate owners of Royal Worcester china – bid £151 million for Wedgwood. The bidders announced that their strategy for Wedgwood would centre on three areas: restructuring management, tighter financial controls, and improved productivity. Wedgwood's management and workforce were united in seeing this bid as a threat to their jobs, and their loud protests succeeded in getting the London International bid referred to the Monopolies and Mergers Commission (on the grounds of the potential threat to competition in the pottery-china market). The M.M.C. usually take three to six months to decide whether or not to recommend to the government that a bid should be allowed. Wedgwood used that breathing space to seek an alternative bidder, so that if it was clear that the firm's independence was bound to be lost, they at least would know who to turn to.

With London International still after them, Wedgwood announced in October 1986 that they were pleased to be taken over by the Irish company Waterford Glass. The price was £252 million. *The Times* described the merger as a 'world beating combination', and suggested that 'if there is any surprise it is that it did not happen long ago'. Waterford's Chairman was written about in glowing terms; no mention was made of the heavy borrowings Waterford needed to finance the deal.

Unfortunately this was to prove an unusual takeover. There are many examples of successful bidders finding disappointment in the performance of the firm they have bought. In this case the problem was with Waterford. In March 1988 Waterford declared a substantial trading loss on its traditional crystal glass side. Excessive production costs and stock write-offs caused it to shed 1,000 workers. Waterford also forced Wedgwood to accept its share of the 'restructuring', with the loss of 986 jobs despite making record trading profits of £20 million in 1987. So Waterford's heavy cash needs were met by squeezing short-term profits out of Wedgwood. Two hundred and twenty years as an independent company had come to this.

APPENDIX A: Sterling Exchange Rates (1979-1986)

	Dollars to the £	Deutschemark to the £	Yen to the £	£ exchange rate index (1975 = 100)
1979	2.12	3.89	465.5	87.3
1980	2.33	4.23	525.6	96.1
1981	2.03	4.56	444.6	95.3
1982	1.75	4.24	435.2	90.7
1983	1.52	3.87	360.0	83.3
1984	1.34	3.79	316.8	78.8
1985	1.30	3.78	307.1	78.7
1986	1.46	3.18	246.8	72.9

Source: *Economic Trends HMSO December 1988*

Questions

(50 marks; 90 minutes)

1   What company objectives did Wedgwood appear to have during the different phases
    of the period 1967-1986?
    What factors led to these differing objectives?   **(10)**

2   How much would a £10 Wedgwood vase have sold for in the United States and
    in Japan in 1979?
    Given the 15% inflation rate in Britain between 1979 and 1980, how much would
    the vase have sold for in those countries in 1980, if Wedgwood wished to maintain
    the same profit margins?
    What percentage price increase would that represent to the foreign consumer?   **(10)**

3   The text details the 'savage trading conditions of the early 1980s'.
    To what extent can managements prepare their firms for such circumstances?   **(10)**

4   Discuss the response of Wedgwood's workforce to the introduction of quality circles.
    In general, why do workers not necessarily leap at the chance to show their
    abilities to management?   **(10)**

5   When takeover bids are made, only two groups have real power to stop them –
    shareholders and government. The former usually regard profit on investment as
    their priority, while 1980s governments felt they should only stop bids that would
    threaten competition. Which other groups are affected by the outcome of takeovers?
    Should governments give their interests equal weight as the two that are
    already considered?   **(10)**

87 INTEREST RATES AND THE GROWING BUSINESS

Concepts needed: *Cash flow, Interest rates, Value of the pound,*
External constraints

Having worked for six years as a design engineer, it seemed natural for Sean Parker to want to start up his own business. His customer contacts gave him an idea of the opportunities that existed and his skills enabled him to create an appropriate economic product. So when he met two brothers who, between them, had financial and production expertise, he sounded them out. The brothers, Tim and Aylott Batchelor, were very keen, so T.A.S. Limited was born.

They chose to specialise in the design and manufacture of machines for printing packaging labels. This was because the enormous range of packaging materials used in modern business means that a very wide range of printing machines is needed; as a result, it is hard for established firms to find the economies of mass production that would stop a new firm from getting established.

Having started with £60,000 of equity and £40,000 of fixed rate loan capital, within two years T.A.S. Ltd. had sales of £540,000 at a 10% net profit margin. With fast rising demand, it was a constant struggle to find the extra resources needed: the finance, the managers, the labour, and the factory floor space. It was a relief when, in April, Aylott negotiated a £100,000 bank loan; sufficient to finance the whole of next year's plans. The terms of the loan seemed reasonable (4% over bank base rates) as it meant paying just 11 per cent.

When the Chancellor pushed interest rates up 2% in the following month, the trio thought nothing of it. Yet worries about inflation forced the Chancellor to keep pushing rates up until, five months later, bank rates stood at 14%. This soon applied pressure to the firm's cash flow, as customers stalled paying their bills, while suppliers chased harder for payment. Back in April, the length of credit time taken by customers was much the same as the length given to suppliers – forty-five days. Now customers were stalling until sixty days, while deliveries were being cut off if payment was not made within thirty days. This meant a large cash drain from a sales level that had reached £600,000 per annum.

In the months that followed T.A.S. received further shocks. The first was a marked downturn in signed orders. Customers still talked about placing them, but the uncertainty over the effects of the high interest rates meant that they kept putting off a commitment. With orders sliding down towards an annual level of £450,000 by February, Sean decided to fly out to a Trade Fair in Munich, to try to generate some export business. Looking round competitors' stands, he was perturbed to see that their prices were lower than his, when converted into sterling. This, he realised, was because the pound had risen 8% against other currencies since the increase in U.K. interest rates. He returned home without a single order.

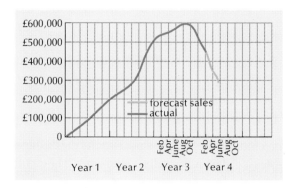

Then, in March, came two fierce setbacks. The first was the loss of two major customers to a German supplier. Months of design work was wasted as the Germans were able to not only undercut T.A.S. prices by 3%, but also to offer longer credit terms. For in Germany the 6% rate of interest meant that offering three months' credit would cost just 1.5% off the profit margin. It became horribly clear that sales would be down towards the £300,000 mark by May. The second blow was the failure of a key supplier – forced into liquidation by the difficult economic position. Although not as drastic as the liquidation of a customer, Sean had been used to a close working relationship with this firm, and its engineers had often come up with design ideas that helped to keep production costs down.

On 30th May – thirteen months after the first increase – the Chancellor pushed interest rates down by 1%. Journalists began to forecast that rates would be below 10% by the Autumn. Too late, unfortunately, for Tim, Aylott and Sean. In mid May they had decided to go into voluntary liquidation; dissolving the company before losses wiped out their original share capital.

Questions

(35 marks; 60 minutes)

1 a Calculate the 'large cash drain' suffered by T.A.S. after interest rates had risen. Assume thirty-day months. **(8)**

   b Explain why the firm's suppliers and customers responded as they did to the higher interest rates. **(6)**

2 In West Germany, the Reconstruction Credit Bank provides £4.5 billion of cheap finance for small firms. The funds are at a fixed rate set several points below the standard commercial rate.

   a To what extent would such a scheme have helped T.A.S. in the situation outlined above? **(8)**

   b Why should small firms receive such favourable treatment from government-backed schemes? **(7)**

3 With the benefit of hindsight, how should T.A.S. have responded to the interest rate increases? **(6)**

FASHION GOES WEST

Concepts needed: Cash flow, Elasticity, Balance sheets, Investment appraisal, Economic policy

'The Americans are crying out for clothes like these,' said Hazell, the fashion journalist. Lucy and Ted looked pleased, but not totally convinced. They still remembered the £40,000 they lost when they tried to market products in the United States last time. Those losses had almost forced their company into **receivership**. Ted, who was responsible for production and finance, recalled this episode with particular horror.

Hazell saw their scepticism and so went into further detail. 'Nothing has hit the young scene over there since punk. High fashion womenswear is worth £850 million in the United States, and any new craze can easily pick up 1% of that.'

Lucy explained that the real problem was financing such a venture. 'At present', she said, 'our monthly cash inflow is balanced by outflows, and we've only got £50,000 on deposit at the bank.' Lucy then jotted down some estimates:

Start-up costs:
  £100,000 (incurred in month one)
Running costs:
  Cost of stock – £16,000 per month
  Transport costs – £4 per item
  (Both these costs would affect the
  month before sale)
U.S. overheads – £10,000 per month

'From day one we'd start incurring those **overheads**', said Lucy, 'but I think we would only start selling clothes from the start of month four. So even if we managed sales of 1,000 garments a month at £40 each, it'd take us over a year to get back into the black. And that is assuming we can get away without giving our customers any credit.'

Ted decided to look more closely at the U.S. fashion market. He found a distribution pattern dominated by big, staid firms.

He wondered if New York would be a good starting point, and so checked on the regional sales pattern. He found that although New Yorkers are only 8% of all Americans, they buy 12% of all new fashionwear. A research report stated that: 'Fashion clothing in New York is price inelastic, but has an income elasticity as high as four.'

As the weeks went by, Hazell convinced Lucy that they should try America.

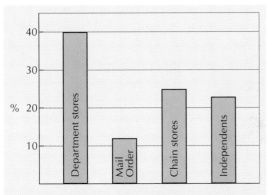

Percentage share of fashion wear for 16–24 year old women. (Total US market)

This was potentially decisive, as Lucy owned 51% of the company's shares to Ted's 49%. She used this lever to persuade Ted that they must have a go.

Ted prepared a business plan, including a cash flow forecast and a thorough investment appraisal, which they took to their accountant. Having looked at the balance sheet (see Appendix A) the accountant expressed concern: 'Borrowing all the extra funds would put you in a very difficult position if the United States move fails. Can you increase the equity capital?' Neither Lucy nor Ted wished to.

Taking this **constraint** into account, the accountant modified Ted's business plan to make it seem as professional as possible to the bank. When Ted and Lucy went there, they were delighted to find the manager happy about the financial side, though he seemed concerned about the **protectionist climate** in America since the U.S. trade deficit was so high. Happily, within a few days a loan was agreed and the expansion could begin.

APPENDIX A: Balance Sheet (as of yesterday)

	£000	£000
Fixed Assets		
Machinery [1]	45	
Property	95	140
Current Assets		
Stocks [2]	40	
Debtors	10	
Cash	50	
Current Liabilities		
Creditors	65	
Overdraft	10	
Net Current Assets		25
Net Assets Employed		165
Shareholders Funds		
Share Capital	50	
Reserves	60	110
Long term loans	55	55
Capital Employed		165

Notes: (1) Assuming ten year straight line depreciation.
(2) Including £20,000 of stock written down by 10% for being over twelve months old.

APPENDIX B: Discount factors

At 10%:		
end of year 1	–	0.91
end of year 2	–	0.83
end of year 3	–	0.75

Questions

(100 marks; 2.5 hours)

1   Explain the meaning of the following terms (emboldened in the text):

       receivership
       overheads
       constraint
       protectionist climate   **(12)**

2   **a**   Set out a cash flow forecast for the first six months, assuming that they start their American expansion today.   **(10)**

    b   What aspects of this forecast would you feel lay the firm open to the greatest risks? Explain why.   **(8)**

3   From the information given, outline where you would recommend the firm should concentrate their distribution effort. Detail the further data you would want to find out to check that recommendation thoroughly.   **(10)**

4   Explain the meaning and implication of fashion clothing being 'price inelastic, but with an income elasticity as high as four'.   **(8)**

5   On the assumption that the firm's U.S. venture lasts three years, and that interest rates are 10%, assist Ted by carrying out a 'thorough investment appraisal' of the project. (The information in Appendix B may help.)   **(15)**

6   Identify the elements of a balance sheet that may have caused the accountant concern, and suggest the positive aspects of the balance sheet that might have convinced the bank manager.   **(12)**

7   Apart from the protectionist measures, how else might the United States government act to try to reduce its trade deficit? How might these actions affect Ted and Lucy's U.S. business?   **(15)**

8   What pressures and problems are likely to affect the firm managerially as a result of their expansion plan?   **(10)**

89 OVERTRADING IN JEWELLERY

Concepts needed: Small firms, Cash flow, Profit, Variances, Sources of finance, Marketing strategy

Claire had always loved jewellery and with the help of her grandfather could make rings and earrings before the age of thirteen. By the time she reached sixth form, her production sideline was generating a useful income from her fellow students. After a year's foundation course at art college, Claire decided to turn full time.

Although she could produce all types of jewellery, Claire's favourite items were rings and necklaces. She had experimented with high quality silver gemstone rings, but found these hard to sell. So she decided to concentrate on costume jewellery, using the flexibility of her one-woman business to respond quickly to changing fashions and musical tastes. When 'Take That' became the group girls screamed for, Claire's were the TT rings and Mark Owen chains.

Even though her business had been growing fast, she was in no way prepared for what hit her when 'Blade' arrived. The Blade twins' blond hair and good looks made them stars even without their great dancing and singing. Claire had chanced upon them just before their first Number 1 record, when it was still possible to meet them without bribing the bodyguards. They had loved her suggestion of sword-shaped 'Blade' earrings and a neckchain. She designed and made them just in time for their first appearance on *Top of The Pops*. As their single and album raced to number one, Blade's management signed a deal with Claire to provide the jewellery for sale as official merchandise on their hastily arranged British tour.

Occasionally in the past, Claire had needed to bring an old friend in to help meet a large order. Never before had she hired unknown staff to work with her in the small workshop. Overnight, everything had to change. The initial order for

Blade earrings and chains was for 40,000 of each – within three weeks. This was as much as she had produced in the whole of the previous year. Thank goodness, she told herself, that I negotiated such a profitable deal.

Each item would be bought by Blade Management Incorporated (BMI) for £1.25, but the materials cost was only 10p and she had always costed her labour time at 25p per unit. Other unit costs usually came to no more than 5p, so there was plenty of contribution for covering the overheads plus the fixed cost of designing and making the mould in which the jewellery was produced.

Through her tutor at art college, Claire quickly brought in three new workers. None had experience, but all they would need to do is pour powdered gunmetal into the moulding machine, take the finished rings out, then give them a vigorous polish. More of a constraint was the lack of machine capacity and physical space. After setting up her new staff at their posts, Claire scurried round commercial estate agents trying to find bigger premises. Within two days she found an adequately sized unit in a smart business park nearby. At £1,500 per month rent and rates, it was more expensive than she wanted, but impatience led her to accept it.

In the two days it took before succeeding, several problems had occurred in the workshop. The student workers had no idea what to do. For some time they carried on producing rings they knew to be sub-standard (all of which were later scrapped), then decided to wait for Claire's return.

Even with her greatest endeavours, it was ten days before the new workshop was operational, with its two new moulding machines – each costing £10,000. The machinery suppliers had given her two months' credit, but the materials for the 80,000 units had to be obtained with cash that Claire did not have. Fortunately the bank manager proved very helpful, extending the business overdraft to £10,000 without even asking to see her books (the loan was secured, however, on her parents' house).

The contract was completed only after Claire had switched to two-shift production at the new factory unit. This required higher pay for the night-shift workers and the recruitment of her old friend as the night supervisor. To find the funds to pay the wages, she had to go cap in hand to BMI for a 20% interim payment. Claire was, again, fortunate to get cooperation. Without it, lack of funds would have meant no wages and therefore no workforce.

When, three weeks late, she delivered the full order, she found BMI desperate for still more product. They paid her immediately and asked for a further 60,000 rings and 40,000 necklaces within two weeks. This caused still more feverish work, with each shift extended to ten hours and with weekend working as well. Again cash proved terribly tight, as the bill for the machines became due.

A visit to the bank manager led to a full discussion of how she was handling the finances and administration of the business. The manager was horrified to realise that Claire was operating without budgets or a cash flow forecast. He insisted that she should take time out from the production process to work out exactly what her cash inflows and outflows had been since the start of the 'Blade' boom, and then forecast the coming three months. He also wanted a full calculation of the actual profit generated by the first contract. Only then would he consider a loan or an overdraft extension. The bank manager said sternly: 'You are suffering the symptoms of overtrading: expanding too rapidly from a low capital base and with an inadequate management structure'. He recommended that Claire should hire a small firms consultant to come in for a couple of days and make recommendations on how to proceed.

Although her diversion into accounting held the completion of the job back by five days, it probably saved her business and her parents' home. It persuaded her to take on an office manager who would handle the administration and the finances, while she focused upon design, production and sales. Blade's success proved far more long-lasting than anyone had imagined, and when, three years later, the twins' popularity faded after a failed film production, Claire's business was well enough diversified to cope.

APPENDIX A: Actual production costs on first Blade contract

Wages and salaries	£48,000
Materials	£12,800
Other direct costs	£ 3,000
Fixed costs	£ 1,200
Overheads	£14,000

Questions
(50 marks; 90 minutes)

1 What factors make small firms such as Claire's more flexible than large companies? **(4)**

2 **a** What profit was made on the first Blade order? **(4)**

   b Calculate the variances from the costs Claire expected for labour and materials. For what reasons did these cost overruns occur? **(8)**

   c Given the profit made on the order, why did Claire run into such severe cash flow problems? **(8)**

3 Outline the internal and external sources of finance that Claire's company made use of. **(8)**

4 Write a report to Claire, as her small firms consultant, making detailed recommendations for action under the following headings:

   4.1 Financial controls
   4.2 Personnel and management structure
   4.3 Marketing strategy **(18)**

STATISTICAL ANALYSIS

Concepts needed: Time series analysis, Seasonal adjustment, Contribution, Value of the pound

Jenny had inherited the large country house from her father. It had been very run down, but the Loan Guarantee Scheme had helped fund its renovation and transformation into a smart hotel. Its site (just outside Edinburgh) made it ideal for the large foreign tourist market attracted up to see Scotland.

From the start, marketing activity had been concentrated on overseas travel agents, especially in America. Their initial direct mailing of a sumptuous, glossy brochure had certainly brought in a lot of custom, but with their second trading year just ending, Jenny was worried about the cash flow position. Following a two year interest rate 'holiday', from next month they would have to start paying for their loans, which looked difficult given the projected profits.

| | Year 1 | | Year 2 | |
	Revenue	Direct Costs	Revenue	Direct Costs
April	£30,000	£25,000	£27,000	£27,000
May	£36,000	£30,000	£34,000	£31,000
June	£46,000	£34,000	£43,000	£35,000
July	£74,000	£45,000	£73,000	£46,000
August	£79,000	£47,000	£76,000	£48,000
Sept	£57,000	£42,000	£52,000	£42,000
Oct	£48,000	£35,000	£45,000	£38,000
Nov	£30,000	£29,000	£30,000	£33,000
Dec	£32,000	£30,000	£32,000	£33,000
Jan	£22,000	£27,000	£19,000	£28,000
Feb	£17,000	£25,000	£13,000	£26,000
Mar	£34,000	£31,000	£31,000	£33,000

After opening in April, the first Summer season had been marvellous, with each of twenty rooms full at £100 each. She had known that things would quieten down in the winter, but was shocked at how bad takings actually were. In their first February, average room usage was just three per night; cash flowed out of the company bank account like red ink. Now, exactly two years after opening, the time had come for a review and perhaps a rethink of strategy. Jenny arranged a meeting with her fellow Directors: her chef husband Allan and their accountant Finance Director Chang-Wei.

Chang-Wei began with a presentation of **raw data** on monthly revenues and direct costs for the past two years. She emphasised that they were not profit figures since they did not take into account depreciation or the **interest that had been accruing**.

> *'What were those other costs you mentioned?'* asked Allan.
>
> *'The depreciation was £40,000 each year, and the interest was 15% on our £200,000 loan,'* came the reply.

After some pressing of calculator keys, Allan declared that the recent position was not at all bad. They had only made a loss in the second half of the financial year – as in their first year of trading. Chang-Wei's shake of the head signalled her disagreement with this analysis.

Allan felt it time to put forward his theory.:

> *'I read an article in* The Sunday Times *about the effect of the pound's exchange rate against the dollar. It said that the **pound being so strong** against the dollar last year made it expensive for Americans to come here – so they stayed at home. That would explain why we did so disappointingly. After all, from the start half our revenue has come from Americans. Anyway, I found some figures on this from the library that seem to confirm* The Times' *view.'* (See Appendix A.)
>
> *'As the pound is now slipping against the dollar, I feel confident that business will pick up soon. So we don't need to change our strategy.'*

Jenny was pleased to hear such optimism, but wanted to discuss her fears. She explained that she now doubted whether they could ever get enough business from the tourist market during the lean, November–April period. In which case perhaps they would have to aim for the business traveller. Unfortunately the leisurely, country house atmosphere that she knew the Americans loved would have to be compromised for the sake of the fast-moving modern executive. Would they lose their tourist trade as a result? And in any case, did they want to end up running the kind of impersonal hotel that business people seem to require?

> *'There is one other possibility', continued Chang-Wei, 'which is that something has gone slightly wrong with the day-to-day management of the hotel. This might have led to costs creeping up, and even to customers going away feeling slightly disappointed. How much of our custom is repeat business, Jenny?'*
>
> *'Very little; much more important for us is customer satisfaction leading to word of mouth recommendation. I ask every visitor how they heard about us and keep quarterly records of their answers. A higher and higher percentage of our clients have heard of us from friends. That must be good.'*

After she had gone, Allan spoke bitterly about Chang-Wei's insulting reference to their management of the hotel. He then went off to phone their advertising agency.

Allan was a great admirer of their tasteful designs, and felt sure that their appointment a year ago would prove a cornerstone of the hotel's future success.

**APPENDIX A: Quarterly data on the number of foreign visitors to the U.K.
(all figures in thousands)**

From:	America	Europe	Other
April–June Year 1:	938	2475	635
July–Sept Year 1:	1283	3200	1135
Oct–Dec Year 1:	672	1988	599
Jan–Mar Year 1:	519	1704	524
April–June Year 2:	846	2484	683
July–Sept Year 2:	1201	3301	1043
Oct–Dec Year 2:	710	2050	600
Jan–Mar Year 2:	552	1802	530

Questions

(50 marks; 90 minutes)

1   Explain the meaning of the following phrases (emboldened in the text):

   raw data

   interest that had been accruing

   pound being so strong   **(9)**

2   Chang-Wei's failure to prepare data that could be easily interpreted was a major reason for the inconclusive nature of the meeting. Calculate the revenue and cost data as Moving Annual Totals, and comment on their usefulness in assessing Allan's statement that: 'the recent trading position was not at all bad'.   **(15)**

3   A further need is to forecast future profits, in order to see how serious the position is. Over the coming first quarter (Apr-June) of year 3, direct costs are forecast to be: fixed – £60,000; variable – one third of sales revenue.

   a   Calculate an eight quarterly moving average of past sales revenue and use it to project the trend figure for sales in the first quarter of the coming year.   **(8)**

   b   The following seasonal adjustment factors have been calculated from the data given above. Use them to forecast the actual revenue for the first quarter of the coming year.   **(2)**

   1st quarter: 0.86   3rd quarter: 0.88

   2nd quarter: 1.68   4th quarter: 0.60

   c   Use this, plus the above cost data, to forecast the hotel's profit/loss in the coming three months.   **(6)**

4   To what extent does the information in Appendix A support Allan's view that the disappointing revenue last year was due to Americans 'staying at home'?   **(10)**

91 DE LOREAN CARS – 'FROM COW PASTURE TO PRODUCTION'

Concepts needed: Productivity, Elasticity, Value of the pound, External constraints, Government intervention

On 3rd August 1978, Mr. John De Lorean announced agreement with the Labour government on a financing package for the establishment of a new sports car factory in Belfast, Northern Ireland. De Lorean, an American former vice-president of General Motors (the world's largest car producer), was to invest £20 million, with government funded bodies such as the Northern Ireland Development Agency (NIDA) putting in £45 million. NIDA would have an equity stake worth £15 million, and would also provide grants and loans.

Sceptics pointed out that the Irish government had already turned the scheme down, believing it to be too risky. Their doubts hinged on the sales forecasts being put forward for an untried product, and on technological factors. De Lorean's prototype called for construction methods never before used in the motor industry.

Mr. Roy Mason, the Northern Ireland Secretary of State, was understandably jubilant, however. It had long been his belief that the sectarian violence in Northern Ireland was connected with the high unemployment. Indeed violence and economic underdevelopment seemed to form a vicious circle. Now he could announce a factory to be sited next to one of Belfast's largest Catholic housing estates, where male unemployment stood at 35%. Its projected employment of 2,000 people could help break through that circle.

De Lorean announced that:

> *'We aim to move from cow pasture to production within eighteen months.'*

Some regarded his choice of this **'greenfield' site** as risky, because the lack of local car production meant that his workforce would be completely inexperienced. De Lorean countered this by stressing the potential benefits of a workforce with no traditional **restrictive practices**.

The car, to be designed by the Italian Giugiaro, would have a body shell of glass fibre-reinforced plastic bonded to a stainless steel outer skin. Although technologically novel (and therefore potentially troublesome) it conformed to an essential element in De Lorean's marketing proposition. He was famous in the United States as the man who quit General Motors, and then exposed that company's practice of 'built-in obsolescence', i.e. they used materials and components with a relatively short life-span, so that customers would need to replace their car regularly. De Lorean had long promoted the notion of an 'ethical' car that would last fifteen years, not five. He claimed that this new car would be completely rustproof, and therefore the body could last for ever. It was to be marketed in the United States alone, as that was where De Lorean's standing meant that dealers were prepared to invest in the project. And at an anticipated $14,000 it would be priced below General Motor's Corvette – the biggest selling sports car in the United States. Hence the expectation of sales of 30,000 cars a year.

By August 1980, 'technical problems' had caused sufficient delays for De Lorean to have to warn his U.S. dealers that the car's launch would have to be put back from November to early 1981. It also meant that extra funds were needed, which the firm managed to get from the (by now, Conservative) government.

On 21st January 1981, De Lorean drove one of the first finished production cars off the assembly line. He announced that a batch of 700 cars would be delivered to U.S. dealers in April. Cars were said to be coming off the line at a rate of three per day, rising to thirty per day by the end of the following month. The U.S. dealers' worries about the supply delays were compounded by the company's ever escalating view of the car's price tag. In August 1980, De Lorean declared that his pricing strategy was that the car should sell for just under $20,000 – about the same as the Corvette. Now, in January 1981, he was speaking of 'the mid $20,000s', i.e. around 20% more than the U.S. produced rival. A major Kansas City car dealer said that the price was pressing up against the threshold at which consumer resistance could be expected: 'If it goes above $24,000 we have a problem'. De Lorean blamed the price escalation on higher inflation in the United Kingdom than in the United States, and the unexpected strength of sterling (see Appendix A).

By the end of January it was plain that the De Lorean Motor Company (DMC) had a major cash crisis. Successive governments had already invested £70 million in the project, and now the firm wanted a guarantee of a £10 million bank loan to 'help resolve a short term **working capital** requirement'. The problem was that a series of production hitches had delayed the launch by six months. So continuing production expenditure, a wage bill of over £100,000 per week, plus steady stockbuilding were all draining cash at a time when none was coming in. In February the government provided the £10 million bank guarantee, but stated that no more public money would be made available to the project.

The crisis of confidence in DMC during January evaporated by May. Motoring journalists gushed over the 2.8 litre V6 engine, the gull-wing doors and the fifteen year life-span of the bodies. They referred to the 12,000 cars expected to be sold in the United States during 1981 at $25,000 each, and the resultant royalties of £2.4 million that the U.K. government could expect to receive (£185 on each of the first 90,000 cars, and £45 on each subsequent one). Throughout the media there was a feeling of admiration for DMC's achievement in creating a car factory from nothing; and a fervent wish that its success would boost Belfast. So when, on 22nd May, the government announced a guarantee of a further £7 million, it received little criticism for changing its mind on increasing its financial commitment.

By August 1981 more than 2,000 people were employed at the Belfast plant. The firm claimed fifty to sixty cars were being built per day. Demand in the United States was said to be phenomenal. Yet in early 1982 DMC was put on a three day week and output was halved from 400 to 200 per week. It emerged that low demand had led to a stockpile of 2,500 unsold cars. De Lorean blamed this on the fierce recession in the U.S. market for new cars; some of the dealers felt that the very poor standard of finish on the cars was the key factor.

The true market potential of the De Lorean car began to come under serious scrutiny. DMC's construction, production and cash flow difficulties had always been presented to the public in the context of an apparently guaranteed level of demand. It had been suggested that the firm's U.S. dealers had placed firm orders for the first two years' production (40,000 cars). Also, the original government investment had been made after the McKinsey **management consultancy** had forecast demand for 30,000 units per year. What had not been revealed was that McKinsey had analysed the likely price elasticity of the car. At approximate price parity with the Corvette, demand should be for 30,000; but at $25,000 for a De Lorean against $20,000 for a Corvette the McKinsey formula forecast demand of just 15,000 units. Furthermore the forecasts were based on a healthy U.S. car market, whereas 1981 proved the worst in twenty years. Sports car sales were hit especially hard as recession mentality took its grip on sales of luxury items. Of the 7,000 cars built by DMC in 1981, only 3,000 were actually registered to owners.

With DMC's problems becoming evermore public knowledge, rumours began to be reported in the press about De Lorean's 'Concorde lifestyle'. For the head of a publicly funded business in severe financial difficulties, his high profile in New York's social scene was disturbing. Especially as it became clear that De Lorean himself had never invested much capital in the project: a later Report by the Public Accounts Committee of the House of Commons showed that his total capital investment amounted to less than £1 million. On 28th January 1982 the Labour M.P. Bob Cryer said bitterly:

> *'This particular venture appears to be a rip-off for the directors and a disaster for the workers.'*

The following day 1,100 redundancies were announced at the plant, bringing the workforce down to 1,500. But this could not prevent the firm from insolvency. On 19th February, 1982 the company went into voluntary receivership. It owed £31 million to its suppliers and had an unsold stock of 3,000 cars. The Receiver said he would keep the business going and look for a buyer. The hoped-for upturn in U.S. demand during the Spring sales peak failed to materialise, however, and wave after wave of redundancies cut the workforce down to a few maintenance staff by the Autumn. With no buyer for the firm and no customers for its products, virtually all the government's investment was lost. Attempts to retrieve some from John De Lorean (on grounds of fraudulent diversion of funds) faltered in the United States courts.

To Mrs. Thatcher's government it was proof that governments should not get involved directly in business activity. The Labour opposition preferred to think of it as an example of how greedy and cynical entrepreneurs can be. Perhaps all it proves, however, is that the internal constraints upon the successful establishment of a new manufacturing firm are troublesome enough; the external factors make it a matter of luck as well.

Sources: *The Financial Times; The Guardian; The Times*

APPENDIX A: UK & US Exchange rates and Inflation rates 1978–1982

	US $ per £	UK inflation %	US inflation %
1978	1.90	9.0	6.8
1979	2.10	13.0	11.4
1980	2.30	18.0	13.6
1981	2.05	12.0	10.4
1982	1.75	8.0	6.4

Sources: *HMSO Annual Abstract of Statistics; U.N. Statistical Yearbook.*

Questions

(60 marks; 100 minutes)

1 Explain the meaning of the following terms (emboldened in the text)

'greenfield' site;

restrictive practices;

working capital

management consultancy **(12)**

2 a Outline the risks involved in the De Lorean project that could have been foreseen at the start. **(8)**

b Given these, discuss whether there was any justification for government financing. **(8)**

3 During 1981, an average of 1,500 workers were employed at DMC to produce 7,000 cars. How did this productivity level compare with that anticipated in 1978? Why may this shortfall have occurred? **(12)**

4 a According to McKinsey, what was the price elasticity of the De Lorean car? **(4)**

b Discuss the factors that may have influenced De Lorean's decision to price the car at $25,000. **(6)**

5 Examine the external constraints faced by DMC. To what extent were they the cause of the project's downfall? **(10)**

THE FORD STRIKE – 1988

Concepts needed: Trade unions, Multinationals, Stocks, Them and us

The U.K. market was booming in 1987, with sales rising 7% to two million cars for the first time. Ford took an increasing share of this growing market (up from 27% to 29%), with its Escort, Fiesta, and Sierra models in the top three places in the U.K. sales league. Ford U.K. annual profits were set to beat £350 million.

Encouraged by **low inflation** in Britain, and keen to match the three year pay deals signed by Ford's German, Spanish, and Belgian workers, Ford U.K. set out to agree a similar scheme with its unions. In October 1987, Ford offered a 4.25% per annum pay rise to its employees. This was rejected as 'insulting', and during the negotiations that followed, **unofficial industrial action** lost Ford production of 26,000 cars (worth over £200 million). On 7th December, the company announced its final offer:

1   6.5% in the first year of a three year deal.
2   Rises in line with inflation for the second and third years.
3   In return, Ford demanded radical **changes in working practices**, including the introduction of team-working, flexibility between skilled and unskilled workers, acceptance by skilled workers of semi-skilled workers as their supervisors, and acceptance of temporary workers to meet seasonal peaks in demand.

The unions arranged a secret ballot of all workers on this offer; they recommended its rejection. On 22nd January 1988 the results showed 90% of Ford's manual workers against the offer. Eighty-seven per cent of employees voted. Although surprised by the scale of their majority, the unions quickly declared that a national, all-out strike would start the following Monday, unless management improved on their 'final' offer. It was to be the first national strike at Ford since an eight week strike in 1978. Management hastily increased their offer to 7% in the first year, and 2% above inflation in the second and third years, but the union considered this an insufficient improvement.

As the deadline approached, the Ford unions became increasingly confident of their position. The leader of the Amalgamated Engineering Union (AEU) described management as 'desperate' for a settlement. There were two reasons for this confidence: first was the realisation that buoyant demand meant that Ford's stock levels were too low to keep the showrooms supplied for long. The other factor was more fundamental: that Ford's development since 1978 of a fully integrated European production system left them very vulnerable to strike action. For although Ford U.K.'s plants accounted for less than a third of Ford of Europe's 1.6 million cars a year, the United Kingdom was Ford's only supplier of certain key

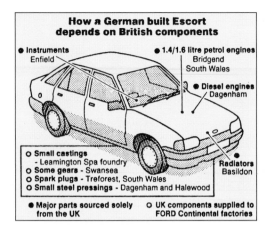

How a German built Escort depends on British components

● Instruments
Enfield

● 1.4/1.6 litre petrol engines
Bridgend
South Wales

● Diesel engines
Dagenham

○ Small castings
   - Leamington Spa foundry
○ Some gears - Swansea
○ Spark plugs - Treforest, South Wales
○ Small steel pressings - Dagenham and Halewood

● Radiators
Basildon

● Major parts sourced solely
   from the UK

○ UK components supplied to
   FORD Continental factories

components. Ford's Dagenham plant, for instance, was the sole producer of the 1.6 diesel engine used in Sierra, Escort and Orion models throughout Europe.

As a multinational with major plants in Britain, Germany, Belgium, and Spain, Ford's strategy had been to maximise economies of scale by concentrating output of components on particular sites. This also enabled them to use local labour to its best advantage – hence the highly paid, highly skilled German workforce produced the gearboxes, a particularly complex item. The components would then be shipped to the assembly plants located in each of the major production sites. As far as possible, Ford aimed to transport components from one country to another, rather than finished cars.

At the same time, Japanese competition was forcing Ford to review existing practices. The start of production at Nissan's highly efficient Sunderland factory in mid-1986 hastened this review. There were two key areas Ford wanted to improve:

1 the rigid job demarcations between skilled and unskilled workers, and between one skill and another;

2 excessive stock levels; the company wanted to move towards the Kanban (Just-In-Time) system used increasingly in Japan; increasing reliance on prompt, frequent delivery instead of buffer stocks would cut Ford's working capital requirements significantly.

Surprisingly, an emergency meeting of both sides on Sunday 31st January led to the announcement that the strike was to be called off. Ford had further improved their offer, and the unions believed that the new package should be recommended to their members in a new ballot. At the local, shop-floor level, Ford's **shop stewards** were furious at the acceptance of the new offer, and criticised their union leaders openly. The new ballot produced a 60% vote to reject the offer, and the strike was on again.

The all-out strike started on Monday 8th February 1988, and was unanimously supported – even at plants which had voted to accept the offer. The *Financial Times* reported that the Labour Party spokesman 'maintained that the 7% increase…did not represent a fair share of the company's rising prosperity when compared with the increased payments made to directors and shareholders'. The Conservative Minister for Employment warned that 'strikes destroy jobs'.

On the hastily formed picket lines, discussion was of the £350 million profit made by Ford U.K. in 1987. One striker said:

'It's a question of whether we get a bit of the cake, and how we get treated. But it isn't all about money. Some people have to ask

permission to go to the toilet ... (and) they're taking away the incentives for trained people like me'.

The Ford management emphasised that the key issue was whether their U.K. factories would be profitable enough to warrant continued investment.

Within one day of its start, the strike forced Ford to lay off 2,500 workers at Genk, Belgium. Not even the plant's management had realised before that they were totally dependent upon daily deliveries of sheet metal parts from Dagenham. By Friday, the Genk factory's 7,200 workers producing 1,400 Sierras a day were told they would be laid off due to non-availability of body panel reinforcement brackets from Dagenham. Similar cut-backs were reported at the massive Saarlouis plant in West Germany, and at Cologne and in Portugal. Ford's management had to face up to the fact that even one minor item missing on a vast assembly line could halt all production.

On Tuesday 16th February, management offered to drop the three year pay deal in favour of a two year one in which the second year rise would be 7% or 2.5% above inflation, whichever was the greater. Other elements of the package included a 9% improvement in pensions, better sick pay, and 100% lay-off pay. The company also agreed that the changes to working practices would not be imposed against local opposition – an important concession to the shop stewards.

On the union side, there was acceptance of quality circles (discussion groups), and of the principle of reorganising the factories so that shop-floor workers could work in teams, instead of being individual cogs in a large wheel. Ford's Personnel Director denied that the revised offer was a climb down, though he acknowledged that both sides in the collective bargaining process had misread the strength of shopfloor opposition to the original deal.

On Monday 22nd February, the Ford workers returned to work after 70% voted to accept the new offer. Ford declared that they had lost about £200 million of output during the strike, in addition to the £300 million lost through unofficial action between October and February. The workforce considered themselves victorious, but one year later Ford announced that Sierra production was to be transferred from Dagenham to Genk, and that redundancies would be inevitable.

Sources: *The Financial Times; The Guardian; The Times*

Questions
(60 marks; 100 marks)

1 Explain the meaning of the following (emboldened in the text):

   low inflation
   unofficial industrial action
   changes in working practices
   shop stewards   (12)

2 Outline the main strengths and weaknesses to Ford of being a fully integrated
   multinational enterprise.   (12)

3 Calculate:

   a   the increase in the number of Ford cars sold in the U.K. between 1986 and 1987; (5)

   b   Ford's expected profit per car sold in 1987.   (3)

4 Discuss the value of the Kanban stock control system to a company like Ford U.K. (10)

5 What evidence is provided of a 'them and us' divide between Ford's management
   and workforce? What reasons do there seem to be to make one more optimistic
   about the future?   (8)

6 Consider whether the Ford workers were justified in their actions.   (10)

93 THE IRISH SAWMILL

*Concepts needed: Balance sheets, Ratios, Pricing strategy, Value of the pound,
Trade unions*

The Rosscrae Sawmill had been established in the heart of Ireland for sixty years. The town of Rosscrae lay near to a range of mountains from which the wood was felled and transported by independent operators. The wood was then stripped of its bark and sawn into a range of lengths and widths by machine. The sawmill distributed its product to about twelve timber merchants in the region, and through its own factory gate wholesale depot.

The mill's layout and mechanisation had once seemed very advanced, but had come to look primitive. Much of the equipment was twenty years old and had long since been depreciated to zero in the company's accounts. So the balance sheet value of the business was very low, whereas the return on capital employed appeared huge (see Appendix A). Despite the appearance of success provided by the high rate of return represented by the £IR 27,000 profit made last year, the firm faced severe problems.

When the Rosscrae Sawmill (RS) began, wood was a very cheap commodity. So the key to economic success was to maximise output with minimum labour or energy inputs. As a result, the mill's designer had thought nothing of installing cutting equipment that – on average – wasted 50% of the raw material.

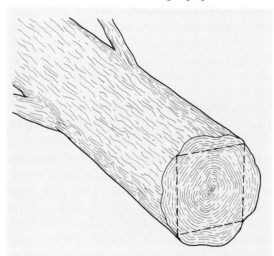

With wood becoming a scarce and expensive raw material, this machinery was wasting too much to be economic. No less seriously, the rough finish to the wood left by the large-toothed mechanical saws meant that the firm's output was inferior to its competitors. These included not only Irish sawmills but also, increasingly, imports of high quality timber from other European Union producers such as Norway and Germany. The Dooley's cost-plus pricing policy gave no flexibility to compete head on with these rivals.

Counteracting these difficulties was the loyalty shown by the firm's sixty employees. Their average length of service was twenty-two years, and for the last three years they had accepted pay rises below the rate of inflation without complaint. This had much to do with the 20% unemployment rate that Rosscrae shared with much of the midlands of Southern Ireland.

The Dooley family had always owned RS, but whereas the firm's founder John Dooley had been a bold and entrepreneurial man, the two grandchildren who now each held 50% of the shares took a short-term, cautious view of the business. Both

Frank and Jim enjoyed the large houses they had inherited, and aimed to generate enough profit from the business to keep themselves comfortably off, rather than risk investing in modernisation that, if unsuccessful, might threaten their lifestyle. Now the slide in the RS market share even threatened to send revenue below its low break-even point.

The Dooleys realised that investment in modern cutting machines along the same production line would improve quality, and therefore halt the erosion in market share. Yet the huge increase in depreciation and interest charges would increase fixed costs so much as to make the new, higher break-even level hard to achieve. So the only viable option was the much more expensive one of replacing the whole layout with a fully computerised modern system that would not only ensure quality, but would also make much better use of the raw material. By using 80% of the wood, these systems would cut variable costs per unit, and would therefore make it easier to operate profitably.

They had costed out the options, and found that the semi-modernisation would cost £IR 700,000 and the complete job would cost £IR 1,600,000 (1 Irish pound £IR = 90 pence sterling). Given that the machinery they would be buying would have a low second-hand value, they were not willing to borrow enough to fund such levels of investment. This left them with three options: to put the business into voluntary liquidation; to sell it; or to continue as they were, hoping that a local building boom or a slump in the value of the Irish pound would save them.

Their accountant told them that liquidation would probably generate more than one might expect from looking at the balance sheet. The main reasons for this would be:

1   The property would fetch 40% more than its current book value.
2   The scrap value of the machines written down to zero in the books would be £IR 7,000.
3   However, the stock might be sold for £IR 4,000 less than the balance sheet valuation.

Armed with this information, the Dooleys put an advertisement in *The Irish Times*:

'For Sale – Long Established Timber Mill And Wholesaler'

They received many inquiries, but only two firm offers: for £IR 100,000 cash; and for £IR 50,000 cash plus a 10% shareholding each in the new business.

To evaluate the latter bid, the Dooleys needed to look at the new owner's plans for the Rosscrae Sawmill. These proved to be in line with their own ideas for full implementation of new technology. Computerised scanning systems would calculate how to cut up each tree trunk in such a way as to maximise revenue (which would usually mean minimising wastage). Then the computer would instruct the automated saws to cut the timber up in that precise way. All the managers would have to do is to ensure that the computer was storing correct information on the value and selling price of every possible cut of timber; and to monitor stock and demand levels to make sure that the system was not turning out

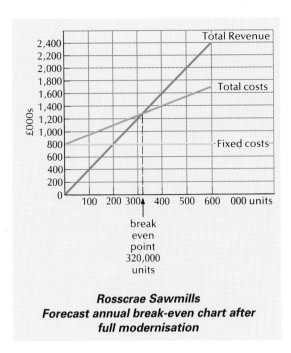

Rosscrae Sawmills
Forecast annual break-even chart after
full modernisation

thousands of 'economic' one-metre lengths when the demand was for lengths of three metres.

As the bidder's break-even chart shows, the expensive machinery would cut manpower and material costs so much as to make the business look viable. With the prospective owner already having a chain of eight timber yards in the Dublin area, extra output could easily be absorbed. The Dooleys were not certain, however, that the bidder would find it easy to achieve their forecast of doubling unit sales from their current level of 200,000 per annum.

APPENDIX A: *Rosscrae Sawmills – latest balance sheet*

	£IR	£IR
Property	30,000	
Machinery	6,000	36,000
Stock	45,000	
Debtors	35,000	
Cash	4,000	
Creditors	26,000	
Overdraft	4,000	
Net Current Assets		54,000
Assets employed		90,000
Loans	8,000	8,000
Share capital	10,000	
Reserves	72,000	82,000
Capital employed		90,000

Questions

(100 marks; 2.5 hours)

1 Calculate the rate of return on capital employed achieved by the Dooleys last year. Explain why it may be a misleading indicator of their financial efficiency. **(10)**

2 The text shows the narrow production and financial orientation of the Dooleys' thinking. What pricing and distribution strategies might they have adopted to provide higher, long-term demand levels? **(12)**

3 If they put the business into voluntary liquidation, what pay-out could each of the Dooleys expect? **(12)**

4 How might the business benefit from a slump in the value of the Irish pound? **(15)**

5 If the bidder offering a 10% stake achieves its sales forecast,

   a What income should each of the Dooleys receive (assuming full distribution of profits)? **(5)**

   b How long will it be before the Dooleys receive more than they would from the other bidder? **(5)**

   c What other factors should the Dooleys take into account before deciding between the options available to them? **(15)**

6 How might the workforce view the Dooleys' deliberations? **(8)**
   To what extent might they be helped by belonging to a trade union? **(8)**

7 Some environmentalists believe that the need to preserve scarce resources requires man to limit the increase in economic growth and prosperity. Others believe that growth in affluence and technology will enable environmental problems to be handled with more efficiency. How does this case lend weight to the latter argument? **(10)**

ROLLS ROYCE – THE GAMBLE THAT FAILED

Concepts needed: Profits, Value of the pound, Product life cycle, Government intervention

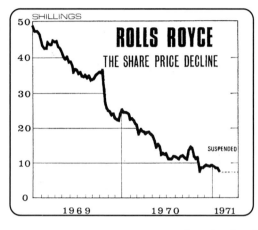

Early in 1969, Rolls Royce shares traded at £2.50 each, so that two hundred shares could be bought for five hundred pounds. Two years later, those same two hundred shares were worth just £14. In the meantime, one of the world's most famous companies had collapsed.

Although best known for its cars, over 90% of Rolls Royce turnover was from the manufacture of engines for civil or military aircraft. The aero-engine market had been a prosperous though unexciting one, but was just entering a new phase in the 1960s. With world-wide passenger air travel trebling between 1960 and 1970, airlines were calling for much larger jet planes. Boeing responded by announcing the development of its 747 (Jumbo) Jet, and Lockheed introduced the Tristar. Both aircraft would need engines capable of generating double the power of previous models.

The American Boeing and Lockheed companies worked on this development with U.S. aero-engine manufacturers. This threatened Rolls Royce with the prospect of missing out on a key market for the future, for the British firm had allowed its product range to become rather outdated. As its image lagged behind the U.S. engine producers, Rolls realised that to break into this new market would require a technologically superior product.

In 1966, Rolls announced the RB211 engine, which would use an innovative new material called carbon fibre to provide a lighter yet more powerful engine than the new U.S. ones. With the lightness would also come fuel efficiency, giving the vital customer benefit of longer flying range at lower cost per mile.

In September 1966, the Rolls selling drive got underway. From then until March 1968, there were always at least twenty Rolls Royce executives in America. Their airfares alone came to £80,000. By Spring 1968, the airlines were ready to place their orders for the new, wide-bodied jets. The RB211 looked very attractive against its U.S. rivals, for Rolls boasted that it was less noisy, more fuel efficient and – since the pound's **devaluation** in 1967 – priced at $55,000 below the $630,000 charged by General Electric of America.

While orders were being negotiated, Rolls discussed the financing of the next stage with the Labour government. For although five years had been spent on **Research & Development** for the RB211, Rolls estimated that a further £65 million would be needed to get it into production. Government approval for a grant of £47 million was clinched by the announcement of an order for 540 engines from Lockheed. The order (it later emerged) was at a fixed price and included severe penalties for late delivery. Rolls had to get the first batch of RB211s from the drawing board to Lockheed by early 1971.

The government Minister responsible, Mr Tony Benn was later to say:

> *'They felt their survival as a company depended on a new engine.*
> *We backed them, but they set the prices and negotiated the contract.*
> *The government did not have the expertise to check the figures of the*
> *most experienced aero-engine company in Britain.'*

By early 1970, Rolls Royce management was aware of serious difficulties with RB211 development. Getting it from the R & D phase into volume production involved the company in its biggest ever organisational task, and this placed great strains on its financial and physical resources. Failures of coordination between designers and the production department meant costs escalated due to work having to be redone. This problem was compounded by the inability of the cost accounting team to cope with their workload – so no-one was quite sure what costs were being incurred.

They also ran into a severe technical hitch. When completed engines were first tested, the engineers were especially interested in the performance of the carbon fibre used to make the fan blades – the heart of the jet. Tests on power output went well, but then came the shock. When planes take off or land, they often fly through flocks of birds. These can get sucked into the jet, so Rolls set up a test to simulate this. The carbon fibre blades shattered, causing the engine to fail. For some months the design engineers tried to get over this problem, but eventually they abandoned carbon fibre for a metal (titanium) that despite being costlier and heavier, was well-tried.

In November 1970, Rolls asked their bankers and the new Conservative government for extra help to finance a development cost that they now estimated at £135 million. The banks agreed to £18 million and the government to £42 million, on condition that independent accountants checked the accuracy of the estimate. In the following months Rolls made various confident statements such as this January 1971 announcement of R&D work on two new engines, the RB202 and the RB410:

> *'At a time when the world's aerospace industries are passing*
> *through a recession, Rolls Royce feels it is vital to continue*
> *fundamental research in those areas that may produce big orders in*
> *the longer term future.'*

Within a fortnight, *The Financial Times* reported rumours that Rolls was in financial difficulties. The paper pointed to three pressures on Rolls' cash position:

1 Overspending on the RB211.
2 Rapid increases in development spending on its military aircraft engines.
3 The need for more working capital to fund aircraft manufacture.

The next day, on 4th February 1971, the Chancellor of the Exchequer announced to the House of Commons that Rolls Royce had asked its **debenture** holders to appoint a Receiver to supervise the liquidation of the company. The reason for this was that the loss of resources already committed to the RB211 project plus the losses that would arise on fulfilment of its contract with Lockheed would exceed the company's **shareholders' funds**. The government, in a reversal of its previous policy of non-intervention in industry, was to take over the essential assets of the business. It soon became clear that this meant nationalising all the company apart from the profitable car division.

In a more detailed report to the House on 8th February, the Chancellor explained that the launch costs of the RB211 had reached £170 million. This was £35 million more than the estimate given four months previously. In addition, Rolls expected a production loss of £60 million on delivery of the 540 engines for which fixed prices had been contracted. Finally, £50 million would be lost under penalty clauses if Rolls Royce was six months late in its delivery times (which it regarded as an optimistic rather than a pessimistic timescale).

The government came under pressure from many directions. The American firms Lockheed and T.W.A. warned that if the government let the RB211 contract fall through, it would cause a serious loss of confidence in Britain's aerospace industry. Rolls Royce creditors were left with £65 million of unpaid bills. Many of these creditors were small suppliers for whom Rolls Royce was their biggest customer. Trade unions and M.P.s were worried about the loss of jobs, thought by some to be as high as 40,000 if the government refused to honour the RB211 contract. Partly to deflect these pressures, Conservative backbenchers attacked Tony Benn for committing government funds in the first place.

Attention then switched to the Receiver, an accountant who was now in charge of Rolls Royce. His biggest short-term problem was that suppliers stopped sending parts, threatening profitable production of cars and military engines. He assured people that all supplies received since his appointment on 4th February would be paid for in full, but some creditors still held out to try to obtain a promise that the earlier bills would be paid.

Slowly the Receiver's persuasive powers returned things to normal. He invited bids for the car division, and – crucially – managed to renegotiate the RB211 contract with Lockheed.

On 23rd February, the government owned Rolls Royce (1971) Limited was formed to take over the Aerospace division, at a price to be agreed later when the Receiver had completed a valuation of its assets. Two months later Rolls Royce Motors was sold for £40 million.

Although the Rolls Royce share price had touched 1 penny on 9th February, the Receiver proved able to generate considerable sums from the liquidation. Eventually, spread over several years, shareholders received a total payout of over £1.40 per share.

More importantly, the longer term proved Rolls management correct in believing that the RB211 was crucial to the future of Britain's aerospace industry. The engine was to form the basis for most of Rolls Royce's civil aircraft sales during the 1970s and 1980s, and is likely to continue doing so for much of the 1990s. Since 1971, Rolls has taken care to base new engines for new aircraft on the proven technology of the RB211, and to ensure that they never slipped so far behind the competition that they needed a huge leap forward to keep up.

Sources: *The Financial Times; Rolls Royce: 50 years at Crewe; The Times*

Questions

(60 marks; 100 minutes)

1 Explain the meaning of the following terms (emboldened in the text):

    devaluation
    research and development
    debenture
    shareholders funds   **(12)**

2 Identify the major mistakes made by Rolls Royce, and suggest the problems they overlooked or underestimated in the decisions they took.   **(12)**

3 **a** If Rolls management had known in 1968 the cost details given to Parliament on 8th February 1971, and assuming their financial objective was to break even on their first 540 engine contract, what price (in sterling) should they have charged originally?   **(5)**

   b By how much did Rolls underprice the engine in dollars, given that the exchange rate in 1968 was $2.40 to the pound?   **(5)**

4 Use the text to help you explain the role of the Receiver in a company liquidation.   **(6)**

5 What light does this case shed on the cash flow, new product development, and extension strategy implications of Product Life Cycle theory?   **(10)**

6 Discuss the implications of the Rolls Royce case for the issue of whether or not governments should intervene directly in industry.   **(10)**

95 THE RISE AND FALL OF LAKER AIRWAYS

Concepts needed: Gearing, Marketing strategy, Cash flow,
Government intervention, Deregulation

Freddie Laker started his freight airline in 1948 with £38,000 of borrowed money. It soon received a huge boost from the 1949 Berlin Airlift, for which his aircraft were hired round the clock to fly in food supplies. By the 1960s, it was a well enough established airline to be able to **diversify** by starting up a fleet of aircraft for the packaged holiday market – Laker Airways. The success of this move led Laker to announce in 1971 his intention to challenge the major transatlantic carriers by forming a no-frills, low price, London-New York 'Skytrain'.

At that time no passenger airline was allowed to operate on any route without government approval. The convention was that on major routes such as London-New York, each country was allowed to have two carriers. This was considered to be sufficient to provide competition, yet with enough control to ensure that competitive pressures did not force the companies to cut back on costly safety measures. So TWA and Pan-Am battled with British Airways and British Caledonian for market share. Alone of the four, British Airways was state owned.

During the 1970s Freddie Laker became a well known figure as he battled to get Skytrain accepted by the British and U.S. governments. To do this, he had to take out expensive court action to prove that the existing arrangement was a **cartel** that acted against the public interest. Only in 1977 did the first Skytrain fly from Gatwick, in a blaze of publicity in Britain and America. Prices were half those of the other carriers, and customers liked the fact that no reservations were possible; you just turned up on the day you wanted to fly, and bought a ticket as you would when travelling by train. Such was Laker's popularity that the Labour government that had fought him in the courts knighted him in the 1978 Honours List. Sir Freddie was born.

The demand for Skytrain was such that travellers in the summer months found that they had to wait for days to get a seat. As Laker's base airport (Gatwick) was

not yet fully developed, this could be uncomfortable. The cramped conditions did not seem to put people off, however, as the prices were so low.

By 1980, Sir Freddie had a 17% market share on the London-New York route, plus 23% and 30% respectively on his new London-Miami and London-Los Angeles flights. This success led him to order ten Airbuses, with a view to using these European-built planes to break open the highly regulated, high fare European airline market. The purchase was financed by a £130 million loan (in

America, in dollars). The first Airbus was delivered in 1981, but no European government would agree to let him fly to their airports.

In the early 1980s, three factors affected the transatlantic airline business:

1 Whereas the initial impact of Skytrain had been to increase the number of people who wished to travel across the Atlantic, by 1980 an economic recession halted that growth in market size.

2 Having allowed Sir Freddie to break the cartel, the United States government then deregulated all air travel in 1978. This allowed many new, low fare U.S. airlines to start a London-New York service.

3 Between 1978 and 1980 the cost of fuel oil doubled in the wake of the supply shortages that accompanied the Iranian Revolution.

As a consequence of these factors, all the original four transatlantic carriers were trading unprofitably. Pan-Am, which had plunged into heavy losses, decided to fight back in the summer of 1981 by offering a stand-by ticket priced at just one pound above Skytrain's. The other three followed, so now Laker had competition that offered better comfort and a Heathrow base, for only one pound more. Laker cut prices further to try to restore its advantage, but the rivals followed Laker's prices down in a classic price war situation. This would damage the profits of all the carriers in the short term, but the major airlines knew that their revenue from First and Business classes would make it easier for them to survive than it would be for Laker.

Major Airlines – Fare Structure Winter 1981/2

Single	London–NY	London–LA
First Class	£917	£1268
Business Class	£315	£684
Economy	£124	£169
Stand-By	£90	£131
Laker Skytrain	**£89**	**£130**

Sir Freddie continued to make confident pronouncements about how loyal his customers were proving, but the increasing volume of traffic on the other airlines suggested differently. It was also significant that he introduced the option of booking reservations in advance, perhaps to assist cash flow. By the Autumn of 1981, rumours spread in the financial markets that Laker Airways was unable to meet the interest payments on its loans. As these leaked out, passengers became more reluctant to book onto Laker flights. By January 1982 it was public knowledge that the banks that had lent Laker £220 million were desperately looking for a solution.

On 3rd February, however, a beaming Sir Freddie announced that his cash crisis had been saved by £60 million of fresh loans. He said:

'I couldn't be more confident about the future.'

Within thirty-six hours, though, the banks had forced him to call in the Receiver to supervise the liquidation of the company's assets. Six thousand Laker passengers were stranded with worthless tickets as Laker aeroplanes leaving from Gatwick were recalled in mid-flight. At Gatwick, the British Airports Authority impounded a DC10 aircraft to cover the company's unpaid bills for landing and parking fees.

Journalists rushing to Companies House to look up Laker Airway's company accounts were shocked to find that despite the legal requirement that up-to-date accounts should be filed there for all limited companies, the most recent for Laker Airways was from March 1980. These showed just £23 million of shareholders funds, and that the firm was 90% owned by Sir Freddie and 10% owned by his (former) wife.

They also revealed that on March 31st 1980, Laker forecast that it must make forty-one million dollars of loan repayments and hire purchase instalments during the coming twelve months – a tall order for a firm that had never made an operating profit of more than £2.5 million (about $5 million) in a year. Appendix A shows a summary of Laker's five year financial record up to March 1980.

The Times reported that:

> *'Bankers said Laker's losses were running at £15 to £20 million a year. It owes banks £230 million, with a further £40 million owed to unsecured creditors. Assets were estimated at about £250 million*...*
> *...New figures showing worse than expected ticket sales, combined with disappointing forecasts for cash flow in the months ahead were the final straw. No-one could be confident that Laker would pay the bills...By any standards the company was extraordinarily highly geared...the banks showed a considerable lack of banking* **prudence.'**

* This proved a considerable over-estimate, as the second-hand value of aircraft during a recession can fall sharply.

On the day the collapse was announced, there was an extraordinary outburst of popular support for Sir Freddie. However, his announcement, just one week later, of the formation of a new People's Airline was very poorly received by a public that had assumed that he had been ruined personally. Newspapers contrasted the losses of his ticket-holders with his 1,000-acre farm in Surrey and 85-ton yacht. Yet Sir Freddie's earlier successes ensured that he kept the respect of many people.

Two years later, his work in breaking the transatlantic cartel was to receive praise from Richard Branson when setting up Virgin Atlantic.

Sources: *Companies House; The Financial Times; The Times.*

APPENDIX A: Summary of the Laker Airways Balance Sheets (1976–1980)

	£000s (as at March 31st)				
	1976	1977	1978	1979	1980
Fixed Assets	29,700	27,800	44,900	82,900	146,300
+ Net Current Assets	−1,100	−1,800	−1,800	−7,800	−11,700
= Assets Employed	28,600	26,000	43,100	75,100	134,600
Shareholders Funds	3,500	4,300	5,800	13,900*	23,200*
+ Loans and HP debts	25,100	21,700	37,300	61,200	111,400
= Capital Employed	28,600	26,000	43,100	75,100	134,600

* including £3.3 million of unrealised foreign currency gains in 1979; in 1980 this figure increased to £4.6 million (it proved an illusion as the value of the $ weakened in1981).

Questions

(60 marks; 100 minutes)

1   Explain the meaning of the following terms (emboldened in the text):

   diversify
   cartel
   prudence   (9)

2   When MPs discussed the liquidation in Parliament, some suggested that the blame lay primarily with state regulators and state subsidised airlines. What justification is there for this view?   (12)

3   Calculate Laker Airways approximate gearing level in 1981. What was the significance of this in the events of 1981-82?   (9)

4   From a marketing point of view, how had Laker left his firm vulnerable to a price war by 1981?   (10)

5   As things became difficult, Sir Freddie was reduced to making bold but misleading statements about his sales and cash flow. This was to keep confidence high. How can loss of confidence make a difficult cash flow position impossible?   (8)

6   Western governments used to feel that passenger transport should be regulated by strict government controls and inspections. During the late 1970s and 1980s the mood shifted in favour of deregulation. Discuss the main issues raised by the freeing of passenger transport from state intervention.   (12)

96 THE NEW DESIGN TEAM

Concepts needed: Restrictive practices, International competitiveness,
Contribution, Seasonal adjustment, Decision trees,
European Union

The Dralux Textile Company produces fabrics for curtains, furniture and clothing. Its origins lay in the mass production of plain materials such as the grey serge used for school uniforms. In recent years it has paid a lot more attention to design. A Design Director was appointed eighteen months ago, and given a £500,000 budget to spend on staff and equipment. He purchased a modern CAD (Computer Aided Design) system with four terminals, and then hired four top designers. The team spent three months talking to the firm's trade and retail customers, and getting to know the firm's manufacturing skills and facilities. Then work could begin in earnest.

After Board-level discussion, it had been decided that the first priority for the team would be to develop a range of new, top quality, top price curtains. The Directors believed this to be a growth market and that the **competition** was more **fragmented** in this market than in the others – especially in the upmarket sector that was to be targeted. Dralux charged an average factory-gate price of £3.50 per square metre for its curtains; the team was set the target of adding sufficient value to the product to justify a £6.50 price tag for the new products.

The team took two months to come up with new designs and a range of fabrics they liked. Certain modifications were needed to the production machinery to cope with the complex patterns, but it was possible to launch the new range in the second quarter of the current financial year. Trade buyers were delighted with the products, and market research showed that consumers agreed.

Yet sales were not as high as expected (see Appendix A). More worryingly, a large percentage of sales were substitutes for traditional Dralux lines. It emerged that the Directors had misread the market. Several of the rival brands were produced by the same Yorkshire company, which was operating a tough policy of full-line forcing (if retailers want to stock the manufacturer's top-selling line, they must also stock the rest of their range).

Although the Managing Director made plain her disappointment at the failure to meet the sales targets, the Design Director felt sure that the launch had been worthwhile:

> *'Even though quarterly sales for the new products were 20% below*
> *target, given that they make a contribution of £2.80 per square metre*
> *compared with £1.20 for the older lines, I'm sure we've still made*
> *money out of this. And the provisional figures for this quarter look*
> *set to be the best in the company's history'.*

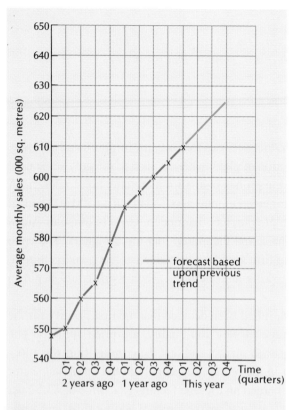

Times series graph showing four quarter moving average of Dralux curtain sales

[Graph y-axis: Average monthly sales (000 sq. metres), from 540 to 650. Legend: forecast based upon previous trend. X-axis: Time (quarters) Q1 Q2 Q3 Q4 for 2 years ago, 1 year ago, This year.]

While the arguments about the success or otherwise of the curtains project continued, a more important matter had to be settled at the November Board meeting. Due to the liquidation of a competitor, sales of clothing linings had been surging ahead. So the Directors had to decide whether to buy the site next door to their linings factory, and expand capacity by fifty per cent. At present it is working at 95% of full capacity (400,000 units), which leaves insufficient margin for error or breakdown.

The linings sell for £6.00 per unit (10 square metres), variable costs are £4.00 per unit and fixed costs are £400,000 per annum. The site next door would cost £500,000 for a five year lease; luckily it is available for immediate use. Extra overhead staff would add a further £100,000 per year to fixed costs.

If Dralux proceeds, research has shown that there is a 0.4 chance that – on average – **capacity utilisation** will be 90% of the new total over the 5 years. Also forecast are a 0.3 chance of 80% utilization and a 0.3 chance of 70% utilisation.

One other matter was down on the agenda for the November meeting. The Company Secretary wanted the Board to agree a policy regarding the European Union's proposal to change the trade restrictions governing international trade in textiles. The E.U. Parliament was conducting a consultation exercise among firms affected, and it seemed sensible for Dralux to take its chance to influence the new legislation.

In the past, European countries had worked within a world-wide agreement on tariffs and trade, which allowed for the use of important quotas on certain types of materials or clothing. This had generally been used by the developed countries to limit the amount of 'cheap labour' imports coming in from the Third World. Now there was a move to prevent this kind of discrimination, on the grounds that poorer countries would never catch the rich ones up if they were prevented from exporting the goods they could produce competitively.

The new rules would also aim to remove the different national rules governing labelling, fire-resistance, and other **non-tariff barriers** to trade within the E.U. The new Europe-wide rules were supposed to be in place by 1992, but no one in the industry had ever believed the complex issues would be sorted out by then.

The Finance Director put a strong case forward that Dralux should press for the retention of import quotas on products such as linings, 'in order to protect the five hundred jobs we provide in Rochdale'. The Production Director was insistent that German moves to force all curtain fabrics to be treated with fire-resistant coatings were a way of stealing a competitive advantage: 'They've got the technology to do it easily, whereas it would cost us a fortune in new equipment'. Only the Design Director seemed optimistic about the changes. He suggested that Dralux should accept that:

> *'The new law will probably look after consumer interests rather than ours, so I think we should just accept that we must make sure that our **products** are sufficiently well-**differentiated** to let us keep our prices up, whatever the competition. That way we can pay for any new machinery we need.'*

APPENDIX A: Dralux Curtain Sales

| | (in thousand square metres) | | | |
	1st quarter	2nd quarter	3rd quarter	4th quarter
3 years ago	480	570	450	690
2 years ago	490	610	470	740
1 year ago	540	630	490	760
Current year	560	660	550	810*
(of which, new lines)	–	(80)	(120)	(160)

* Provisional

Questions

(100 marks; 2.5 hours)

1 Explain the meaning of the following terms (emboldened in the text):

    fragmented competition
    capacity utilization
    non-tariff barriers
    product differentiation   **(12)**

2 Why might a firm avoid entering a market where the practice of full-line forcing is being carried out? Should such practices be of concern to consumers?   **(10)**

3 Few firms have a Design Director on the Board. Discuss the wisdom of this, especially for firms operating in internationally competitive markets.   **(12)**

4 To help settle the debate about the success of the new curtain products, it is necessary to calculate their impact upon total sales and contribution.
   With that in mind:

    a Calculate the seasonal adjustment factors for the 2nd, 3rd and 4th quarter (show workings).   **(8)**

    b Apply those factors to the extrapolated figures shown on the graph, in order to forecast what sales would have been like if the new designs had not been launched.   **(8)**

    c Calculate the effect of the launch on contribution over the nine months available so far.   **(12)**

5 **a** Draw a decision tree of the issue of whether or not to acquire the site next to the linings factory.   **(6)**

    b Calculate the effect of the decision on profits over the next five years. Then indicate the expected values on your carefully labelled diagram. Indicate and state your decision on numerate grounds alone.   **(12)**

    c Explain any factors that might lead you to feel uncertain about your decision.   **(10)**

6 If you were the Managing Director, what conclusions would you draw from the discussion about the European Union rule changes? Outline the policy you would press your fellow directors to agree.   **(10)**

A GENERAL APPROACH TO ASSESSED CASE STUDIES

People tend to offer different advice on the ways in which assessed cases should be tackled, and the style which may suit one individual may not be right for another.

Assessed case studies take two forms: the unseen and the pre-issued. The two types require somewhat different techniques, although in the examination hall the pressures will be very similar, and the pitfalls equally dangerous.

The unseen case study

The AEB's Paper 2 is a good example of the unseen case.

Read the rubric on the cover page carefully. Very few candidates do this, but there might be special instructions which you must follow. Then, on turning over the exam paper:

1 Read the case quickly, just to get the general 'feel' of the organisation, its personnel and its problems.

2 Examine the questions quite thoroughly. It is possible that they might be connected, and one might have an impact on another. In the Cambridge 9730 examination the questions are printed before the case study itself, as a way of encouraging candidates to read them first.

3 Re-read the case, this time more carefully, perhaps highlighting points which relate to the questions, or marking '1', '2', '3', '4' etc in the margin, depending on which part is relevant to which question.

4 Answer the questions in turn, relying on the mark allocation as an indicator of how much time to spend on each.

5 Remember the skills which are being examined (see page 11), and put them into practice. Try to get into the shoes of the people about whom the case is written. For instance their age, background and experience may be relevant to the way they react to circumstances and the prevailing business environment. Use the material in the case as evidence to support points of analysis and evaluation, and don't be afraid to use theoretical concepts where they are appropriate.

The pre-issued case study

The Cambridge Double Module examination is an example of this type.

1 Use the case as a base for revision. This means identifying overall topic areas for study up to the examination. It does not mean trying to identify specific questions.

2 Make certain you know the meaning of everything in the case. Particularly if English is not your first language, there may be a word or phrase which has a subtle meaning that you are unaware of. The examiners will be conscious of such difficulties, but it is impossible to predict them all. Don't be afraid to ask for help.

3 Technical terms will often form a basis for questions in the examination itself. It is important not only to be able to understand their textbook definitions, but also to be able to explain them within the context of the case study, where their meaning might be subtly altered.

4 Question spotting is particularly attractive in numerate areas, partly because it appears to be easier to see what the examiner is going to test, and partly because many candidates are uneasy about handling numerical data, and therefore want an insurance policy! In fact it is just as dangerous to attempt to anticipate a numerical question as it is any other. The examiner will be well aware that the material will be seen well in advance, and so he or she will change things, or perhaps add more numbers in the questions so that rehearsed answers do not receive a disproportionate reward.

5 When it comes to the examination itself, the precise wording of the questions must be very carefully watched, because it is almost certain that during the weeks beforehand the main areas of the syllabus to be tested will have been correctly identified. It will therefore be a great temptation to regurgitate answers to rehearsed questions rather than the ones which actually appear on the paper. Otherwise, the techniques which have already been outlined for handling the case study in the exam room apply whether it is preissued or not.

An example of an assessed case study

In June 1993 the AEB set the following case in Section A of Paper 2 of their Advanced level Business Studies examination. A copy of both the paper and the mark scheme can be obtained from the AEB's offices in Guildford, Surrey.

STABLE FINANCE

In some ways the problems had started with the milk quotas imposed by the European Community in 1987 to prevent the over supply of milk, but William Provender reckoned the quotas were simply the final straw. In his opinion the difficulties had started much earlier – on the death of his father in 1979 – when he and his brother Benjamin had inherited the 120 acre Home Farm. William and Benjamin had disagreed about the way to run it almost from the first moment. William was keen to continue the family tradition in farming, but Benjamin was far more interested and increasingly involved with the antiques trade. The land at Home Farm was used to produce arable crops, although the soil was really too wet to guarantee acceptable levels of profit. Indeed from 1980 onwards profits steadily declined. This was partly due to geographical factors, but it was also a result of the different personalities of William and Benjamin.

William and Benjamin Provender

Although the two brothers got on well enough, their different interests meant that making decisions about the future of Home Farm was both difficult and extremely lengthy. William wanted to move into dairy farming, which was highly profitable given the price support then on offer from the European Community, and which in any case suited the farm's geography. Benjamin, on the other hand, argued for staying with arable production, which they both knew and understood. Any change would only delay his desire to move into the antiques business full-time. In the end, however, the declining profitability of arable production, and the attractiveness of the dairy option persuaded Benjamin that it was the right move. Unfortunately the delay in making the decision had a profound effect.

Dairy farming

The change-over involved the construction of a calving shed and a milking parlour. This was completed by 1987, but it required a considerable outlay, resulting in a shortage of capital to purchase a dairy herd. Consequently the farm was not producing milk at a critical moment; the time when the EC decided to limit milk production by the introduction of quotas. The new system meant that each farm was allowed to produce a certain amount of milk – its quota – based on existing levels of production. Zero output, as in the Provender's case meant no quota, and although it was possible to buy a quota from another farmer who did not need it, this was very expensive and therefore prohibitive to the Provenders..

The Crisis of 1993

Having missed the chance of a milk quota, the brothers continued to farm as before, but profitability went into serious decline, and the long term view for arable farming looked bleak as the European Community continued its reform of the Common Agricultural Policy. Added to this was the brothers' quite different approaches to farming. By 1993 it was necessary to look at alternatives.

Plans for the future

William and Benjamin decided that there were three practical alternatives which they should investigate:

Project 1   Keep Home Farm, but convert it to organic production;
Project 2   Change the farm into a small working unit using animals which would have been kept on an English farm in the past, and open it to paying visitors;
Project 3   Develop the farm into a livery and riding stable.

Project 1: Keep Home Farm, but convert it to organic production.

The advantage of going organic was the price premium which could be earned on the farm's output. In order to qualify, however, the farm would need to use no artificial fertilizers on the fields for three years. During that time output would fall, and prices would remain low as at present. Given the small scale of the farm there was some doubt that it would be able to sustain both brothers even when the price premium was earned. In any event there was no guarantee that the premium would last indefinitely. There might also be the possibility of a 'set-aside' payment which the European Community was making to farmers who did not use all their land for production, but again such a payment could not be guaranteed.

Project 2: Change the farm into a small working unit using animals which would have been kept on an English farm in the past, and open it to paying visitors.

This option attracted both brothers. William could continue to run the farm at present, while introducing new breeds for tourists to enjoy. The visitors would in effect subsidise the farm's output so that it would not have to be so efficient in terms of output as it would otherwise have to be. Benjamin liked the idea because he felt he could use his knowledge of the antiques trade to acquire old farming implements. There were, however, marketing considerations; the reaction of neighbours, especially to the increased traffic and the problems of parking; and there would have to be alterations made to the farm's outbuildings.

Project 3: Develop the farm into a livery and riding stable.

The farm's location, within an hour of London, made it an ideal spot for well-off commuters. The countryside was pretty, and many people kept horses or ponies. Consequently a large and ever growing number of farms in the area had turned over to livery stables. These stables looked after the animals for the owners for a set fee each week. As an extension of the livery, many also offered riding, either in the form of lessons and/or 'hacks' – rides into the countryside.

The brothers were not that knowledgeable about horses, but they knew Lucy Girth, who was. Lucy had recently been forced to leave another local stable and was looking for work. Stable lads would also be needed, but there were opportunities to employ them at very cheap rates under government training schemes. There would have to be a considerable capital outlay for the horses and ponies, and for the provision of loose boxes. In addition the fields would require new fencing to reduce their size. There were marketing implications as well, although at present demand appeared to outstrip supply.

Financial information:

	Project 1	Project 2	Project 3
Capital outlay	£37,000	£40,000	£106,000
Net Cash Flow			
Year 1	£8,000	£22,000	£59,000
Year 2	£8,000	£22,000	£59,000
Year 3	£8,000	£22,000	£59,000
Year 4	£12,000	£22,000	£59,000
Year 5	£12,000	£22,000	£59.000

Both brothers realised that changes had to be made, but they feared that as well as their current information being imperfect, their predictions for the future were also fraught with uncertainties. The days of the gentleman farmer were well and truly over …

a   Explain why, in supermarkets, organic produce costs more than non-organic produce.

(6 marks)

b   Apart from financial considerations, what factors would the brothers have to take into account if they chose Project 3? *(12 marks)*

c   i   What is the net present value for Project 2 at a discount rate of 10%   *(5 marks)*

Discount values (Net Present Value of £1)

Year	10%
1	0.9091
2	0.8264
3	0.7513
4	0.6830
5	0.6209

ii   Study the following diagram:

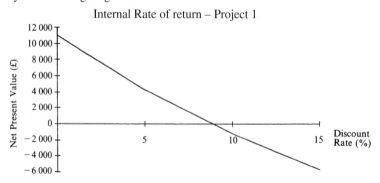

Internal Rate of return – Project 1

What do you understand by the term 'internal rate of return'?   *(3 marks)*

iii   What does the curve in ii tell you about Project 1?   *(3 marks)*

iv   Assuming the projects return a positive cash flow equally throughout the year, apply the pay back method to all three projects, and on these calculations decide which is the best.   *(4 marks)*

v   Identify one advantage and one disadvantage of the pay back method.   *(2 marks)*

vi   Name one other method of investment appraisal apart from pay back, discounted cash flow and internal rate of return.   *(1 mark)*

d   Explain the impact of good motivation on organisations. Use examples from the case study wherever appropriate to illustrate your answer.   *(14 marks)*

Question (a) Explain why, in supermarkets, organic produce costs more than non-organic produce. (6 marks)

The mark scheme for question (a) (i)

As a candidate it is important to identify the way the examiner will be awarding marks. It may be on the basis of levels – that is to say the skills which were outlined on page 11, or it may be on the basis of points made, with some explanation.

In the case of this particular example the notion of cost in a supermarket obviously refers to the price. Price is determined by the interaction of demand and supply, and so it is fairly straightforward to see that two marks would be available for identifying and explaining demand conditions, two for supply conditions, and two for bringing them together.

In the example of a student's work which follows there are errors of English spelling and grammar which have deliberately not been corrected.

A student's response

Organic produce are more expensive in shops because the farmers don't use artificial fertilizers therefore the crops are smaller in size and they have to sell a lot more to compensate for loss of profits. Also in the supermarkets you are paying for the luxury of the goods. Because peoples habits have changed – healthier living is now the trend – not everyone can change and conform to these needs. So the organic farmers can charge higher prices so in fact the consumers are paying for the convenience of the service. They also know that not everybody can afford to have a vegetable garden and produce organic food, because of lack of space and time

Organic food cost more than non-organic, because they know when everyone starts producing organic produce the smaller farms are going to lose out, because the bigger farms are going to produce more and take away their profits. The answer opens with a simple comment about supply.

Examiner's comment

The answer opens with a simple comment about supply.
Very quickly the candidate moves into demand, talking about the 'luxury' of these goods.
The aspects of demand are well developed.

At this point there is an attempt to return to supply again, which just about justifies the second supply mark.

The final mark

The obvious shortcoming to this response was the inability of the candidate to pull demand and supply conditions together. Four marks would be awarded for getting the demand and supply elements correct.

A second student's response

Organic produce costs more than non-organic produce because of the extra difficulty of growing the produce to the same standard as non-organic without the use of any man-made chemicals. The production of organic produce uses the theory of product differentiation in order for a higher price to be charged. Product differentiation is when a company makes its product have a unique selling point from the competitors products and therefore consumers who wish to make full advantage of this unique selling point have to pay more.

As I first stated organic products are more difficult to grow and the more work that you put into the production the more value is added to the product.

Consider the mark you would award, then turn to page 300 for the actual mark.

Question (b) Apart from financial considerations, what factors would the brothers have to take into account if they chose Project 3? (12 marks)

The mark scheme for question (b)

Unlike the first question, the high number of marks available suggests that this part will be marked on the skills displayed. As the number or complexity of the skills increases, so more marks can be awarded. In this example we might have:

Skill level 1
If the candidate has simply identified one or more factors, up to four marks would be available.

Skill level 2
This level would go further than simple identification, and would credit explanation of relevant factors. A further four marks would be on offer if this level was reached.

Skill level 3
At this stage the candidate will give a detailed explanation. The distinction between a simple explanation and a detailed one is perhaps a fine one, and so it is well worth teasing out all the possible aspects in order to ensure moving to the highest possible level.

When using this type of mark scheme, it should be remembered that once a particular skill level has been reached it is not possible to fall back, as it were, to a lower one. So in this case, once a candidate has offered any explanation beyond simple identification he or she automatically moves to skill level 2, and it is assumed that the skills in level 1 have been demonstrated. As a result, reaching level 2 will earn a minimum of five marks – four for level one, plus one for level 2. Indeed, once an answer has moved into the higher level it is assumed that the middle of that next level will usually be reached, and so a level 2 response will probably be awarded six or seven marks. Such is the premium placed on skills displayed as opposed to simple fact regurgitation.

In this particular question it is important to note that the words 'Apart from financial considerations' are used, so the possible responses would include: the market conditions, the state of the economy, market research, government training plans, the personal plans of the two brothers, and so on. Any points relating to aspects of costs would be considered irrelevant.

A student's response

Other factors that the brothers have to take into account are the competitors. As it states in the case-study that a large and growing number of farms in the area are being turned into livery stables. So it seems that the market idea is becoming saturated and the brothers profits or expected profits shall be even lower.

Also at the moment stable lads are cheap and easy to come by, what would happen if pressure groups saw this as a form of discrimination and requested the law to change. This would mean that stable boys would be able to choose where they want to work and the brothers would be in another tight spot. Also Lucy might go and work where the pay is better.

Also the brothers have a limited knowledge of horses. They would have to hire someone who could be trusted and had quite a vast knowledge of horses and stables and riding lessons.

Also the location of the farm. Only well-off commuters could get there so from the start they are limiting themselves to rich people. Some rich people aren't prepared to travel that distance just to take their children riding. And most well-off people have country homes which are near stables anyway and are unlikely to change.

There would need to fence the horses in. The size of the area would have to be to a certain standard or else they would lose consumers.

The present demand appeared to outstrip the supply. By the time the brothers set up and find employees the demand might have decreased. The brothers would be in the same position as they were in the beginning.

Examiner's comment

The candidate has made a valid point about competition and is therefore into level 1 It has not been explained sufficiently to move into level 2 at this point. This is a slightly outrageous assumption. Can the law really be changed this easily? Probably not. However, there is some explanation here, so level 2 is reached. This paragraph is valid and adds to the level to of explanation.

This paragraph appears to suggest some strange thinking about commuters, but there is a glimmer of value on the point about not changing.

The final paragraph does add a little, although it is not expressed at all well.

The final mark

Although it was a pretty woolly response, it clearly got into level 2. Placing it at a particular point within that level is where the skill of the examiner comes in. In this case it was better than average, but by no means outstanding, and so seven marks would be appropriate.

A second student's response

If the brothers opted to choose option three they would have had to consider a number of non-financial factors, in my opinion these would've been:-

i   Although the brothers would both own and control the livery and stables due to their lack of knowledge concerning horses they would have to give whoever became the manager of the stables the majority of power in how the business was going to be run in order for them to have any chance of success. If the brothers were unwilling to do this their chances of being successful would be minimal and they would most likely end up losing everything.

ii What are the firms long term objectives? If the brothers want the firm to run at a reasonable profit which would enable them to survive comfortably then they could quite easily have choosen option 1 or 2 but by choosing number three it seems quite clear that the brothers are interested in long term growth.

Question (c) (i) What is the net present value for Project 2 at a discount rate of 10%? (5 marks)

Discount values [net present value of £1]

YEAR	10%
1	0.9091
2	0.8264
3	0.7513
4	0.6830
5	0.6209

The mark scheme for question (c) (i)

This is essentially a calculation question, and so if the final number is correct, five marks would automatically be awarded. But if is not, then one mark would be available for any single line which is; two marks if the lines are correct, but they are not totalled, and three marks for a figure of £83,396. If that number is arrived at then the candidate has obviously forgotten to deduct the initial cash outflow. The correct calculation is as follows:

Cash outflow	£40,000	1 mark

Net cash inflow
Year 1   £22,000 × 0.9091 = £20,000
Year 2   £22,000 × 0.8264 = £18,181
Year 3   £22,000 × 0.7513 = £16,529
Year 4   £22,000 × 0.6830 = £15,026
Year 5   £22,000 × 0.6209 = £13,660

Present Value of Inflows   = **£83,396**

A student's response

22000 × 0.9019 = 20000.2   Year 1
22000 × 0.8264 = 18180.8   Year 2
22000 × 0.7513 = 16528.6   Year 3
22000 × 0.6830 = 15026   Year 4
22000 × 0.6209 = 13659   Year 5

83395.4
(−)40000.0
43395.4

Examiner's comment

This answer is perfect and therefore scores the five marks. It is clearly laid out so that even if the final total was wrong, marks could still have been awarded for the correct process.

A second student's response

	cash out (£)	Net cash (£)	Discount factor	NPV (£)
Now	40,000		1	
Year 1	Unknown	22,000	0.9091	20,000.20
Year 2	"	22,000	0.8264	18,180.80
Year 3	"	22,000	0.7513	16,528.60
Year 4	"	22,000	0.6830	15,026.00
Year 5	"	22,000	0.6209	13,659.80

Net Present value = 20,000.20 + 18,180 + 16,528.60 + 15,026,00 + 13,659.80 − 40,000
= **43,395.40**

Question (c) (ii) Study the following diagram:

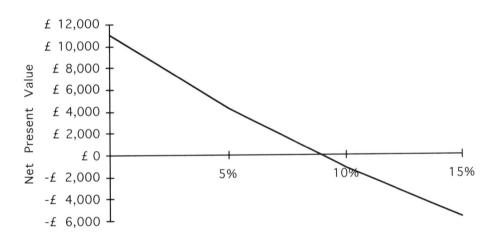

Internal rate of Return - Project One

What do you understand by the term 'internal rate of return'? (3 marks)

The mark scheme for question (c) (ii)

Internal rate of return is the discount rate which, when applied to a project's projected flows, will yield a net present value of zero. This rate is then compared to the company's 'criterion rate' (i.e. the rate the company sets for all similar projects) to see if it is worthwhile.

Although there are three marks available, which might suggest marking on the basis of 'points', it is often the case when an explanation is required that the examiners will reward answers on the basis of how effective it is. In this case someone who displays a simplistic notion of the concept or can give a limited description of the diagram will get one mark, a good notion of the theory or an accurate analysis of the diagram would get two marks; and three marks would be available for someone who offers a clear analysis which might be illustrated with figures from the diagram itself.

A student's response

The internal rate of return refers to the amount of profit that would be received. This means how much profit the brothers would make after the convertion to inorganic produce in relation to how much profit they are making now.

Examiner's comment

Quite clearly the candidate has no idea of what internal rate of return is. It is slightly surprising that the diagram itself does not provide more of a clue to the correct answer. As it stands, however, this response would not attract any marks.

A second student's response

The internal rate of return is an accounting calculation which is made to show what percentage of the initial sum of invested is made as a profit for a average year through which the investment operates

$$\text{I.r.r.} = \frac{\text{average annual profit}}{\text{sum invested}} \times 100$$

I.r.r. is used to measure the profitability of a single investment is similar to return on capital employed but it consider one investment whereas return on capital considers the firms totall performance.

Question (c) (iii) What does the curve in (ii) tell you about Project 1? (3 marks)

The mark scheme for question (c) (iii)

This question will be marked on the basis of points identified from the diagram. The ones which could be used are:

1   That if the discount rate is zero the NPV would be £11K
2   That the discount rate that yields a NPV of £0 is about 8%
3   That any discount rate >8% yields a negative NPV
4   A simplistic statement would be to the effect that as interest/discount rates rise, the NPV falls
5   At 10% Project 1 has a lower NPV than Project 2.

A student's response

The discount rate of return in relation to the net present value would be 9% at £0. So as the discount rate increases the net present value decreases. So the curve shows that Project one is not a very good scheme to invest in.

Examiner's comment

Given that the candidate's response to part (i) was so weak, this is quite a good attempt. It does show that by keeping calm and describing what can be seen, some marks will always be available. In this case only one mark for the '9% at £0' observation.

A second student's response

The curve tells me that their is a strong relationship between the discount rate and the Net present value of project 1. As the discount rate shows how the value of the pound decreases with time it would be reasonably accurate to say that as time passes by project 1 will become less and less profitable.

Question (c) (iv) Assuming the projects return a positive cash flow equally throughout the year, apply the pay back method to all three projects, and on these calculations decide which is the best. (4 marks)

The mark scheme for question (c) (iv)

Once again this is a straightforward calculation, although the decision as to which one is 'best' could be based on wider factors such as the initial cash outlay or a higher final return. The slight difficulty with the question is that two of the projects pay back in the same year, and so fractions of years are required to make the answer precise. Of course any candidates who said that such predictions could never be that accurate would attract full marks because they would be displaying solid Business Studies knowledge applied to a calculation. The numbers themselves are as follows:

Project 1 – in year 5 (January)   – 1 mark
Project 2 – in year 2 – 0.81 = 9.72 months (21 October) – 1 mark
Project 3 – in year 2 – 0.79 = 9.48 months (14 October) – 1 mark for calculation+
                                        1 for identifying 'best'.

A student's response

Project 1
Cost = Returns = no of years
£37000 £8K+£8K+£8K+£12K = £36000
Therefore pay back period for project 1 would be <u>4 years 4 months</u>.

Project 2
cost £40000

Therefore payback period <u>1 year 5 months</u>

  46000
  <u>22000</u>
   8000

Project 3
cost 106000

Therefore payback = <u>1 year 2.5 months</u>

 106000
 <u>59000</u>
 47000

So on these calculations project 2 would be best.

Examiner's comment

From the very start it is clear that the candidate has little idea of how to carry out the calculation. It is surprisingly frequent for the word 'therefore' to appear when there is no justification for it within the answer itself.

Note that there are calculations dotted around with no explanation. It is vital for all numerical work to be clearly explained so that credit can be given wherever possible.

The final mark

The candidate did identify the 'best' year based on the figures which had been calculated. This would earn one mark. The exact calculations were wrong, although the year was correct in each case. Given the right year the examiner would probably award one mark for that, giving an overall score of two.

A second student's response

Option 1

initial investment = £37,000

contribution up to end of year 4 = (£8000 x 3) + (£12,000) = £36,000

monthly contribution in year 5 = $\dfrac{£12,000}{12}$ = £1,000 per month

outstanding investment cost at the end of year 4 = £37,000 – £36,000 = £1,000
monthly contribution in year 5 = £1000
∴ payback is <u>4 years and one month</u>

Option 2

initial investment = £40,000

contribution up to end of year 1 = £22,000

monthly contribution in year 2 = $\dfrac{£22,000}{12}$ = £1833.33

outstanding investment cost at end of year 1 = £40,000 – £22,000 = £18.000

months taken to payback in year 2 = $\dfrac{\text{outstanding investment}}{\text{monthly contribution}} = \dfrac{£18,000}{£1833.33}$ = 9.8181

∴ payback is in one year and nine point eight month or <u>approximately one year 10 months</u>

Option 3

initial investment = £106,000 contribution up to end year 1 = £59.000

contribution per month in year 2 = $\dfrac{£59000}{12}$ = £4916.67 per month

outstanding investment at end of year 1 = £106,000 – £59.000 = 47,000 pounds

months taken to payback in year 2 = $\dfrac{£47,000}{4916.67}$ = 9.559

∴ payback is in one year a 9.6 months (<u>or one year 10 months approx</u>)
Option three has the best payback although it is only slightly better than option two's.

Question (c) (v) Identify one advantage and one disadvantage of the payback method (2 marks)

This is very straightforward: there will be one mark for each. Given only one mark, it is important that only one marksworth of time is allocated to the answer! Possible points include the following advantages: simplicity, ease of calculation and easily understood, and disadvantages include that it ignores the time value of money and the cash flow after pay-back.

A student's response

The advantage of this method is that you can see (after how many years) the scheme would have paid for the initial outlay. This allows the decision maker to chose a scheme that suits him best and is the better of the ideas.

A disadvantage of this scheme is that it does not take into account that the machine might become obsolete and need to be updated before it has even paid for itself.

Examiner's comment

The first paragraph outlining the advantages appears to make no sense at all, other than simply to describe the obvious. The disadvantage is better, although put in rather simplistic terms. Both the advantage and the disadvantage are rather too fully expressed for the number of marks available.

The final mark

One mark would be awarded for the disadvantage.

A second student's response

Payback's advantage is that it shows how soon a firms initial investment outlay will be recouped. But a disadvantage is that payback doesn't consider the investments profitability after 'payback' has been achieved.

Question (c) (vi) Name one other method of investment appraisal apart from payback (1 mark)

The mark scheme for question (c) (vi)

A single mark is on offer for identifying one of: average rate of return, annual rate of return, cost benefit analysis, accounting rate of return or simply writing 'ARR'.

A student's response

Average rate of return

Examiner's comment

This is clearly correct, and therefore gets the mark. Note that the answer does not have to be 'dressed up' in any way for the mark to be awarded.

A second student's response

Cost benefit analysis

Question (d) Explain the impact of good motivation on organisations. Use examples from the case study wherever appropriate to illustrate your answer. (14 marks)

The mark scheme for question (d)

As usual the last question on the case study moves from the particular to the general. The case material offers examples of how *one* business organisation operates and the question asks the extent to which this demonstrates how *all* businesses work.

It is important that any answer contains evidence from the case, but also material drawn from theory. Very often it is the theory which provides a structure around which the answer can be written. In other words if the theoretical concepts are quoted first, then examples from the case can be more effectively used to illustrate them.

So in this example good motivation speeds up and improves decision making throughout any organisation and engenders an enthusiasm for the firm and any project which is current at the time. It makes people more willing to co-operate and accept positive criticism. It also leads to higher profitability because there is greater output at lower unit costs, fewer industrial disputes, and good industrial relations. This in turn leads to easier recruitment and less need for inspection, fewer returns and lower guarantee claims.

Within this theoretical framework, the case offers some illustrations. For instance, Bill was keen on farming, while Ben was not. This resulted in slow decision making on the milk quota and thus a loss of profits. Furthermore the decision on milk was also affected by the brothers' knowledge of existing processes and an unwillingness to change. Ben's interest in antiques affected things as well. It certainly delayed the changes, but also it made Project 2 far more attractive.

As far as the actual marking is concerned, this will be carried out on the basis of skill levels. As usual the lowest level will be simplistic, and will probably do no more than lift extracts from the case or will relate basic theory. Such an answer will get between one and five marks. The next level will combine theory and practice, but again not very convincingly, and will earn between six and eight marks. To get between nine and eleven marks the answer will have to be considerably more detailed, and will display careful thought which lifts it above the ordinary. Finally, to earn between twelve and fourteen marks the response will question some of the assumptions made, such as the connection between good motivation, good decision making and high profits.

A student's response

The brothers were both motivation, only when it came to their decisions. When William had finally been able to persuade Benjamin it was too late. The government dealt out milk quotas on existing levels, they were therefore given no quotas. If the conversion occurred earlier on they might have been given a quota. This shows the impact of bad motivation on an organisation.

Good motivation on the organisation seemed only to be achieved before 1979, when their father was still alive. This resulted in the farm doing alright. Therefore it can be seen that good motivation in an organisation will have a good effect on the business.

After the 1993 crisis the brothers were motivated and determined to get themselves out of

Examiner's comment

The answer starts very poorly. It does not even make any sense in terms of the English used. It then goes on simply to repeat what is already stated in the case. Nevertheless it has moved into level 1. The second paragraph is using evidence from the case to support the argument, although the evidence is certainly somewhat superficial. It is still clearly level 1 The candidate makes this situation so by deciding to look at the projects 1, 2 and 3 they were able to see their situation. On reaching a decision they could then make a new decision and thus both parties would be motivated.

Therefore being motivated the profits would be high as can be seen in the case study the profits were low which means that the brothers weren't equally motivated.

Although there are differences in ideas they could have compromised and tried to sort out the problem from the start because by the end they have lost large amounts of potential profits.

So good motivation in an organisation leads to large profit margins, good objectives and good consumer relations.

So overall project two would have been a good project to take on because both seem to like it and could be motivated in the scheme.

some amazing assumptions about profitability and motivation. The standard of English remains poor, which makes it difficult to work out exactly which points are being made. The remainder of the answer follows the same line of argument, and ends with a reference back to project number 2, which seems to come out of the blue.

The final mark

This really was a very poor answer. The only way in which it scored at all was in its description of the case study material. It did not involve any theory, despite that being quite clearly part of the question. The answer did not raise itself out of level 1, and would be worth only four marks.

A second student's response

Motivation of the workforce can be the making or breaking of an organisation. Motivation describes the willingness to work and general attitude with with a member of staff will go about their duties. According to theorists such as Herzberg, Maslow and MacGregor each individual has different motivational requirements and they can be demotivated more easily than motivated.

According to Herzberg and Maslow staff will perform much better if the enjoy and have an interest in the work that they are doing, if we consider the case in the text this idea is supported as the text says "...This option attracted both brothers. William could continue to run the farm...Benjamin...could use his knowledge of...antiques" so when the brothers were going to be involved in tasks which interested them they were more than happy to put in more work and effort. If we contrast this with an example in the text where both brothers were demotivated due to an unsavoury working atmosphere you can see how a business can suffer the adverse effects caused by demotivation, I cite "...from 1980 profits steadily declined...it was...a result of the different personalities of William and Benjamin'

When we look at the uses of motivational theory in large organisations it is obvious that the Japanese owned institutions are light years ahead of most British firms, maybe this is why we also 'lag' behind in terms of productivity and management worker relations. Japanese companies use motivation of their foundations in an attempt to build a successful company whereas British firms use motivation as an extra. A highly motivated workforce can transform a run of the mill company into a market leader. If the staff want to work hard as the have pride (and enjoy) in their job then they will try their best at it, this will result not only in them being quicker but producing better quality products which can be sold at a higher price than previous models.

As well as improved quality and productivity you can also instill a sense of totall commitment to your company in a highly motivated worker as he or she will want to do well for themselves and the company and do whatever the can to enhance the firms reputation.

Motivating a workforce is a skill that managers should have but many don't when you consider the difference between your company being internationally competitive or fighting for survival then maybe it is worth investing in.

Marks for second student's examples

Question (a)

One supply point and one demand point are made. Thus two marks can be given.

Question (b)

It is clear that the candidate intended to come back to this Question but never had time, or simply didn't get around to it. In any event it was very superficial and did not get beyond level one. Two marks.

Question (c) (i)

This is a wholly correct answer, and therefore worth five marks.

Question (c) (ii)

No marks. There is nothing of relevance here.

Question (c) (iii)

It is possible to identify a point of description worthy of one mark, although the notion of profitability is slightly worrying when talking about investment appraisal.

Question (c) (iv)

This is an excellent answer worthy of the full four marks.

Question (c) (v)

The advantage is credit-worthy, but not the disadvantage, and so it is worth one mark only.

Question (c) (vi)

This is correct. One mark.

Question (d)

Certainly there is a theoretical structure within this response, and a sound attempt to relate theory to the material in the case. From the marking point of view it is really a question of deciding whether it falls within level 2 or 3. It is probably at the top end of level 2 and would be awarded eight marks.

SOURCES OF INFORMATION FOR BUSINESS ASSIGNMENTS

Name, Address and Telephone Number	Type of information
Advertising, Institute of Practitioners in 44 Belgrave Square London SW1X 8QS Tel. 0171 235 7020	Good library on advertising; hold reports on measuring advertising effectiveness
Advertising Standards Authority (ASA), Brook House, 2/16 Torrington Place London WC1E 7HN Tel. 0171 580 5555	The role of the ASA in policing advertising standards
Advisory, Conciliation and Arbitration Service (ACAS) Library and Information Service, Room 111 27 Wilton Street London SW1X 7AZ Tel. 0171 210 3613	Human resources, especially legal requirements, redress and employee relations
Banking Information Service 10 Lombard Street London EC3V 9AP Tel. 0171 626 8486	Helpful on business plans and preparing requests for loans
British Franchise Association Thames View, Newtown Road Henley-on-Thames Oxon RG9 1HG Tel. 01491 578049	Useful contact for recent case studies of new business start-up
British Standards Institution 2 Park Street London W1A 2BS Tel. 0171 629 9000	Information on BSI Kitemark, BS 5750 and BS 7750 (environmental assurance)
Central Office of Information Hercules Road London SE1 7DU Tel. 0171 928 2345	Facts on government policies and advertising
Central Statistical Office (CSO) HMSO Publications Centre 51 Nine Elms Lane London SW8 5DR Telephone enquiries: 0171 873 0011 (24 hours) Telephone orders: 0171 873 9090 (24 hours)	Government statistical publications such as the Annual Abstract of Statistics and Social Trends

Name, Address and Telephone Number	Type of information
Chambers of Commerce, Association of British 9 Tufton Street London SW1P 3QB Tel. 0171 222 1555	For address of your local Chamber of Commerce
City Business Library 1 Brewers Hall Garden London EC2V 5BX Tel. 0171 638 8215	Excellent secondary material on markets and economic data
Commission for Racial Equality Elliot House 10-12 Allington Street London SW1E 5EH Tel. 0171 828 7022	Legal requirements and obligations to employees
Companies House 55-71 City Road London EC1Y 1BB Tel. 0171 253 9393	Annual accounts of all limited companies available publicly
Companies House Crown Way, Maindy Cardiff CF4 3UZ Tel. 01222 388588	Annual accounts of all limited companies available publicly
Confederation of British Industry (CBI) Centrepoint, 103 New Oxford Street London WC1A 1DU Tel. 0171 379 7400	Data on business performance nationally
Consumers' Association 2 Marylebone Road London NW1 4DF Tel. 0171 486 5544	Publishers of *Which?* magazine – covering many issues in marketing ethics and honesty
Data Protection Registrar Wycliffe House, Water Lane Wilmslow Cheshire SK9 5AF Tel. 01625 535777	Responsible for operating the Data Protection Act
Design Council 28 Haymarket London SW1Y 4SU Tel. 0171 839 8000	For the role of design in boosting business export potential